A MESS
OF GREENS

Waiting to be slow simmered, these collard greens could just as easily be turnip, mustard, creasy, or other leafy greens.

ELIZABETH S. D. ENGELHARDT

A Mess of Greens

SOUTHERN GENDER
AND
SOUTHERN FOOD

The University of Georgia Press
Athens and London

Portions of this book appeared earlier, in different forms, as "Writing That Old Moonshine Lit," *Journal of Appalachian Studies*, Vol. 13, Issue 1 & 2, Spring/Fall 2007, copyright 2009 by the Appalachian Studies Association; "Beating the Biscuits in Appalachia," in *Cooking Lessons: The Politics of Gender and Food*, edited by Sherrie A. Inness, Rowman and Littlefield, 2001; and "Canning Tomatoes, Growing 'Better and More Perfect Women,'" *Southern Cultures*, Winter 2009, copyright 2009 by the Center for the Study of the American South, and are reprinted here with permission.

© 2011 by the University of Georgia Press
Athens, Georgia 30602
www.ugapress.org
All rights reserved
Designed by Mindy Basinger Hill
Set in 11/15.5 Garamond Premier Pro

Printed digitally in the United States of America

Library of Congress Cataloging-in-Publication Data

Engelhardt, Elizabeth Sanders Delwiche, 1969–
A mess of greens : Southern gender and Southern food / Elizabeth S. D. Engelhardt.
p. cm.
Includes bibliographical references and index.
ISBN-13: 978-0-8203-3471-4 (hardcover : alk. paper)
ISBN-10: 0-8203-3471-5 (hardcover : alk. paper)
ISBN-13: 978-0-8203-4037-1 (pbk. : alk. paper)
ISBN-10: 0-8203-4037-5 (pbk. : alk. paper)
1. Food habits—Southern States—History. 2. Food—Social aspects—Southern States—History. 3. Cooking, American—Southern style—History. 4. Women—Southern States—Social life and customs. 5. Southern States—Social life and customs. 6. Southern States—Social conditions—History. I. Title.
GT2853.U5E64 2011
394.1'20975—dc23   2011012367

British Library Cataloging-in-Publication Data available

For my mother, BETTY WHITMIRE DELWICHE,
whose macaroni and cheese recipe it really is

CONTENTS

ACKNOWLEDGMENTS

ix

INTRODUCTION
Whose Food, When, and Why?
Longing for Corn and Beans

1

CHAPTER ONE
Moonshine: Drawing a Bead
on Southern Food and Gender

21

CHAPTER TWO
Biscuits and Cornbread: Race, Class, and
Gender Politics of Women Baking Bread

51

CHAPTER THREE
Canning Tomatoes:
Growing "Better and More Perfect Women"

83

CHAPTER FOUR
Will Work for Food:
Mill Work, Pellagra, and Gendered Consumption

119

CHAPTER FIVE
Cookbooks and Curb Markets:
Wild Messes of Southern Food and Gender
165

CONCLUSION
Market Bulletins:
Writing the Mess of Greens Together
193

NOTES
205

BIBLIOGRAPHY
235

INDEX
259

ACKNOWLEDGMENTS

I VOLUNTEER with a leadership group for at-risk girls in West Virginia. Whether we are dining around a campfire or at a picnic table, no meal at High Rocks begins without a round of "gratefuls," in which anyone is free to offer thanks to anyone or anything that happened during the day. Having grown up around a southern table whose meals started with a blessing, gratefuls feel a lot like saying grace, except they have a better sense of humor. Inevitably, gratefuls range from the serious to the silly. Book writing, for me, amasses the same range of thanks.

First and foremost, I am grateful to the people around the region who left their stories and recipes to history and who became the subjects of this book. I am amazed by their resourcefulness and courage. Included with them are the librarians and archivists who helped preserve those documents—and without whom my research would have suffered. I especially thank Andrea Cantwell and the staff at the University of Arkansas, Shannon Wilson and the staff of Berea College's Hutchison Library, everyone at Mississippi State University's Special Collections and University Archives, staff at the Southern Historical Collection at the University of North Carolina at Chapel Hill, Boyd D. Cathey and the staff at the North Carolina State Archives, public librarians at the Chattanooga Public Library, Henry Fulmer and the rest of the South Caroliniana Library, and volunteers at the Henderson County Genealogical and Historical Society.

My academic home, the Department of American Studies at the University of Texas at Austin has hosted both quirky meals and my quirky projects. I am deeply grateful to be around the table with Bob Abzug, Cary Cordova, Janet Davis, Steven Hoelscher, Randy Lewis, Nhi Lieu, Stephen Marshall, Jeff Meikle, Julia Mickenberg, Naomi Paik, Mark Smith, and Shirley Thompson, as well as staff members Stephanie Kaufman, Cynthia Frese, Ella Schwartz, and the incomparable Valeri Nichols-Keller. Thanks always go to my mentor, Frances Smith Foster. It has been enormously helpful and inspirational to be a member of the Southern Foodways Alliance. My new co-conspirators in the sister organization, Foodways Texas, are ready for me to be done with this and turn to our next projects; they inspire me as well. Students, graduate, undergraduate, and especially the members of the *Republic of Barbecue* team, made me an altogether better scholar, and I am grateful to them.

The Writers' Colony at Dairy Hollow, in Eureka Springs, Arkansas, knew they gave me a fellowship to work on this project. So did the University of Texas, through the Dean's Fellowship program. The lodge at Charit Creek in Tennessee and the fine home of Jessica Swigger in Cullowhee, North Carolina, gave me the same luxury, albeit less formally. I officially thank all of them.

Very great appreciation goes to John T. Edge and Marcie Cohen Ferris. Not only are they fellow members of the Southern Foodways Alliance, who were among the first to hear me talk about this research, but also, they and other anonymous readers helped make this book manuscript much better than it would have otherwise been. I am also grateful to the tag team of Erika Stevens and Laura Sutton who, along with the rest of the University of Georgia Press, shepherded this manuscript along its way. I thank editors at *Southern Cultures* and the *Journal of Appalachian Studies*, as well as anthologists Sherrie Inness and Ronni Lundy, all of whom read and helped improve earlier, smaller portions of this work. Psyche Williams-Forson and Carolyn de la Peña both helped me at crucial points in this research, with friendship and inspired intellectual conversation.

Most importantly, Betty and Bob Delwiche, my parents, and Imogene Eaker, my godmother, were always game to answer my strange food questions (including "Did you ever eat fiddleheads?"; "Where exactly did the solder go on the can?"; and "In which cemetery is that female moonshiner buried?"). Jennifer Steadman, Julie Clarenbach, Jolie Lewis, Cynthia Riley, and Jaime Madden took me out for many a hike or walk after too much southern food or too much writing about southern food. Although Cynthia might consider adopting a name that begins with a J, I am grateful to all of them.

Finally, I want to thank my fifth-grade school picnic. To celebrate "pioneer days" in the mountains of North Carolina, it featured girls packing baskets of homemade food on which boys bid. That made me annoyed enough to start asking *why* women were expected to cook and have their worth judged by their food skills—and apparently enough to write a book about it years later. More importantly, though, the picnic made me ask my grandmother, Iva Sanders Whitmire, to teach me to cook her famous fried chicken and to bake biscuits. We stood in her kitchen, laughing, talking, and cooking—and for that lesson, which completely turned my ten-year-old's feminist anger into equally feminist appreciation, I am profoundly grateful to her and to the public school system of Hendersonville, North Carolina.

A MESS OF GREENS

INTRODUCTION

Whose Food, When, and Why?

LONGING FOR CORN AND BEANS

IN THE 1760S, ancestors on my mother's side of the family landed in Philadelphia and started down the Trans-Allegheny trail, heading for South Carolina. By the 1790s, they had moved up into the North Carolina mountains to a series of communities in Transylvania and Henderson counties—Quebec, Toxaway, Brevard, Hendersonville. Most of them never left. They worked in timber, tannin, and the later paper factories; kept boarders; had small general stores; and generally did what they could to survive. They helped found churches and build schoolhouses; they farmed in small ways and kept garden patches. For more than two hundred years, my family practiced and perfected late-summer, southern meals to share. Surely they cooked real southern food done right. Clearly, it must have been authentic and pure; the nostalgia we feel for it, uncomplicated.

From the Fourth of July through Labor Day, with birthdays and visits in between, any weekend could bring a reason to gather, talk, and eat. The get-together could take place at a picnic shelter up in the forest (whether Pisgah, the Nantahalas, or the Smokies), beside the lake at Camp Straus (where present and former employees of the local paper company could play), or simply in the kitchen of my grandmother, Iva Sanders Whitmire (1907–2001). Regardless, certain foods always made an appearance. Green beans, picked and snapped earlier in the day and then cooked long and seasoned with ham, graced the table. Silver queen corn joined the beans; both were almost always from Uncle Jerry and Aunt Betty's garden. Tomatoes thickly sliced and watermelon sliced even thicker added color. Fried chicken was piled high, hot from the cast-iron skillet, lightly battered, pan fried, and juicy. From the same skillet came fried okra and fried squash. Biscuits with homemade apple jelly or blackberry jam accompanied the meal. Canned by my grandmother, Uncle Joe, or Uncle Jesse (who was not my uncle in terms of blood but in every other way), the jellies and jams always had handmade labels. Each year's batch held stories of hidden, pick-your-own farms or discoveries of patches by the side of the road. Late summer meals often meant the first taste of flavors that kept us company all winter.

Potato salad and slaw filled large bowls in summer, cutting down on heat in kitchens. My family was particular not only about how to dress the slaw—Duke's mayonnaise, vinegar, milk, salt, sugar, and pepper—but also about how to cut the cabbage. We used a paring knife (my grandmother's blade was almost gone from years of sharpening) to flake off the small bits of cabbage between thumb and knife blade. It took at least half an hour to do a head of cabbage this way. Chopping, slicing, or—heaven forbid—using a food processor was frowned upon. Although I have asked my mother and aunts, no one knows if this came from a desire to achieve a particular taste or if it was the only knife my grandmother had and, thus, how she always did it. Whatever the reason, we all agree the slaw somehow came out better that way—the final arbiter of any family's favored food practices.

On special occasions, the day ended with homemade peach ice cream—my dad, the chemical engineer, supervised that job, his knowledge of ice and rock salt in combination outweighing his perceived-as-unfortunate childhood outside western North Carolina. The freestone peaches came from down the mountain in South Carolina, and the ice cream was cranked by hand with cousins and uncles all taking turns. Electric cranking ice cream mixers have been moderately tolerated in later years—but, to my family's mind, the kitchen counter, computerized, mechanized appliances that whir and buzz and automatically freeze the ingredients hard have nothing to do with real peach ice cream. Pitchers of cold, sweet tea sat nearby to refresh the tired and impatient ice cream makers.

Variations of that meal were being enjoyed by families at the next picnic shelters over, by mountain residents in earlier decades, and by southerners across the region. Your family may have similar memories and menus. A closer look at the meal, though, reveals four dilemmas that are at the heart of this book—and they are why I am telling you so much about my own particular family traditions here at the beginning of a project whose chapters are not so much about my personal history as they are about a broad story of food and gender in the southern United States during a crucial transition period of the 1870s through the 1930s.

The turn-of-the-century South existed in a troubled relation to emerging national markets and visions of a new America. Convulsed by the legacies of Reconstruction and solidifying the era of Jim Crow, southerners interacted against a background of mob violence and lynching. Women of different races came together in kitchens—often as servants and mistresses—but also as people with shared tastes and ingredients. Meanwhile, much of white America was gripped by nostalgia for the plantation South—the blockbuster movie *Birth of a Nation* swept the country and "Mammy's cooking" became a central image of the nostalgia. Corporations responded, creating figures such as Aunt Jemima and Uncle Ben to bring the plantation into kitchens across the country. But much of the celebration involved a mythic South, like that in the following decades' *Gone With the Wind*, existing more in the cultural imagination of the time than on the ground. Actual southern communities faced devastating environmental change brought by textile mills, the soil-exhausting sharecropping economy, and the exportation of raw materials such as timber, paper, cotton, and tobacco, which made for a painful transition to a money economy.[1] Questions of class and social hierarchies in this new economy played out on the pages of community cookbooks produced by various churches, women's clubs, and charitable organizations; in the booths of curb markets and club exhibits; and in the letters and photographs exchanged across the region. A combination of climate, stubborn individualism, economic necessity, and regional pride held together "the South" even as race, class, and gender threatened to pull it apart—and writers of novels, short stories, and poems recorded the tensions. As today's South and the United States as a whole ever more fully enter global markets and engage shifting definitions of region, race, class, and gender, the 1900 South comes along with us. We can see how this particular past informs the present in that seemingly simple family meal that nonetheless hides complicated questions of defining the South, balancing technology and nostalgia, recognizing racial and ethnic diversity, and deploying gender in its dishes and foodways.

DEFINING THE SOUTH

First, my family's favorite summer meal was simultaneously local and regional—as a result, it helps us ask how the South gets defined, by whom, at what time, and why it matters. If pressed, members of families like mine might describe themselves with several adjectives: "North Carolinians," for instance, because there is pride of state here. The 1960s-era War on Poverty established the federal Appalachian Regional Commission and coined a term for an identity. In the intervening decades, my family has slowly adopted the word "Appalachian" to connect our experience with those of other mountain residents. In addition, "American" might be listed. Perhaps because of my family's mountain roots, which meant divided loyalties in both present and past politics and a strong sense of inclusion for all, we have never been a Confederate flag–waving crowd. Yet I did grow up knowing that I was not Yankee or Midwestern or from some generic place, so the adjective that is mostly unsaid, but that gets applied to us and shapes our senses of self even when we resist it, is "southern."

In the meal, you see visible expressions of our background regional identity. Fresh sweet corn and green beans were part of our celebration, but they would fit just as well on tables in Alabama, Texas, or Virginia (or possibly my father's native Wisconsin, for that matter, but more on that in a moment).

Watermelon did not grow especially well in the mountains but came to us from other southern fields. Our preference for South Carolina peaches could just as easily have been filled by the fabled Georgia peach or the Texas varietals. The methods of cooking—frying cornmeal-dipped okra and mixing fresh and home-canned foods on the table—spoke to larger regional food practices. Even the foodways, the practices and customs around providing, preparing, and sharing the food, with the emphasis on female cooks and family-food-centered celebration, placed this particular meal in the U. S. South.

Yet, if you quizzed members of the family about where we are from, the most likely answer would be more specific: "the mountains of North Carolina" or even "the mountains of western North Carolina." A subtle change, putting "mountains" first emphasizes how important they are in terms of loyalty and love of place. At the same time, making mountains the most important part of the phrase recognizes the marginalization of Appalachia and its foodways from the rest of the state and the region. North Carolina has never quite known what to do with its mountains—geographically far from the state capital, they often are far down on the state's priority list as well. For my family and others, the mountains are the most relevant identity possible. Yet the shared meal reflected that less than it could. While garden vegetables cooked in a kitchen no more than five hundred yards from where they were grown achieved a degree of closeness that local food advocates champion, even more local foods could have been on the table but were not. I could have listed heritage items that in combination made the location of our meals in the Blue Ridge Mountains undeniable. Foods foraged from the particular mountain environment have long been part of my family's table—ramps, hickory nuts, persimmons, mountain trout, and wild berries—and we still eat many of them. Traces of the local were present: the ears of corn and mounds of beans, although they spread across the country (even to Wisconsin's gardens), hinted at deeply buried local connections as my family lived in the heart of Cherokee land, whose tribal origin story of Selu was one of corn mother and companion beans.[2]

Although Tennessee food scholar Fred Sauceman claims such foraging connections are hallmarks across the South—that, indeed, "Southerners have pickled watermelon rinds, made wine out of corn cobs, stewed mudbugs, killed spring lettuce with vinegar and bacon grease, and sautéed dandelion greens, thereby creating America's most diverse indigenous cuisine"[3]—those items were not on the table at my family's summer celebrations. Did we choose to downplay the economic pressures that led to such resourcefulness? Perhaps, more simply, we celebrated abundance and good times. Either way, the meal pointed to aspirations in addition to nostalgia; in other words, it was both what we believed we were and what we (perhaps subconsciously) wished to become, members not of a marginalized group, but fellow North Carolinians, southerners, and Americans, eating a recognized, even storied, cuisine. The meal and, indeed, this book are more about such aspirations and the stakes involved in the food choices. As chapter 1 explores, the wild Appalachian, outside capitalist norms, mobile, free and unpredictable, was a source of great anxiety in the early century—for people within and out of overlapping communities of Appalachia, the South, and America. Choices made even today hint at the consequences of old anxieties.

I could have described a different but equally historically southern meal. The greens my family ate most often were turnip, mustard, or creasy, not collards. My grandmother most preferred to boil her cabbage rather than make slaw. They ate dove and lots of squirrel, only rarely having pork barbecue or buttermilk-soaked fried chicken. The dessert was less likely to be peaches and more likely to be fried apple pie made with tart dried apples and little sugar. Biscuits, as chapter 2 explores, were relative newcomers to the mountain table. They relied on ingredients not indigenous to the high mountains, but they sat undeniably in the center of the family table, whereas cornbread was relegated to supper or breakfast. Family members canned tomatoes or ate them fresh, but they rarely fried the green ones. Just as my godmother remembers first hearing that she was Appalachian in the 1960s, the celebration of fried green tomatoes as a signature southern food coalesced around Fannie Flagg's book of that name as late as the 1980s. In other words, scholars (including me), media, advertisers, and artists not only excavate food practices, we actively shape them as well. Our definitions of "true" southern foods change and evolve constantly, as some foods are lifted and celebrated while other equally common ones stay in the background waiting for their day. *A Mess of Greens* balances on shifting ground, resisting what cultural studies scholar Tara McPherson calls the flawed lenticular logic of never seeing the contradictions of southern societies simultaneously (her term refers to the vintage postcards, called 3-D or lenticular, which change images depending on how you turn them).[4] Buried in food choices are stories of race, class, gender, and social power that are the topics of this book.

Finally, readers in Louisiana may argue that I cannot claim the meal was southern without gumbo on the table. Kentuckians want burgoo. Coastal southerners might insist on shrimp and oysters, or at least rice, in the meal. Elsewhere, I have agreed with southern food scholars like John Shelton Reed who argue that barbecue and its variations work like the cheeses of Europe to map the diverse southern food *terroir*, the deep connections between food and place, most precisely. Given the diversity of food and place across the region, then, does the "southern" in southern food hang together enough to be useful? Cultural and social historians from Henry Shapiro and Allen Tullos to the newer Global South anthropologists and literary scholars such as James Peacock, Kathryn McKee, and Jennifer Greeson have all struggled with the ways the South both coheres and fragments. For the purposes of this project, I follow the lead of scholars such as McPherson and Patricia Yaeger who argue that people recognize the differences but still act as if the whole hangs together.[5] The imagined South is the South, as it were, powerful and contested. Southern food exists, even if we fight over what counts.

Thus, while "southern" or "mountain" or "Deep South" or "coastal" food might seem timeless (or at least stable over hundreds of years), in fact, they were very much contested and being worked out in the post-Reconstruction era that is the time period of this project. The following chapters explore West Virginia, Kentucky, Tennessee, North Carolina, Georgia, South Carolina, Mississippi, and Arkansas foodways. Virginia and Alabama make appearances. Louisiana and Florida get admittedly short shrift, and, although I have written elsewhere about Texas, my current home state receives little attention here. I sincerely hope other books follow to fill in stories from those states. Since my goal is not to write a broad history of all the food stories that could be told (I am not even certain that project is possible), I have chosen five moments and five food practices that together illuminate the intimate connections of food, gender, and region.

In the course of writing my first book, *The Tangled Roots of Feminism, Environmentalism, and Appalachian Literature*, I started noticing the times food worked as a code in women's letters, diaries, novels, and short stories.[6] It communicated messages about morals, religion, individualism, and education. For instance, choosing to ferment instead of shipping the corn crop, or deciding to serve hot breads like cornbread rather than cold sliced breads or beaten biscuits could gain a family the reputation of being unhygienic, morally suspect, uneducated, and even ungodly. Aspiring instead after new stoves, cookbooks, and well-equipped kitchens signaled women fighting for the modern American soul. In other words, food "means" more than sustenance, and those meanings shift over time and place. Although everyone must eat, which might suggest food transcends gender, the histories of women and food mean that, on the contrary, food is richly gendered. As ideas of community, region, and nation hang together and fall apart, shifting in meaning depending on who is talking (for instance, about "America," "the South," or "Appalachia"), local people in local places are defined by and participate in defining the local, national, and global societies in which they live; this is the cultural work of societies. For women, especially, food does this cultural work. Breaking the codes of food begins with its uses, preparations, and costs but ends with the social histories of race, class, gender, and place that hide in the recipes, ingredients, and food practices we embrace and use to define ourselves.

AUTHENTIC TECHNOLOGY

Turning back to the family's summer feasts, nostalgia and romanticism could easily emphasize their local and homemade parts, while equally present processed ingredients faded into the background. But technologies and consumer-culture innovations were thoroughly embedded in the meal—from the ice needed to freeze the ice cream, to the Duke's Mayonnaise in the slaw and potato salad, to the White Lily flour used in the biscuits. Today, I generally make my own mayonnaise, in a simple combination of fresh egg yolks, lemon juice, oil, and salt. But no matter how good, no matter how unprocessed or basic my version may be, our family nostalgia is instead for the commercially produced jar from the grocery store.

The history of Duke's turns out to be precisely the point, though. Founded in 1917, the original company used recipes for mayonnaise and sandwich spreads from a woman named Eugenia Duke, a South Carolinian who apparently needed to make some money by her own means. She began selling sandwiches to soldiers stationed outside Greenville. Out of the popularity of her products, Duke's Sandwich Company formed. The company marketed sandwiches and spreads to upstate textile workers. Many of Duke's early customers were mill women without time or kitchens to fix their own meals, so traveling dope wagons, similar to today's taqueria trucks, selling Duke's sandwiches were a blessing. A second company sold Duke's Mayonnaise. Although it was later bought by a Richmond, Virginia, parent company, even today the product is made in Greenville and marketed regionally. Both companies' Web pages celebrate the contributions of Mrs. Duke, but neither gives her much of a voice.[7] As chapter 3 explores in the story of early-century tomato-canning clubs, women and girls eagerly embraced the science and technology of commercial food production. Subsequent years have threatened to erase their contributions or make them into safely contained images (such as Mrs. Duke silent on the Web or girls behind 4-H displays). *A Mess of Greens* unearths such industrial stories despite our own seeming eagerness to force women and girls into the domestic spaces of our collective memories.

A similar reassignment has happened to the food the women and girls cooked. As much as southern food gets celebrated as the product of southern women (black and white) cooking in home kitchens, the region was fertile territory for the founding and expansion of food corporations—Duke's was accompanied by White Lily and Martha White Flours, Coca-Cola, and Pepsi, to name just a few. Mrs. Duke was not the only professional woman involved in early food companies. Still other women like the mill workers who first bought Duke's spreads created market demand for products. Their daughters and granddaughters became the brand-loyal consumers like the women in my family, recognizing and valuing the southern industrial food products. National food scholars in the tradition of Harvey Levenstein and Donna Gabaccia are right to say transportation, urbanization, and market development were delayed in the South. Such delays led to an emphasis on home-cooked, regionally specific foodways, and hence, the persistence of a unique southern food culture.[8] The southern food story's paradox lies in how assiduously the South worked to catch up, and how much its corporate food products and their consumers helped solidify the reputation of that southern cuisine that has persisted in the global marketplace. Southern food, not to put too fine a point on it, is more of a thing than "Yankee food" or "Midwestern cuisine" or even "American food." In John Egerton's words, "For as long as there has been a South, and people who think of themselves as Southerners, food has been central to the region's image, its personality, and its character."[9] By focusing on the 1870s–1930s era of economic growth and transformation, *A Mess of Greens* examines how people rearranged and rebuilt southern identities within these new technology- and market-driven worlds. A central claim of this book is that this is the crucial era to study if we are to understand food and gender in the twenty-first-century South.

At the same time, the story does not follow a straight line. With the establishment and shoring up of segregation in the South, race and class continually pushed against each other. The era's food story developed in fits and starts. For each articulation of anxiety or resolution of tension, another came into prominence. Moonshine tensions were still in full development while biscuits-versus-cornbread battles arose, and tomato clubs shared space with both. In the final chapters, the mill girls who sacrificed nutrition to keep their homes and dignity and the women who shared conversations at curb markets, in cookbooks, and by notes sent with seed exchanges were enmeshed in ongoing debates about authenticity and labor. Thus, *A Mess of Greens* roughly begins in the 1870s and continues to the 1930s, but individual chapters' timelines overlap to keep from flattening the complexity of the gender and food stories.

WHOSE SOUTHERN CULTURE? WHO IS SOUTHERN?

I could just as logically discuss my family's late summer regional and local meal as a national and transnational experience. For example, the soybean oil used in the mayonnaise, the milk used in the ice cream, the salt used to freeze the dessert, and the corporate headquarters of the grocery stores used to purchase ingredients not from Aunt Betty and Uncle Jerry's garden likely came from outside the mountains and the South. Going further, the equipment to produce and transport the foods most certainly was built elsewhere on the continent if not overseas. But also, the people at and behind the meal exhibited crucial diversity in the story. My Dad from Wisconsin, with Belgian, French, and Polish ancestors, sat at the table. The family genealogy down to my Mom blended Scots-Irish, German, and English elements. The extended family included Native American ancestry; and, as scholars have demonstrated again and again about the small-town South (and yet as many white families feel may have been true for others but not themselves) African American families in the same towns with the same last names were usually not coincidences.[10] Whiteness, too, was a much shifting concept. During most of the time period of this project, my family would have been viewed as a separate race, since "Appalachians" were not then counted with other white Americans.

Certainly, black cooking techniques influenced the recipes on the table, even if my family and many other Appalachian white families were too economically marginal to follow other middle-class white southerners in hiring African American kitchen help. As scholars Psyche Williams-Forson and Frederick Douglass Opie have argued, the okra, the chicken for a special meal (called, as Williams-Forson reminds us, the "gospel bird" to commemorate its role on special occasions), even the cooking method of frying foods in the South were stories of race as well as gender in the kitchen. What looked like a quintessential southern drink, iced tea, was a distant reminder on the table of British colonial trade routes to India and China and the Atlantic slave trade triangle of Caribbean sugar, African labor, and European and U. S. capital.[11] Southern communities, far from being as isolated as the myths said, long traded wildcrafted ginseng with China and Korea, had Greek, Jewish, and Asian community members, and early on relied on labor of Latino immigrants.

In popular accounts, stories of southern food frequently focused on elite white and enslaved or poor black foodways.[12] *A Mess of Greens* joins other southern scholars to instead examine the broad middle—poor whites, farm families, middle- and working-class African Americans, southerners who made up the numerical majority. However, this book is about these same southerners precisely because they were not automatically included in the tent when southern food was defined, discussed, and developed. At the same time, the turn of the century was an era when people were forced into one or another category, and great anxiety clustered around blending, mixing, and passing in new capitalist social structures. As chapter 4 explores, much of the southern food story in the early century was about absence and lack of food, starvation, pellagra, and the grotesque diseased southern body among people for whom the new systems were supposed to bring prosperity and coherence.

Forgotten food stories, daily decisions outside haute cuisine or nostalgically drawn plantation quarters, drive the chapters of this book. *A Mess of Greens* recovers stories of people, in other words, for whom food was both very high stakes in terms of having enough, balancing time and nutrition, and positioning self and family in the racial, class, and regional hierarchies of town, state, and nation.

GENDER MATTERS

Returning one more time to the summer meal, dramas of gender played out before, during, and after the actual eating, if only we pay attention to see them. While today my aunt and uncle share the labor of the garden supplying the meal, gardens in the late nineteenth century were often seen as the domain and responsibility of women. Gardens extended domestic space, and in a gender-divided society, they were quite different from farms. More than that, the responsibility of planning, directing, and coordinating meals from either the historical or present-day gardens fell mostly on women's shoulders. As southern food scholar Marcie Cohen Ferris puts it, even while there may be family variations, "Throughout the region's history no two areas have remained more conservative than the food southerners eat and the gender of those who cook it."[13] Kitchen space, recipes, and conversations were very much women's domain at the family meal with my grandmother's slaw, biscuit, and fried chicken recipes, aunts bringing specialty desserts, and even my generation of female cousins hanging out in the kitchen while male cousins wandered outside.

At the same time, we can overplay connections between food and femininity. The reign of celebrated male chefs and male-dominated food businesses was in full operation at the turn of the century, but it is hard to explain if we assume women have the only natural connections to food production. If we overemphasize the private, home connections between women and food, then we do a disservice to black women for whom home kitchens were often not private, domestic spaces. Instead, women working as domestics found their public workspace in the intimate home of someone else—and they rarely (if ever) received the full privileges of white women there. Families then and now contain almost infinite configurations of men, women, girls, and boys—making varying choices about gender roles within and beyond the family table. Across the South, what Ferris rightly calls a rigid patriarchal ideology proved again and again to be fluid, especially within intimate family, neighborhood, and local structures of power. Just as "the South" was a largely imagined, hard-to-define term, femininity in the South was as well. When women taught other women and girls about daily food preparation, supply, and presentation of food for the family, they performed a political act. Once we stop viewing these acts as natural, we can tease out the dynamics embedded in the lessons.

Competing with the domestic messages about women and food, the turn of the century brought about the full-scale invention of the female consumer—in magazines, cookbooks, and mail-order catalogs, as well as at corporate demonstration booths at county, state, and even world's fairs. Nationally, people took interest in the individual choices women made with family money. Although different women had widely varying amounts of disposable income, almost every woman in the country spent some money on food at the turn of the century. Corporations knew this; popular media targeted this; reformers used it; and individual women learned to navigate a new landscape of capitalism and marketing while they fixed dinner every evening. Innovations in food technology (some in response to Upton Sinclair's Progressive text, *The Jungle*), such as refrigerated rail cars, national distribution systems, sanitary and safe canning processes both for individuals and corporations, joined innovations in advertising and national marketing to usher in an era of great changes in what Americans grew, purchased, cooked, and ate. The Progressive and clubwoman's movements emphasized women's active participation in the changes.[14] In a time in which everything from the general store to basic senses of how to be men and women was in upheaval, food stood at the epicenter of the struggles.

In cookbooks, especially community ones, morning gossip, and private letters, communities emerged. Food provides a lens to see the places communication happened even if we can no longer decipher the specific messages. These communities are the subjects of chapter 5, which brings us to three sites where women debated, resisted, and created alternative spaces for themselves. At the same time, women across the South, especially economically and socially privileged ones, deployed gender to enforce economic and racial structures of power—this too was reflected in foodways. In portraits of female moonshiners, models of femininity almost erased become visible again. When combined with science, technology, and marketing, gender promoted new cooking practices such as canning, and often did so by making cultural, moral, or ethical judgments about women as consumers. Ones who did not have enough money, for whom promises of industrialization failed, stared back at mainstream culture, indicting their judges and serving as cautionary tales of too easily accepting new models.[15] An attention to the food they ate and the relative value given to their ways of eating reveals differences between women living in North Carolina's mountains, Mississippi's agricultural belt, and Kentucky's long-established towns, and even between women around the table for late summer, mountain celebrations.

FIVE FOOD STORIES, CHAPTER BY CHAPTER

Questions of definitions haunt not only the family meal but also this larger project in food studies—first, where was the South (was it local, regional, global, national, imaginary)? Second, what was the role of technology, capital, advertising, and nostalgia (what counted, what was too much, who decided and when)? Third, who was the South (who counted, when)? And finally, how were women defining themselves, enforcing social hierarchies, and passively receiving such judgments?

Food studies emerged in American studies research because both explore material culture, historical changes, and literary discourses and give us traction on the above questions. Because food both intimately connects and divides genders, races, classes, and regions, food makes history and culture palpable and palatable. People talk about food even when they are not intending to—in letters, diaries, photographs, novels, short stories, and poems—and they talk about themselves when they intend to talk about food—in advertising, recipes, advice manuals, and cookbooks. Pairing a feminist theoretical approach (that looks at race, class, and gender in individuals and institutions) with an American studies methodology (that uses a flexible, interdisciplinary definition of texts), this book brings sources back in conversation with each other. It also makes visible the social relations and exercise of social power behind the sources.

Rather than get lost in cataloging variation across the region and individuals or attempting sweeping comprehensive statements, I focus on five moments in the southern food story. Using archival materials, letters, diaries, literature, photographs, government records, and cookbooks, *A Mess of Greens* pairs specific food items or practices with particular communities in the U. S.

South from the 1870s until the 1930s in order to tease out how diverse women used food to negotiate their own changing southern and American identities. Whether in the characterizations of moonshiners, the choice between biscuits and cornbread for the family meal, records of girls' tomato clubs, the specter of the starving and diseased body in mill literature, or the hidden archives of curb markets, local cookbooks, and market bulletins, this book explores issues of power involved in the nation's evolving fascination with, nostalgia for, and creation of social hierarchies in and about the South, despite—or because of—its ever increasing integration into national markets and cultures.

Chapter 1, "Moonshine: Drawing a Bead on Southern Food and Gender," examines the parade of females in popular moonshine literature about Tennessee, Kentucky, North Carolina, and Georgia. Substantial enough to constitute a genre of fiction, moonshine literature heightened the stakes in the politics of food by bringing gender, place, and class into ideologies of lawlessness and vice. National debates—about New Women, rebellious teen girls, and the consumer and capitalist culture pressing on them—played out in the pages of magazines and novels as the economies of turning corn into liquor were deliberately overlooked. The moonshine debates foreshadowed motivating issues behind biscuits and cornbread, tomatoes, and pellagra; the freedom embedded in the wild moonshiner was echoed in the pockets of hopefulness in community cookbooks, curb markets, and market bulletins. *A Mess of Greens* starts with moonshine because in the lawless and the out-of-bounds, we can more clearly see the tensions and the stakes involved in what makes it to the dinner table.

The second chapter, "Biscuits and Cornbread: Race, Class, and Gender Politics of Women Baking Bread," explores how in the southern mountains the choice a woman made between cooking biscuits or cornbread for her family was that between, on the one hand, high culture, moral uplift, and Progressive hygiene and, on the other, ignorance, disease, and unending poverty. Further, the beaten biscuit recipe championed by reformers to counter Appalachia's perceived lower class was a bluegrass and coastal South recipe with its own racial politics, while cornbread recipes relied on minimal labor and local ingredients and equipment. Unpacking the two recipes through letters, diaries, and handwritten accounts reveals deeply gendered and deeply classed battle lines of culture.

Chapter 3, "Canning Tomatoes: Growing 'Better and More Perfect Women,'" further engages the rhetorics of science and technology as it analyzes a popular program that introduced farm girls to capitalist markets: the girls' tomato club movement in Mississippi, North Carolina, and South Carolina. Handwritten girls' club narratives and Department of Agriculture reports illuminate how new methods of canning and food preservation brought together women of different classes and races to think of a garden vegetable as technology, money, education, and citizenship. Corporate and national food companies simultaneously embraced and belittled the five hundred thousand rural girls (at the program's height) putting food away while finding themselves in the new domestic science.

Chapter 4, "Will Work for Food: Mill Work, Pellagra, and Gendered Consumption," examines where girls and women who could not afford to be in tomato clubs landed: the piedmont mills that hired sharecropping, mountain, and tenant farming girls but did not provide them with enough legal means to feed themselves. The chapter argues that much of the story of southern food in the early twentieth century was one of lack and absence. Looking at the grotesque bodies of pellagra victims in southern labor literature broadens the discussion even further as consumer choice proved deadly complicated to navigate. The "pellagrin" (the era's term for a pellagra sufferer) in strike novels haunts the southern food story, reminding us of the dangers of romantically glossing over what was broken in the food and gender systems.

Finally, chapter 5, "Cookbooks and Curb Markets: Wild Messes of Southern Food and Gender," explores the role of collaborative cookbook authorship and curb market gossip. Cookbooks from the region both reflected and shaped the audiences for which they were produced; the chapter wrestles with interpreting the sometimes surprisingly ethnically, religiously, and monetarily diverse moments in the texts. Often dismissed as gossip if noticed at all, the conversations around the edges of the region's new curb markets made space for politics and education, as women became experts in their own and their communities' lives.

By reading the cookbooks and accounts of early curb market days closely, we can unearth unexpected conversations and hidden collective communities that have been obscured from view by the gender and race politics of the twentieth-century South. The process is partial and exploratory, requiring a metaphorical embrace of the "mess" in the dish of greens, but it rewards us with voices from women transitioning into and resisting the modern South as the 1930s came to a close.

The conclusion examines a curious collaborative book from the mid-century by garden writer Elizabeth Lawrence. In it, a repository of hidden knowledge from the South's agricultural market bulletins, seed savers, and women's letters is recovered. Languages of food, gender, and place extend from Lawrence and other mid-century daughters of women in moonshine literature, biscuit-and-cornbread battles, tomato clubs, and strike novels. The market bulletin friendships give us a bridge to our present-day world of southern food and gender. *A Mess of Greens* ends, then, with new languages worked out in the hidden spaces of southern cultures, gender, and foodways.

CONCLUSION

Even as I began this introduction with the claim that much of what follows is not personal, that is not strictly true. Nor could it be. Food is intimately personal, entering our bodies, impossible to avoid, and providing both pleasure and struggle. If, as 1970s feminism taught us, the personal is political, then food, that most personal exchange, is always political, too.[16] I entered this project with my family on my mind—not because we are right or central (or even that I am right or central to my family—in fact, I am certain my mother, cousins, and other family members will take issue with some of my extrapolations). But I began with us because we are gloriously complicated—just as every other family is. For me, family stories can drive my research interests, leading me to wonder, for instance, why every woman in my family is supposed to know how to make cornbread but only the gifted biscuit makers are celebrated—and then to go in search of a battle over that very question that played out in

Kentucky during the 1870s through 1930s. Just as often, my scholarly research interests have unexpectedly added to the family stories—as when the tomato club research I began in Mississippi led me to the North Carolina archives of Jane McKimmon and a picture of my great-great-grandmother posed with her own tomato club, a moment from her life none of us knew previously. My personal definition of southern food, then, is both significant and meaningless without all the other definitions. What I can do as a scholar—and what I hope you as a reader of this book will join me in doing—is ask what is at stake in the changing definitions. Let us try to understand what else is being said when someone asks for a second helping of cornbread, carefully writes out a treasured recipe, opens a jar of garden tomatoes, or sneaks a sip of white lightning.

Almost inseparable in today's cultural imagination, mason jars and moonshine were not always so tightly connected. Photograph by the author.

CHAPTER ONE

Moonshine

DRAWING A BEAD ON SOUTHERN FOOD AND GENDER

MANY FOODS AT THE TURN of the century were suspect, according to the United States government. For instance, the same laws that tightened the regulation of alcohol and created what would be the federal Food and Drug Administration (FDA) also targeted non-licensed and adulterated butter and cheese, as well as any number of patent medicines. Yet, the one we remember, the one whose bad reputation remains intact (taboo and technically illegal), is moonshine. It may seem counterintuitive to start this book on southern foodways with a food item that for years existed largely outside the bounds of socially acceptable consumption. However, in the 1870s, the era in which we begin, only a few decades had passed since moonshine was first declared illegal—and the laws and their enforcement were still evolving.[1] Thus, at the time, it was not clear that moonshine would remain outside social boundaries. In addition, as the region emerged from the chaos of the Civil War, agriculture and industry were profoundly disrupted in the southern states. What could be made at home and what could be eaten out of fields that had been burned or decimated, what could and should be sold in fragmented markets with scarce currency, and who could be responsible despite new codes of gender, race, and class, all needed renegotiation. Thus, it also was not clear what other foods and practices might join moonshine as beyond the realm of the acceptable. Moonshine, then, with its position on the borders, its practices and people outside the boundaries of society, was perfectly positioned to reveal the tensions and anxieties driving early twentieth-century southern food activism.

Moonshine casts a long shadow on southern foodways. While traces of actual moonshiners, especially female, nonwhite, and ones who are not portrayed as mountain hillbillies, are relatively elusive in the historical record, authors during the era busied themselves with fictional portrayals of moonshining. Novels, short stories, and magazine pieces filled the national media of the time; moonshine stories seemed to clutter the pages of every publication, including high-class *Harper's Monthly* and the *New York Times,* dime novel presses like Beadle, technical journals like *Scientific American,* and religious and philanthropic publishers like the Russell Sage Foundation.[2] Tensions and anxieties specifically around women and moonshine clustered into three roughly chronological categories: first, gendered Progressive rhetoric about activists and career women (most apparent in stories between the 1870s and 1910s); second, the invention of the teen girl and resultant struggles over what to do with her (in stories dating from the 1880s to the 1920s); and third, early twentieth-century consumer culture and its failures (applicable in stories written in the 1910s to 1930s). Questions raised by the figure of the Progressive Era's New Woman in the South animated the beaten biscuits crusade; the unsettling teen girl received attention from the tomato club organizers; and the problems of consumerism in the South drove portraits of food-based disease in southern labor fiction, each a subject of a chapter to follow. Finally, the wildness, hidden secrets, and subversive traditions of moonshine in general carved out spaces the hidden communities of this book's final chapter and conclusion also inhabited.

RECIPES AND REASONS

All you really need to make moonshine is corn, yeast (which can be captured from the wild), water, heat, and cold. Fundamentally, moonshine requires chemical reactions much like those in baking. Twentieth-century distillers added sugar to the recipe, as well as more or less fancy equipment to facilitate the process. From a kitchen batch brewed on stovetop to a giant twelve-hundred-gallon operation in the woods, the basics stayed about the same. Moonshiners mixed sugary sprouted ground corn with a little water and yeast, and added heat. Once it activated, they clarified and strengthened it by bubbling the vapors (generally two times) through copper tubing. Cooling the vapors back to liquid condensed and proofed the alcohol. Despite the reputation of moonshining as primitive, the ingredients and equipment could be expensive—refined sugar, copper tubing, commercial yeast, barrels, copper pots, additives to color the product or add to its bead (the bubbles that signal the proof and kick of the liquor). Many suggest that as the century progressed, the home-brewed liquor of the South became not corn liquor at all, but, rather, sugar liquor with essence of corn—because true corn liquor required patience and safety. One strategy to stop moonshine made it illegal to possess sprouting corn (which, after all, was used almost exclusively for moonshine). This stricture applied both to the moonshiner sprouting the corn and to the mill owners grinding it. Thus, many brewers abandoned corn in favor of purchased sugar. Other, more dangerous twentieth-century practices—bubbling the liquor through car radiators instead of clean copper worms; adding everything from chicken excrement to the contents of a spittoon to fake aging; and pouring in oil or soap at the end to add shine and bubbles—all mean that it is still a very good idea to know and trust the moonshiner before tasting his or her wares.[3] At its best, moonshine tastes smooth and cool before its warmth hits you. The resurgences of craft and small-batch production today mean that we can sample from a range of top-end versions exhibiting a subtlety well beyond the rotgut of myth and song.

Historians give three explanations for why people risked illegal distilling. The first dates back to the 1790s and the United States government's initial major attempt to tax alcohol. That failed policy culminated in 1794 with the Whiskey Rebellion, in which fifteen thousand troops were called out for the first time against the nation's own protesting citizens. Prior to then, one could legally brew liquor and sell it in whatever quantities one wished; thus, the argument that "my great-great-grandfather turned his corn into liquor and no one told him he couldn't" was often technically true. Even if your ancestor was George Washington, the claim could stand, since Washington broke from Thomas Jefferson's attempt to establish grapes for wine and instead went straight to brewing whiskey at Mount Vernon. European colonists consumed great amounts of alcohol—both the great-great-grandfathers and grandmothers, so both private and public demand was high. Later, Scots-Irish who emigrated to the South hailed from the center of Great Britain's resistance to liquor taxation, so they, too, were inclined to continue the earlier protests by defiantly moonshining in their new homes.[4]

The second explanation concerns the economic reality of shipping corn as the nineteenth century progressed: scholar Wilbur Miller calculates a mule could carry four bushels of unprocessed corn, but twenty-four bushels of corn whiskey. Similarly, a wagon could hold twenty bushels of corn, which might have brought its seller ten dollars in the 1890s, but it could carry the equivalent of forty bushels of whiskey, worth around $150. As with any raw material in the American economic system, corn gained intrinsic value the more it was processed or modified. An ear of corn on a farm far away from the market was hardly worth harvesting, but ground, canned, or fermented, it could be shipped more easily and sold at greater profit. Such realities, combined with inconsistent prosecution of those caught, gave powerful incentive to turn to illegal distilling. Industrialization encouraged the practice as people became dependent on cash in hand even as temporary jobs dried up.[5]

Finally, the third explanation acknowledges the seductive persona of the romanticized moonshiner. When educator Daisy Dame came to Kentucky in 1910, she longed to find a man with a Winchester at an abandoned still she visited. In her letters home, most of the local people were ignorant or pitiable; the moonshiner, however, was mysterious, romantic, and fascinating. No wonder some of those locals took on the moonshiner identity in response, such as the young, educated lawyer from the area who, to go on a picnic with the new schoolteacher, agreed to show her his gun and escort her to a notorious moonshining area. From his North Carolina mountain vacation home, Du Bose Heyward wrote in his 1926 novel *Angel* that the moonshiner role did not just attract others but also provided a path to respected manhood. Heyward's character argues, "Your paw, and your paw's paw were preachers, an' so you are a-thinkin' preachin's a pretty fine callin' fer a man ter foller, don't yer? ... well, with the Merritts hit's always been blockadin'; an' they's many an' many in these here mountains what think hit's more o' a man's job than preachin'." Novelist Sherwood Anderson further suggested that the romanticized moonshiner added value to the product, serving as a do-it-yourself advertising campaign. Anderson's narrator in *Kit Brandon* (1936) claims, "In Northern cities and towns they had a kind of illusion about the mountain moon and that helped make a market. They had read books and stories about mountain moonshiners, the gun-toting, hard-eyed mountain man."[6] Dame, Heyward, and Anderson all asserted that the iconic image held enough emotional or economic potential for contemporary southerners to adopt the practice in search of the benefits.

Whether motivated by unfair taxes, economic desperation, or romantic longings, people across the United States turned to moonshining. If we trace evidence through government records, we find moonshining in places as far afield as Missouri, Arkansas, Louisiana, Florida, Philadelphia, Chicago, along the Canadian border, across the Caribbean, and in Texas and other western states. Women and people of color produced and distributed moonshine; people of all classes funded and profited from the practice. The range of groups united to fight illegal alcohol production, consumption, and acceptance hinted at the reach the practice had in United States society: groups such as the Women's Christian Temperance Union, religious groups (especially Baptists), industry lobbyists, factory owners, anti–domestic violence suffragists, and health advocates.[7] Actual moonshining was often violent, dangerous, and damaging to producers, consumers, and even bystanders.

The idea of moonshining, though, landed in Appalachia, where the stereotypes doggedly took hold, but also where the forum of fiction allowed exploration and imagination of new social arrangements through its practice. Nonetheless, being from the mountains and having to counter those stereotypes my whole life, my own conflicted responses to moonshine tempted me to dismiss the body of literature about it even while I gathered it together for analysis. I feared these were all stories of the grizzled, ignorant, slightly noble but misguided, white, male small-time family moonshiner destined either to get his comeuppance or to be enlightened by do-gooders at the end of the story. Even in scholarly circles, when moonshine is discussed, the grizzled moonshiner is pulled out of the surrounding story (whether fictional, historical, or contemporary) as an example of how hillbilly and white-trash stereotypes persist. Although that practice has helped to analyze and dismantle Appalachian myths, we have in the process flattened and over-simplified our readings of the stories, their settings, their eras, and, most specifically to our purposes here, the food practices they portrayed.[8] What images of moonshine and moonshiners can tell us about southern foodways has not been explored. Women in moonshine have been doubly erased, first by a focus on the stereotyped male image and second by the resulting flattened approach. Our aim, then, is to reconnect women in moonshine stories to the rest of the southern food stories.

PROGRESSIVE RHETORIC, GENDER NOSTALGIA, AND NEW WOMANHOOD

If Anderson's "gun-toting, hard-eyed" man stereotypically represented the male moonshiner in literature, he was joined by a helpless, ignorant, innocent female equivalent, passively staring out at strangers. She is the main female in John Fox Jr.'s *Trail of the Lonesome Pine* and almost all of Mary Murfree's short stories; she comes down to us today as the women on porches that people like Loretta Lynn and Dolly Parton avoided becoming. Yet, one group of female characters in moonshine literature exploded the stereotype. What are we to make of women who had careers, refused to be silent, or upended social structures by engaging something as taboo as moonshine? Nationally, these educated, vocal, career women (so striking as to be labeled "New" in the late 1800s) defied separate spheres ideologies of female submission, innocence, and passivity by rejecting domestic femininity in favor of public work, independent choice, and Progressive activism. Historian Carroll Smith-Rosenberg calls the late nineteenth-century New Woman a "revolutionary demographic and political phenomenon" because American men and women responded to her sometimes with excitement, sometimes with fear, but always with the realization that the rules of gender were profoundly challenged at the end of the century.[9] In the final three decades of the 1800s, mainstream discourse alternately embraced and criticized both historical and fictional New Women; moonshine stories focused on her potential instead.

According to Smith-Rosenberg, even when embraced, the New Woman remained "a perennially liminal figure—a figure always outside of the existing social structures and with no way of coming in"; she never became that which mainstream society dreamed all their daughters would be. That was perhaps especially true in the South, where both white and black educated women (albeit from different motivations) were more likely to endorse the ideal of respectable ladyhood rather than single, professional career woman as the key to a public activist role. Southern New Women, then, were often held at arm's distance from the centers of southern societies.[10] Given that moonshine, too, was perennially constructed as outside the rest of America, what better practice to explore how such women fit into society? Authors of the era seemed to think so when they wrote stories combining moonshine with active, strong women and then explored a range of responses to them.

In Lucy McElroy's novel *Juletty*, a southern, female moonshiner illustrates the expanded work roles New Women could perform when the domestic and public were combined around a taboo food practice. Characters in George Creswell Gill's fictional *Beyond the Blue Grass* and in Catherine Frances Cavanagh's nonfictional magazine report, "Stories of Our Government Bureaus," consider moonshining as a serious option for women for whom the promise of a domestic safety net failed.[11] The perceived wildness of communities in which the moonshine was made paired with their imagined marginality to allow thought experiments with alternate definitions of femininity or with expanded social roles available to women.

Lucy McElroy (1860–1901) published *Juletty* in 1901. The novel takes the point of view of an inexperienced revenuer that eventually marries the title character. Hers was a common approach; the revenuer narrator appears frequently in the literature. *Juletty*'s Jack Burton is possibly the dumbest revenuer in the literature, however; almost everyone in the novel fools him—including sheriffs, drunks, and freckle-faced boys. The biggest ruse Burton faces concerns Juletty. A mysterious, auburn-haired figure lurking around the hidden still causes Burton to dream of Juletty. Despite his dreams, Burton believes with such certainty that women are never moonshiners that he convinces himself the moonshiner must be her father, even though the father lies on his deathbed.[12]

Two revelations await Burton. First, to his shock, Juletty is not at all a simple country girl in need of his care—she earns a comfortable living for herself and her family as an educated writer. As her father says, far from being helpless or passive, "there comes papers and books from Louisville every now and then with pieces she wrote in 'em, and she gets a sight of money for 'em, too . . . she runs this place and takes keer of the whole family." Having a successful career, publicly taking care of others, and not depending on anyone to make her way in the world puts Juletty in the role of New Woman. Second, Juletty proves to be the unrepentant moonshiner who bested Burton and the rest of the United States government at every turn. In other words, the most successful moonshiner in the county, the one who foiled revenuers and who ultimately avoided jail time because Burton resigned his governmental position in failure, is Juletty herself. The otherwise curious detail of her writing career effectively means that she moonshines not for mere subsistence but for enjoyment. As she exclaims, "I laid every plan, and saw with my own eyes that they were executed properly! I did not think it wrong then, and I do not think so now."[13] With Juletty, McElroy explored the fun and freedom expanded public gender roles could give all women. Juletty works, manages others, plans for the future of her organization—she is a skilled leader, having fun along the way. At the same time, viewed in the context of New Womanhood, the details of Burton's reactions and Juletty's two careers reveal inherent anxieties around women's work: perhaps women would best men at earning money; perhaps they would defy masculine codes of proper business behavior; and perhaps they would even enjoy breaking the law.

McElroy's novel trades in contradictions and tensions. It explores women's economic and social freedom, but does so in both legal (writing) and illegal (moonshining) ways. It displaces the previously masculine characteristics of wiliness, daring, and independence onto a beautiful southern woman; but it does so by means of an otherwise domestic practice akin to baking. Further, Juletty's independence and equality do not last beyond the story; as Smith-Rosenberg suggests, the New Woman remained liminal, never quite let into society. The final page of the novel is the one moment Burton completely controls, emphasized by his italicized "I": "*I* clasped the real culprit close, and laughed at the thought of her pluck and the wisdom of her plans for evading justice, and reveled in the bravery of her final confession . . . I sentenced her to captivity for life—to the man who had raided her 'Licit Still."[14] By marrying Juletty off to the revenuer, McElroy re-domesticated her into traditional gender roles. McElroy's readers could choose either to embrace or to reject Juletty's former life; regardless, McElroy created enough rhetorical space to highlight the interplay of gender, food, and social hierarchies, pointing out that who cooked what could introduce debates over morals as well as laws and roles.

A small number of stories suggested that, rather than for daring, fun, extra profit, or the challenge, some women turned to moonshine as a social necessity. In those stories, moonshine served as a de facto safety net. Many New Women targeted the consumption of alcohol in society and worked to strengthen the safety nets needed by people (primarily women and children) whose lives were adversely affected by others' drinking. They founded orphanages and schools, lobbied for Prohibition, and created safe houses and retreats for affected people. Some moonshine stories challenged that activism to explore how partial the solutions were. Challenging the easy equation of alcohol *consumption* with social ills, they substituted alcohol *production* as a last resort for women trying to support themselves and their families after society failed them. For instance, most of George Creswell Gill's *Beyond the Blue Grass* is a story of giving certain promising mountain boys an education in accounting so that they can work for the railroad and extractive industries penetrating their mountain communities. Yet it also highlights the cracks in society through which the most vulnerable still slipped. Two characters conspire to alter a land survey to hide the Widow Moseley's still from a stranger who has newly purchased the land. They explain, "Old Joe Moseley died, you know, last winter. He was purty o'nery, but that's no difference now. It's the only way the widder and her two boys has to make a livin'."[15] Gill's characters defend the widow's subsistence operation; they were not justifying, for instance, the actions of women like Juletty. Yet, female moonshiners like the Widow Moseley entered a new public relationship with a food precisely because the domestic world failed to support them.

A magazine article written by Catherine Frances Cavanagh (actively writing, ca. 1895–1915) struggled with a twentieth-century woman making decisions that combine those of Gill's fictional Widow Moseley and McElroy's fictional Juletty but on a larger scale. Ironically, we know more about Mrs. Rose, the moonshiner whose story she documented, than Cavanagh herself. Her work was a rare, woman-authored exposé of government work, one of several magazine pieces she wrote in her career. Although Cavanagh described Rose as "one of the most notorious moonshiners in southeastern Kentucky," she also referred to Rose always as "Mrs."—perhaps signaling her adherence to at least some gender expectations. Rose, Cavanagh clarified, was the widowed mother of a large family. Because her husband was killed "in one of those famous Kentucky feuds," Rose bore sole responsibility for the domestic welfare of her children. Cavanagh wrote that Mrs. Rose's "gang made and sold whiskey in the open, and came as near being a corporation as any moonshine concern could and exist among the independent manufacturers in that wild district," and Mrs. Rose was involved for seventeen years. In Cavanagh's description, moonshining was truly Mrs. Rose's career; the narrative played with the idea of a female chief executive officer of her "corporation." Still, immediately after being caught and sentenced to jail for marketing and selling moonshine, Rose embraced a more traditional domesticity: "Mrs. Rose was employed as a cook when at the jail. When told of her release, she said she was very glad to go home to her children, but that she really had had a nice, peaceable time in the jail, sure of her meals, enjoying her domestic tranquility." In the end, nostalgic womanhood trumped the role of CEO, with jail functioning as the boot camp Mrs. Rose needed to return to an appropriate womanly role. Working for a pardon "in order that she might return home to her large family," she endorsed "domestic tranquility" and all it conveyed successfully enough to win a pardon from President Theodore Roosevelt in 1907.[16] Cavanagh's narrative contained and controlled Mrs. Rose's transgressions with wild moonshine by restoring domestic order—women were mothering widows, not moonshining Julettys, and they neither profited from nor enjoyed alcohol in any of its forms.

Of course, the narratives' professed cultural tolerance and understanding of how women became moonshiners did not always hold true in practice. My godmother, Imogene Eaker, remembers growing up in the 1920s in a town with a woman who may have had much to say to Mrs. Rose or Juletty. Before Bushnell, North Carolina, vanished under the waters of the Tennessee Valley Authority's Fontana Dam in the 1940s, it thrived with a church, school, swinging bridges over the river, and general store. The town also had its own female moonshiner, who lived directly on the path between schoolhouse and church. During revival week, the schoolteacher made his pupils sing hymns in front of her house on their way to mandatory church services. One is tempted to imagine the woman sitting inside sipping some of her product and laughing—and perhaps she did enjoy her chosen career. But in truth, her life must have been incredibly difficult—as a single woman in the 1920s with a daughter to raise in a small town with few economic opportunities besides farming (and that difficult for a woman to do by herself and impossible without the means to own land). No wonder she turned to brewing moonshine on her stovetop.[17]

Such stories explored new ways of being a woman in the South. The early era of moonshine stories negotiated Progressive rhetoric concerning gender, considered the options, voiced anxieties, and imagined adaptations to accommodate new definitions of femininity. Would food become a tool used by women to defy the government? Or could it be tamed? When even former judges in the region argued about moonshiners, "Why should the Government 'parsecute' them for making their own corn into whisky in their own homes, any more than for making their corn into bread in their own ovens?" it is perhaps no wonder that the corn itself acquired a taint.[18] Looking at the moonshine literature helps us understand why activists like Katherine Pettit and May Stone came to the region already viewing corn with suspicion—morally dubious, possibly illegal, certainly not what they could comfortably endorse. Their counter-suggestion, that a wheat-flour biscuit recipe allowed women in the region to rebuild their own domestic safety nets, ushered them into further education, and answered the desperate social issues faced by southerners, is the subject of the following chapter. Moonshine stories here performed important cultural work for the nation by creating career women, active in public life, with control over their own bodies, who existed and even prospered without society coming to a halt. After the turn of the century, however, risk-taking, law-flaunting young women even more unsettling than Juletty, Mrs. Rose, the Widow Moseley, or Bushnell's "fallen" woman burst onto the national scene, as younger, more daring girls occupied the pages of the nation's novels, short stories, and magazines. Fictional and historical teenagers in the moonshine literature exploded the terms of gendered Progressive rhetoric because they were no longer out of the ordinary (almost every family has teenagers at some point). Would they, however, spin completely out of control?

THE TEENAGE UNKNOWN: FIXING THE MOONSHINE GIRL AND THE NATION

Cavanagh's "Stories of Our Government Bureaus," along with its portrait of Mrs. Rose, also portrayed out-of-control teen girls she termed "Mountain Amazons." Cavanagh began, "Women moonshiners are not uncommon; and they fight with the combined energy of wild cat and rattlesnake when they are discovered." Cavanagh supported her assertion with the example of teenage Betsy Simms, "a beautiful giantess," active in moonshining from age sixteen to twenty-two, in North and South Carolina. When finally sent to jail in Raleigh, Simms tried to escape by setting "fire to the door of her room" to attract the jailer (given that the next sentence emphasized her physical attributes, possibly flirting as well). That jailer "was promptly stabbed by buxom Betsy," but she did not disable him enough to escape. She then parlayed her position as "a queen among moonshiners, having at her call a band of strong men, who more than once came to her rescue." Although it is unclear on whether Simms successfully escaped, the narrative nonetheless showed Simms at a very young age leading, masterminding, and controlling "a band of strong men." Simms refused to play by the rules. She never listened to authority (she even stabbed it), she was unapologetic, and she was sexually and physically imposing (as the buxom giantess), "frighten[ing] more than one revenue officer into flight."[19]

As southern societies struggled to define the relationships between womanhood, activism, and food in the twentieth century, a further complication emerged. In 1904, G. Stanley Hall published his influential *Adolescence: Its Psychology and Its Relations to Physiology, Anthropology, Sex, Crime, Religion and Education*, marking a wave of concern, celebration, and even the invention of adolescence. Although Hall spent most of his two volumes discussing teen boys, the troubling teen girl lurked in the cultural background. By the 1930s, she had boldly entered the national imagination, in everything from flappers in popular culture to Nancy Drew in popular literature. Alongside New Women and against passive stereotypes, stood other female moonshine characters—daughters poised between childhood and adulthood. Martha S. Gielow (1854–1933) wrote a novella *Old Andy, the Moonshiner* that, despite its title, put the female teen on center stage in the moonshine literature. The tensions and anxieties Gielow explored foreshadowed the tomato club activists' debates as they considered the implications of putting money in the hands of farm girls.[20]

The teen girl was created in the midst of early century immigration, racism, and consumerism. In the South, migrations of great numbers of residents, codification of Jim Crow practices, and late but vigorous emergence of mill and factory cultures raised the stakes even further. In *Consumerism and American Girls' Literature, 1860–1940*, girls studies scholar Peter Stoneley suggests that girls fiction came into popularity "during successive waves of immigration" and African American emancipation, and he finds the white teenage girl's "volatility becomes a metaphor of class, racial, and ethnic uncertainty; the possibility of 'fixing' her coalesces with the possibility of resolving such social uncertainties." For Stoneley, the tamed or domesticated teenage girl moderated and controlled an unsettled American national body; he argues that successfully controlling the one (the wild teenager) translated to solving the other (a range of social tensions). Expanding Stoneley's model, Ilana Nash, in her study of mass-culture representations of teen girls, *American Sweethearts: Teenage Girls in Twentieth-Century Popular Culture*, adds helpful language for girls' roles in early literature, saying, "either the girl was a quasi-angelic creature... or else she was an exasperating agent of chaos." Nash further investigates how the angel was "praised for her bubbly charm, her obedience to authority, and her chastity," while the "agent of chaos" repeatedly "challenged the boundaries and hierarchies of a patriarchally organized society (one that protected the social, economic, sexual, and political privileges of mature males)."[21] Although neither talk directly about the South nor about food, both Stoneley and Nash argue that stories featuring girls were locations for working out society's nervousness about the early twentieth century.

For the moonshine literature, female teen agents of chaos and purity lived in parts of the South portrayed as simultaneously full of bloody feuds and uncorrupted, noble ancestors. Given that Stoneley's figure of metaphoric race, class, and ethnic volatility and Nash's figures of chaos and angel could just as easily describe a chaotically dangerous and refreshingly new South at that time, the moonshine stories with their southern teenage girls, in their southern-ness and their teen-ness, doubly embodied social tensions of the day. Controlling and fixing the girls, especially by educating them, had the power to control and fix the larger South, a possibility worked out through the foodways in the pages of the moonshine stories. In Gielow's novella, the only father Sal knows (her grandfather) sends the teen girl to school; he finances her education from the family moonshine still. Through Sal, Gielow controls and fixes one teen by educating her into national culture. On the final page of the novella, Gielow claims explicitly that fixing teens would fix the South's race and immigration struggles.[22]

Old Andy opens with Sal running wild. She is only eight, but her grandfather recognizes he has just a few years to earn the money to send her to school. He believes his girl needs to leave the mountains and wild animals that are her only companions in order to live a successful life. By the time she turns twelve and departs for school, Sal has had four years to get used to the idea. She has practiced by planting flowers in straight rows, a none-too-subtle metaphor for her forthcoming domestication. Gielow understated the danger; the sacrifices Old Andy makes reveal his concern over what could happen if Sal runs as wild as the mountain flowers usually grow. Joel Chandler Harris, in "At Teague Poteet's," a parallel story of mountain teens, portrays a girl just a few years older than Sal who is given to "a-gwine a-whoopin' an' a-hollerin' an' a-rantin' an' a-rompin' acrost the face er the yeth." Given how he risks jail to earn money, this must have been what Andy feared Sal would do: run wild across the face of the earth, yell, get angry, and be out of control. Like Andy, Teague announces, "when a gal gits ez big ez you is . . . the time's done come when they oughter be tuck up an' made a lady out'n; an' the nighest way is to sen' 'em . . . to school."[23] Both men believe education could take up the girls and turn them into ladies.

But how would the family afford to transform Sal? Even idealistic Gielow admitted that education costs money. Andy carefully calculates, and Gielow's text lingers over the number of pints of moonshine he distilled, how much he deducted to fund the start-up of his still, and how long the family worked to earn the required fifty dollars to send Sal to the school lady.[24] Moonshine is a necessary, if illegal, evil in the novella; while not endorsed, brewing liquor is the only strategy available for the family to purchase the education that promises Sal's future legitimate prosperity. Moonshine fuels an economic machine, and the novella suggests that if the problem could be solved in a place so lawless as one where cash came from moonshine, then it could be solved anywhere. Gielow carefully constructed and used the wildness of this foodway to drive home her point about education and teen girls.

Old Andy outlines the lady's education he wishes for Sal. He wants her to sew "the putties' frocks . . . the color of them blue bells on the crick side," "larn to cook cake," and "make sound on a thing ... called er pianny"; only as an afterthought does he mention that Sal should learn the history of their family's "ancestors," meaning American history. In other words, reading, writing, and arithmetic were much less important than sewing, baking, and entertaining. Through Andy, Gielow measures Sal's success in terms of her initiation into the female middle class. *Old Andy* emphasizes the consumer goods and skills that marked middle-class life and girls' education (pretty dresses, dainty cooking, and musical accomplishment) and the costs associated with buying that class mobility. Sal trades her wild companions for a lovingly detailed list of objects she acquires while at school: "the little bed off the floor with its snow white sheets—the pictures—the books, and the wonderful revelation of those pages, the stereopticon views of the life of Christ, which she had seen—the tones of the organ," and the "well made calico and the simple sailor hat with a pink ribbon around the crown." Metaphorically, Gielow argues that Sal's education changes her inside and out; she entered school and "the little mountain flower grew and developed with wonderful unfoldment."[25] Even her name changes, as Sal becomes Sarah. Practically, though, her education consists of a series of classed objects and behaviors she layers onto her body. *Old Andy* was published in 1909, the same year North Carolina organized its first tomato clubs. Sal's education neutralized the era's southern class tensions as she embraced the goals and desires of a white middle class, disarming future fracturing of political alliances. Each class could pull for Sal to succeed.

The price is significant, however willingly Andy and his wife pay it. Sarah is kept ignorant of her family's struggle until she happens to read in a newspaper about her grandfather's months of hiding from pursuing revenuers, arrest, and trial. As she runs home to help, she encounters a lawyer who turns out to be her long-lost father.[26] She and her father arrive at the courthouse just in time to deliver an impassioned plea to keep Andy from jail. Quickly, though, Gielow made it clear that the plea went beyond the family drama of the story. Melodramatic, certainly, the meeting of father and daughter moved the story beyond individual to broader cultural issues.

Gielow did not want girls like Sarah to disappear into middle-class life with their new education (written twenty-five years earlier, Harris's "At Teague Poteet's" ends with its main character vanishing into a comfortable life in prosperous Atlanta). Instead, Sarah plans to help other mountain residents join her in her new class position by refusing adoption by her father. He wants to take her "to a beautiful home... where my wife and little ones would love you, and where you can have books and music, and where I could be as a father to you." Instead, she persuades him to pledge successfully to the court, "I will endeavor to reclaim the mountain heights... to right the wrong of neglect to these people of the hills... [and to] carry the light into their darkness with Christian and industrial training"—a plan with which Sarah would help. The single gesture ushers other mountain residents along with Sarah into a modern South, with Sarah and her father working to "lift the cloud that hangs on their arrested progress and give them the sunlight of enlightened citizenship."[27] Gielow's *Old Andy* not only proposed teenage girls were waiting to be tamed or domesticated into mainstream American life, it also followed Stoneley's concept of how such taming could simultaneously resolve the class chaos and tensions in larger society. Setting it in the southern mountains further proposed that the teen girl could usher other white citizens into the national polity and solve racial and ethnic tensions increasingly feared by the middle class.

Gielow's narrative allows for at least two interpretations as the story wraps up in the courtroom. With tinges of social Darwinism, the first is a nativist argument that immigrants and African Americans were simply bad for America. In the epilogue, Gielow explicitly lists the racial and ethnic social tensions she saw wracking the nation: "The high percentage of illiterate native born whites in the Appalachian mountains is a menace to the future welfare of this country. We give millions every year ... for the education of emigrants and negroes [*sic*]. Let us give the same chance to these American children of the Nation." In other words, Gielow argued that "emigrants and negroes" threatened to take over the nation if whites remained uneducated. To avoid what many at the time called "race suicide," Gielow's solution bound poor whites and the white middle class together in alliance through the education of a girl called Sarah.[28]

The second interpretation unites American racial diversity in a single body. In the world of the novella, Sarah is effectively biracial (being half Appalachian and half middle-class white). Writing in an era of belief that Appalachians were ethnically and racially separate from other white Americans, Gielow argued that the infusion of Sal's father's middle-class, non-Appalachian blood explained why "from birth the marked difference between Sal and the other mountain children had been evident to all who looked upon her."[29] Sarah's body implies that other racial and ethnic diversity (such as that of the before-mentioned immigrants and African Americans) could also be united in a single American, the tamed teen. Stoneley's framework of the metaphorical "fixing" of such social tensions helps reveal what was underneath Sarah's biracial identity. While Gielow would likely have been horrified at the prospect of racial intermarriage in the United States, her narrative suggests that racial reconciliation through Sarah's education was possible. Similar to *Juletty*, this narrative has rhetorical space for either reading; the key is the debate itself.

In the novella, the debate centers around the courthouse scene, in which Sarah's father becomes the mouthpiece for Gielow's belief that fixing this Appalachian teen and her family could fix the nation. Gielow wrote on behalf of the Southern Industrial Educational Association (SIEA) of Washington, D.C., an organization actively participating in national debates. The SIEA was "incorporated and organized for promoting industrial education among the impoverished, uneducated mountain people of the Appalachian region."[30] Gielow used the end of her narrative to plead for donations to the cause. Industrial education, with its evocation of training good capitalists, including giving men like Old Andy careers beyond moonshining and turning girls like Sarah into teachers, was Gielow's solution to resolving social tensions.

Stoneley argues that the process of resolving those tensions often involved "buying into womanhood," which, in turn, made the teen girl a consumer item herself.[31] Sarah's father essentially attempts this, until he is persuaded to help save Andy and the other mountain residents instead. Stoneley's line of argument, however, puts the loving list of consumer goods that Sarah acquired in a different light. Unlike Juletty, who hides her money, Sarah wears her middle-class status proudly and attempts to spread it to others. All of this implies an unquestioning faith in the good of capitalism and mainstream United States society, one that the tomato club organizers discussed in chapter 3 mostly shared. By the time Sherwood Anderson created a female character in the moonshine literature, early twentieth-century optimism in the power of capitalism to create social well-being had weakened in the face of trusts, labor violence, and the Great Depression. But *Old Andy, the Moonshiner* could end in 1909 with a hopeful call for how industry and middle-class values would bring economic prosperity and racial peace (albeit perhaps in the form of reinvigorated white labor that would balance the power of immigrant organizing) through the work of properly educated teen girls.

Despite Cavanagh's cynical portrait and the loss of Gielow's style of optimism, by the time Sherwood Anderson penned his portrait of a female bootlegger leading a gang of men down mountain roads and through city streets, all was not grim. Readers could imagine and even admire a lawbreaking, brashly sexual, economically independent, successful southern woman without domestic ties. Though she exhibits features of both, neither frameworks for New Women nor those for teen girls works for such an outrageous character. Kit Brandon begins bootlegging while still in her teens; she "retires" from it in her thirties with fame and celebrity. The sex she has does not automatically result in children, and she refuses to apologize for enjoying it. She transports, helps produce, and even drinks moonshine. Kit refuses taming; rather, stories like hers suggested that her transgressions were precisely what Appalachia and the nation needed. She is a study in modernity, mobility, and consumer goods. The contradictions in her story parallel the difficult dreams in southern labor fiction haunted by the disease pellagra, our subject in chapter 4.

MOONSHINE NATION: MOBILITY, CONSUMERISM, AND *KIT BRANDON*

The new century brought about, if not the invention of, then the thoroughgoing influence of what J. M. Mancini calls a "hybrid, circulatory consumer culture." Advertising reached masses of Americans, through magazines, celebrity spokespeople, and burgeoning movie, radio, and publishing industries.

At the same time, people knew to look out for scams, fads, and fashion; with world wars, violent labor strikes, and lynch mobs also realities, consumers often had to develop strategies to survive in the marketplace. Looking through this third lens of consumer culture at a final set of female characters (who refused to be pinned down by class, gender, education, or even legality), we can see the nation revisiting its changing gender roles one more time through food and place.[32]

American studies scholar Mancini examines early country music (much of which emerged from the South), arguing rural southern hybrid culture paralleled modern, urban culture of the 1920s and developed its own "blurring of fixed social categories" in response to the complications of modern identities. Yet discussions of consumerism often focus on its emergence in urban centers and not in more rural or isolated areas of the nation. Mancini differs, arguing that rather than locating the consumer economy and the resultant modernity it fostered solely in "the clubs of Harlem, the back rooms of the Tenderloin, and the cafés of the Lower East Side," we should also expect it, for instance, "in the hollers of Appalachia." Although she talks specifically of music, another link between those speakeasies, backrooms, and Appalachia's hollers was what people drank (and bought to drink) as they listened to the music. In other words, moonshine lubricated the circulation of consumer culture, which in turn made space for changing definitions of femininity in the later moonshine literature. Anderson's 1936 novel, *Kit Brandon: A Portrait*, looks back to Prohibition and explores the effects of modernity, consumerism, and nation on one woman's life, affording us the possibility to explore gender, class, and nation in a story of moonshine literature.[33] Anderson (1876–1941) not only wrote one of the mill novels that chapter 4 explores, but he also drew attention to Kit's moonshine body and the consumer goods that alternatively cause her pain and free her from her surroundings, foreshadowing the haunting figure of the starved female mill worker, herself both consumed by and longing to consume twentieth-century southern cultures.

Anderson framed his portrait of a young Appalachian woman from east Tennessee who becomes a notorious bootlegger as an interview between the novel's first-person narrator and Brandon. Some years after the main action of the story, Brandon drives them around South Dakota and tells him her story. A multi-layered meditation, the book features narrative gaps, fragmented theories (both signaled by ellipses), and ambiguous speeches. Perhaps the gaps, fragments, and deliberately confounding quotation marks explain why Anderson's final novel remains understudied.[34]

The major difference between *Kit Brandon* and earlier pieces is that Anderson stepped back from the construction of isolated Appalachia, moonshiners, or even "the South" to examine them as exactly that: inventions used strategically by different people at different times. He included tourists, sensational news writers, national moonshine distributors, bored middle-class women, Kit, and the narrator among those who employed stereotypes about the region.[35] *Kit Brandon* suggested that if America could incorporate even a place as wild as Kit's mountain past, then anyone and any place could enter the nation, even through their most taboo foodways, moonshine. Characters like Brandon performed cultural work within and beyond the South as they explored how disposable labor became sophisticated producers and consumers. Through them, Anderson also explored the costs to society and individuals of such a transition. Unlike any of the previous works, Anderson's questioned how blurry the boundaries between legal and illegal, food and drink, and public and private practices really were. For the men and women entering textile mill work in the 1910s and 1920s, the questions of domestic and public, gender and food were similarly up in the air; moonshine rhetoric here stood behind the starving pellagrins who faced the failures of consumerism in the South.

When the novel begins, labor is at its most visible and yet most disposable moment—in the early 1920s. Simultaneously, Anderson's narrator argues, "the illicit liquor business was in its first full flush of success, as was the oil business when the elder Rockefeller, Mr. John D. himself, got in and the steel business when Andrew Carnegie began." Kit recognizes that her family's east Tennessee farm provides no long-term options against such powerful forces; from its failing acres, she watches "life, modern life, with its high-powered swift machines, new comforts, in clothes, houses, food—all of the modern conveniences of life—these passing on by." Further, Anderson signaled doubt that the individual New Woman could fix society's inequalities. He set the story during national Prohibition, at the moment when "politicians were in terror" of the Women's Christian Temperance Union. With his stated hostility to the WCTU and other benevolent activists, Anderson clearly disposed of Progressive rhetoric. Landing in one of the new southern factory boomtowns, Kit tries to be an average working-class woman, "being a factory girl, then a clerk in a store, in a city—it was a five-and-ten-cent store." Still not a New Woman with a career, Kit has little chance of fully supporting herself or her community and no transformative education appears to turn her into Katherine (as Sal became Sarah). Further, Kit's father attempts to sexually abuse her; he is no Old Andy, playing a positive role in the young girl's life, even with moonshine. Anderson rejected the power of education and uplift, calling it merely salve over white liberal guilt.[36] Fixing this teen girl through foodways would not resolve any larger racial, ethnic, and class problems, at least not in expected ways.

Instead, Kit enters bootlegging with her eyes open, hoping to make a lot of money, and she drives the moonshine all over the United States, radically redefining womanhood as she goes. She narrates "her marriage into a famous family of bootleggers in a certain Southern industrial town, her becoming, herself, first a little bootlegger, then a big one. Her becoming a notorious woman rumrunner... this during prohibition, of course... men met, some, she frankly said, even lain with."[37] By the end of the novel, untamed Kit has broken laws, claimed her own sexuality, and beaten men at business and smarts; she has embodied the worst fears of Juletty's revenuer Jack Burton and middle-class society. Although Kit spent time in jail, Anderson did not leave her there with Betsy Simms; instead, Kit got a future. Ironically, the key to the cultural work performed by Kit's story resides in Anderson's repeated invocation of Rockefeller, Carnegie, oil, and steel; channeling their examples, disposable female laborers like Kit could become sophisticated national consumers, emerging from the wild southern mountains to move on the national stage—but they had to break laws and risk respectability just as the robber barons had done.

Radically departing from the earlier moonshine literature's faith in development and capitalism, consumerism in *Kit Brandon* is a self-perpetuating cycle that damages its weakest participants. The novel's critique of capitalism begins in the mountains, as Anderson criticizes lumber and coal companies who had denuded and then deserted mountain communities. By the time Kit is a young woman, textile and furniture factories have replaced coal and lumber companies. This time the resources stolen are human: "A lot of factories had come down out of the North, the Middle West and out of New England into towns of Virginia, North Carolina and Tennessee—to lap up the cheap labor of hill billies and girls like Kit herself, girls who had left their mountain homes." Factories manipulated workers' desire for consumer goods, getting them "wanting what they could not get at home [...] new hats, silk stockings. They were wanting new dresses." Then, companies produced "cheaper, shabbier cloth, but keep the design and the colors. Make duplicates, plenty of them. The big mail-order houses sending the word out too, even to remote villages, to farms. In Paris today, in Beanville, Arkansas, three weeks from now." They sent the message, "Quick, buy copies of *Delineator, Ladies' Home Journal, Woman's Home Companion, McCall's Magazine*. Take home a copy of *Woman's Home Companion*, young woman. Keep up to snuff."[38] Such manipulation of desire (here, specifically feminine desire) set up a cycle in which working-class people took poorly paid jobs to earn money to buy consumer goods, finding themselves trapped in the jobs, wanting even more goods.

As including the marketing strategies of mail-order houses' catalogs hinted, the world of Anderson's novel is crossed with networks of circulating capital, raw materials, people, and intangibles such as desire. Instead of using it as a symbol of Appalachia's isolation, Anderson made moonshine a product of modern consumer marketing, tracing its evolution from relatively uncomplicated local drink to romanticized, complex advertising object. As a young girl, Kit served as lookout at her father's still. Later, Kit and her friends from the factories drink together the "raw, terrible drink [that] burned Kit's throat. Funny to think it might have been made by her own father, back up in the hills." Yet the recipe for this moonshine is not a precious inheritance from a great-grandfather or

George Washington; liquor here is "the story of every big American industry [...] The little makers in the hills, the old type of mountain moonshiner of romance, was being wiped out."[39] It is a thoroughly modern drink, produced for specific markets, quickly and with as much profit as possible.

Moonshine proves the very ingredient that makes Anderson's southern story rigorously contemporary, firmly anti-nostalgic. He provides long lists mixing Appalachian, Midwestern, and eastern states as sources for raw materials and destinations for finished products. Sugar and containers come into the mountains; "workingmen in all the industrial towns" of "the North, Pittsburgh, Youngstown, Akron, Toledo, Cleveland, Detroit, Indianapolis, St. Louis" demand "North Carolina moon, Tennessee moon, North Georgia moon"—some of which is "run" in from the "West Indies Islands" by way of New Orleans and "spots along the Gulf of Mexico." In other words, like other consumer goods, moonshine in *Kit Brandon* is a national phenomenon, drunk all over the country, manufactured all over the country, and shipped all over the country. Equally, *Kit Brandon* is not a story of lawbreakers disconnected from all normal society; the novel explores the layers of a market economy—the same people buying the illegal liquor are the town leaders and the mill owners prosecuting and driving Kit into the business by advertising and producing the consumer items she and other mountain workers desire. Yet the business works because captains of the moonshine industry maintain and export the idea of the lone mountain moonshiner in the southern wilderness; that moonshiner is their advertising campaign. This is where the "gun-toting, hard-eyed mountain man" makes his appearance in the novel.[40] Clients' concepts of remote Appalachia allow the moonshine business to expand, transporting liquor in cars unexpectedly driven by female Kit across the nation.

At first, the stereotype of the grizzled moonshiner works so effectively that Kit passes essentially invisibly, allowing her to complete more and more daring runs. Once those outrageous risks make Kit famous, her physical body slips away under others' ideas of how a moonshiner looks. The national imagination invents her as a female equivalent of the gunslinger, feeling no need to stay faithful to Kit herself. Posters describe "the reputation she was presently to get

... the romanticizing of her figure by the newspapers ... herself heralded as a desperate character, bold, beautiful, dangerous, etc., etc." Kit knows her wanted picture, titled "Kit, the rum-running queen" is "faked" by the "newspapers of big towns that circulated out through the country in which she worked." Those national papers describe "a tall slender young society girl, a debutante"; further, "there was a story of her great wealth. She was a beautiful young society girl who had gone into the game as an adventure." Some of the descriptions focus on Kit's imagined character traits, saying, "She was a dangerous woman, always armed and was said to have killed two or three men"—though the narrator reveals that Kit carries a gun only once in the whole novel. Finally, Kit becomes flamboyant, described by "one of the papers" as having "diamonds set in her teeth."[41] Many of Kit's imagined characteristics, such as her boldness, the diamonds in her teeth, and her willingness to take on other men, unpin her from local and national ideas of womanhood.

Other traits disconnect Kit from ideals of social class. She moves in multiple classes as the romance surrounding her life makes Kit an attractive figure for both "respectable women" who visit "her in jail, wanting her life" and for working-class women who see in her "a mountain girl, ex-mill girl, getting keen [...] Why should the daughters of mill owners, storekeepers, daughters of professional men, novel writers, etc., etc., have anything on you, cotton-mill girls, big department-store girls ... when it comes to handling men?" Both groups of women are inspired by Kit's message to "sharpen your wits. Life's a game. Women know. Working women, particularly."[42] In Kit's life, fixed gender and class roles are not simply blurred or stretched; rather, they are exploded by her moonshining female figure.

But what happens after the explosion? Once unfixed from gender and class, Kit steps into new hybrid identities marked by fluidity and change. Fellow runners and members of the moonshine gang are ethnically and racially diverse, and Kit moves among them with ease. In addition, her desire is no longer shaped by factory owners advertising in women's magazines; a sophisticated consumer, she chooses what and whom she desires, and, a savvy producer, she makes her own rules to acquire those things. For Anderson, the new identities were no longer Appalachian; they were American. Kit is described as like the "Rockefellers, Goulds, Harrimans," a radical, working-class, female, Appalachian, successful American for the early twentieth century. In the midst of the Depression, *Kit Brandon* suggested one did not have to be rich, white, male, or from New England to succeed on such a grand scale. Once famous (or infamous) enough that she has to keep a low profile, Kit reads "books that told about early adventurers in America, the pioneers who went out of the East to open up the West, western railroad builders, builders of bridges, books about men who bound all of America together, by railroad and telegraph lines. The pony express riders of western plains." Soon, "she at times felt herself some such a one," a free, flexible pioneer, not a confined, domestic female. In a moment in the novel at once radical and conventional, Kit becomes the earlier stories' gender role reconfigurations on a grand scale—she embodies American individual heroism. Yet, Anderson, wanting to create a new heroine for mainstream America, seemingly could only imagine her as a male hero in the distant American West.[43]

Unlike McElroy, who retreats into heterosexual romance to end her story, or Gielow, who uses the end of her story to call for donations, Anderson seems at a loss to resolve Kit's story. So he leaves Kit in faraway South Dakota, having "got what she thought she wanted, a swell car to drive, clothes, money to spend," but looking (vaguely) for "some sort of work that did not so separate her from others. There might be some one other puzzled and baffled young one with whom she could make a real partnership in living."[44] What exactly could a retired, notorious female moonshine bootlegger do in South Dakota? Whether read as a risk-taking hero embraced by all classes or a dangerous improper woman, Anderson's character created space through moonshine to debate gender in the 1930s.

For all the difficulty at the end, the narrator clearly admires Kit, and Anderson gives her a powerful symbol of her freedom and mobility—her car—that she manages to hold onto. Kit is hard to separate from her automobiles; no longer disposable labor herself, Kit acquires the ultimate American consumer item, a symbol of freedom and success. The narrator testifies, "she was the best driver I ever rode with, could get more out of a car without hurting the car. Like many modern people, she had got the feel of machinery down into her veins, into all of her body." *Kit Brandon* celebrates the automobile in Whitmanesque terms: "the new thing in man's life, the machine in America so perfect, so intricate. Doing so many marvelous things so marvelously. Youngsters, almost children, driving modern high-speed American automobiles, over American roads—such roads never before known in all the world. Let's begin to sing this." Anderson's song of ourselves (and our automobiles) especially resonates for a woman like Kit, who has "the feel of it, in [her] own body, in [her] hands. The purring thing down in front, under the hood of the car." Kit's motto is "don't cut down on your speed. Aim it! Shoot! Go across at speed! Control with the motor, not the brake" and her philosophy is "if you are going to get smashed you're going to get smashed"—not incidentally undercutting Anderson's attempts to put the brakes on Kit's adventures at the end of the novel. Anderson suggested that one of the sites of the invention of modern industrial life—Ford's assembly line—created a powerful symbol of escape from itself and from limiting ideas of gender, class, race, and food. In 1906, Mary Mullett agreed that "To the honor and the glory of the sex be it recorded, however, that the woman in front of the machine isn't the whole story. There is also the woman behind the machine." Mullett celebrated the female driver's steady hands with their "iron grip" on the wheel, the swift wits, and the "cool nerve which commands even a man's admiration."[45] Anderson's character Kit embraces her automobile just as wholeheartedly.

Rather than studying the novel, however, many scholars merely question whether Kit Brandon was real.[46] That they can find evidence of similar women points out the moonshine rhetoric tapped by Anderson. For instance, one scholar claims "more than a year before *Kit Brandon* was published, [Anderson] had spent several weeks interviewing Mrs. Willie Carter Sharpe, a woman rum-runner from southwestern Virginia whose exploits had become legendary and who was soon to be tried in one of the largest moonshining trials ever held in Virginia." Sharpe clearly inspired Anderson; his description of her in an essay entitled "City Gangs Enslave Moonshine Mountaineers," clearly resembled Kit. Anderson called Sharpe "a mountain child from a neighboring county, [who] as a child had gone down into a southern industrial town to work in a cotton mill"—a story the strike novels also echoed. Sharpe worked in an overall factory and a department store. After a marriage, she "began selling liquor around town, drumming up trade." Soon, Sharpe's "passion for automobiles" and driving skills put her at the head of "convoys of cars on the roads at night, herself in a fast car acting as pilot, government men, not fixed, coming in from Washington, the chase at night, cars scattering, dashing through the night streets of towns, the big business carried right on"—not a bad plot summary of *Kit Brandon*. But another scholar argues the model for Kit came instead from Anderson's newspaper articles written in 1928 about a woman named Mamie Palmer.[47] It is curious that literary scholars through the decades have worked so hard to determine if fictional Kit is real. Their efforts illustrate just how high the stakes were in portraying southern women whose relationship to food had nothing to do with the domestic or the socially accepted.

Kit and her automobile embodied the mobility and freedom to circulate literally in the moonshine nation. Theirs was an enduring partnership, described by Kit as "something of what a husband might be to her."[48] At their best, Kit Brandon and her car traveled through and around southern and national consumer culture, fluidly exploring the freedom of new class, region, and especially gender identities. The final cultural work of Anderson's novel merged the mountains, the South, and America into one large moonshine nation, erasing borders and citizenship, but illuminating the roadways and economies that bound the whole.

CONCLUSION

From the 1870s to the 1930s, stories about moonshine filled the pages of national magazines, catalogs of well-known presses, and columns of large-circulation newspapers. Authors from the South, such as Lucy McElroy and Joel Chandler Harris, writers who wrote almost exclusively about the mountains, such as Martha Gielow and George Creswell Gill, and people who only occasionally considered the South, such as Sherwood Anderson and Catherine Frances Cavanagh, all chose the background of moonshine for their American stories.

Tracing how writers of moonshine literature used their moonshining characters to negotiate and intervene in broad cultural and political debates shows that these characters are not merely buffoonish minor characters confined to stereotype. Characters in moonshine literature used a taboo food practice to explore gender roles during a period of shifting definitions. Moonshine characters wrestled with new gender roles and the implications of active, strong women who were not confined to domestic spaces or domestic foodways. They integrated young, newly invented teenage southerners (even racially diverse ones) into the nation through education while neutralizing potentially explosive gender, race, and class politics. And, finally, they ushered rural citizens into the new consumer economy, not simply as disposable labor but also as sophisticated producers and consumers. By the end of the era of moonshine literature, moonshine characters had performed crucial cultural work for the region. They show us the way into four other moments in the southern food story, those explored in the following chapters.

By the 1936 debut of *Kit Brandon*, the female, empowered, mobile moonshiner, could be "a curious American phenomenon," a "young, pretty, good-looking American woman on the move."[49] Out of an exclusively isolated moonshine imaginary, the safe space where New Womanhood's gender reconfigurations could be contained by marriages between Juletty and Burton and the solution to American racial and immigration politics enacted by the education of Sal, a national community of moonshine people and places emerged. Social, historical, and cultural moments played out in and on the body of the New Woman, teen girl, and female bootlegger—as they took a simple combination of corn, yeast, water, and sugar and turned it into the most taboo of foods, exposing the tensions and anxieties behind biscuits, canned tomatoes, mill food, and other secret food languages.

A scene happening across the region, "4-H club member making biscuits," 1920s, North Carolina. Courtesy of Special Collections Research Center, North Carolina State University Libraries, Raleigh, North Carolina.

CHAPTER TWO

Biscuits & Cornbread

RACE, CLASS, AND GENDER POLITICS OF WOMEN BAKING BREAD

IMAGINE YOU WERE a young mother in the rural southern mountains before the turn of the century. You did not have much ready cash on hand, but you did have a family to feed. For years, your easiest solution was to put together a pone of cornbread while you were finishing the rest of the meal. It served well to sop up the potlikker in the bowls of beans or greens; it was delicious cold with sorghum or honey for a breakfast or snack; it crumbled into buttermilk for a light end-of-day meal. Then, some single women with college educations came to your neighborhood to start a free school. Imagine your reaction when, before offering classes in math or reading or writing, they instead told you that cornbread imperiled the morals, the health, and the future prospects of your entire family. It was almost as if they were on a crusade. This chapter focuses on a particular movement that began in Appalachian eastern Kentucky, one that centered on social salvation through bread. A story of morals, hygiene, class, race, and gender-role alliances hides in the struggles over the choice between cornbread and biscuits.

When I was ten, my grandmother taught me to make biscuits. Sifted flour, buttermilk, baking powder, soda, some salt, and lard (vegetable shortening, in her later days) in mathematical proportion—measured carefully by me, eyeballed from years of practice by my grandmother—all are baked in a hot oven until fluffy and flaky. Biscuits are a deceptive recipe; they rely on an alchemy of ingredients, oven and touch. I may know her recipe, but I am still working on the touch; every time I move, I have to learn a new oven and keep practicing my skills. Still today, a pot of beans or vegetable soup in winter is incomplete without a skillet of cornbread. My mother made cornbread for dinner regularly; in fact, I cannot remember when I first ate it. I have been working on my cast-iron skillet to perfect its seasoning; my mother seems to be able to make good cornbread in any pan that comes to hand, but this is a trick I have not learned.

While the recipes have remained fairly stable over the past century, biscuits and cornbread have shifted in meaning since the 1870s. Today they are, at least for Americans of European and African descent, both quintessential southern and soul foods,[1] hallmarks of down-home or country cooking, and sources of nostalgia for "simpler" times. But when the nineteenth century turned into the twentieth, they had very different and distinct meanings. To some observers, one meant high culture, modern hygiene, and Progressive womanhood. Biscuit baking demonstrated class consciousness, the ability to acquire specialized ingredients, racially coded leisure time for certain women, consumer-marketed equipment, and nationally standardized consumption. Cornbread, on the other hand, symbolized ignorance, disease, and poverty. It could be made with locally produced ingredients, equipment made at home, and brief moments of time seized between other work; even at the turn of the century, it was regionally identified and nationally disparaged. A social history of class, race, and gender hides in the differing recipes and use of cornbread and biscuits.

COLLEGE GIRLS GO (FURTHER) SOUTH

Although university education for select women emerged out of the 1860s and 1870s, a national consensus about what women would do with their educated lives remained elusive. As southern African American intellectual Anna Julia Cooper argued in 1892, women's sphere, which fifty years earlier had been strictly defined as "kitchen and the nursery," was now so all-encompassing that "no plan for renovating society, no scheme for purifying politics, no reform in church or in state, no moral, social, or economic question, no movement upward or downward in the human plane" was outside their purview. The 1890s until the 1920s were the heyday of the Progressive Era—a time of settlement houses, New Women, public libraries, anti-tuberculosis campaigns, "Lifting as We Climb," temperance, and, of course, suffrage. Regionalist women's writing enjoyed great success; many local color authors chose the South as the setting of their fiction.[2] Women like Cooper, Amelie Troubetzkoy, Miss Matt Crim, Emma Bell Miles, Grace MacGowan Cooke, and Maria Louise Pool chose careers in writing. Margaret Morley combined writing with the scientific practice of being a naturalist; still others, like Annie Fields and Martha McCulloch-Williams focused their scientific impulses on cooking and the emerging profession of home economics.

Many women became teachers and activists; May Stone (1867–1946) was one of them. In 1884, Kentucky-native Stone entered Wellesley College, scarcely nine years after it opened. Despite leaving college a year before she was to graduate, Stone gained entrance into the group of socially conscious, educated women looking for careers. She found hers by participating in women's clubs and the club-sponsored "mountain work" in eastern Kentucky. Historian Anne Firor Scott documents the projects taken on by southern women's clubs by 1900: "they organized libraries; expanded schools; tackled adult illiteracy; organized settlement houses; fought child labor; supported sanitary laws, juvenile courts, pure water, modern sewage systems; planted trees; and helped girls to go to college." As if modeling the combination of turn-of-the-century projects mapped by Scott, Kentucky-native Katherine Pettit (1868–1936) joined May Stone in eastern Kentucky to lead the rural settlement house movement, establish libraries, teach elementary school, facilitate girls' applications to college, and plant trees. When the opportunity arose, both women left for what they thought were short adventures in the mountains. Pettit and Stone were middle-class, white, educated women who came to Appalachia with the idea of helping the less fortunate; once they reached the mountains, each chose to stay for the rest of her life. They were not alone in their efforts;

as historians Jess Stoddart, Deborah Blackwell, and Nancy Forderhase have researched, dozens of similar women came to the southern highlands. Some, such as Lucy Furman, combined their activism with writing autobiographical fiction. All were ready to "help"—but what help was most needed was often strangely defined.[3] In the early decades, that help often took the form of cooking lessons.

One of the most well-known experiments run by Progressive women in the South during this era was Pettit and Stone's Hindman Settlement School. Starting their very first summer, when they were staying in tents because the school had no buildings yet, Pettit and Stone kept journals. Far from being private diaries, Pettit and Stone's journals were used for fundraising, read aloud, passed from hand to hand, excerpted, and strategically deployed. Today, they give us a picture of the school's early years.[4] Although Stone took courses at Wellesley, which prided itself for offering rigorous, gender-neutral education, at the school in the mountains, female students were introduced to "domestic science" alongside, and sometimes even before, reading, writing, or arithmetic.

In the early 1800s, advocates of domestic economy, such as Harriet Beecher Stowe and Catharine Beecher, emphasized women's work inside homes. They prescribed kitchen layouts, charted foods to budget and serve, and argued the world could be changed by careful management of the home sphere. By the end of the century, this activism took two related but more public directions. The first was the establishment of cooking schools, demonstration kitchens, and laboratory research to improve the products of the home kitchen. From the famous Boston Cooking School, which had much to say about the dangers of ill-prepared food, to the domestic training kitchens at settlement houses, historically black colleges, and women's clubs, which aimed to professionalize the role of household servants and maids, a generation of women debated gender roles in the modern kitchen. Such women produced cookbooks, reports, and training manuals, many of which argued there was hardly a social ill that could not be improved by professionalizing the home kitchen. Annie Fields, for instance, felt that cooking encouraged temperance and countered the evils of drink. In the report *How to Help the Poor*, she argued "that cooking schools and the knowledge of cheap and savory preparation of food must soon have their effect on the percentage of drunkards no one can question... [T]his question of food underlies all." As food scholars Harvey Levenstein and Laura Shapiro have documented, the solutions proposed by activists like Fields often vilified immigrant, ethnic, and regional foodways, in favor of a bland, northeastern, WASP-ish food tradition, something fully operational in the struggles over cornbread.[5]

The second, related approach brought the problems of the world into the home through reformers locating settlement houses in the public center of communities struggling with massive social change. The most famous of the reformers was Jane Addams; her Hull House settlement brought activist women into urban Chicago's immigrant communities and pioneered a system of two-way learning and listening between activists and residents. Links between Hull House and Pettit and Stone were both intellectual and personal; they shared staff and correspondence on the developing concept. Hindman, however, was an early, rural incarnation of the settlement model. Residents and teachers lived, worked, cooked, and learned together on the grounds, which meant no domestic practice was too private for Pettit and Stone to investigate.[6]

According to Pettit and Stone, they were summoned in 1899 by a letter sent from the Reverend J. T. Mitchell to the State Federation of Women's Clubs in Kentucky. Although Stone and Pettit educated both men and women, cooking lessons for women were a core element of their mission from the beginning. Mitchell requested they "conduct... meetings of wives, mothers, housekeepers, young ladies and little girls. Lectures and lessons in cooking and homemaking should be made particularly enthusiastic and then the intellectual and moral features can be made interesting."[7] Not only were women defined by Mitchell, Pettit, and Stone in the categories of wife, mother, and housekeeper before all others, but also cooking and homemaking were presented as *the* path for southern mountain women to follow to reach the intellectual and moral positions occupied by Pettit, Stone, and their teachers.

COOKING LESSONS

According to evidence from their letters, diaries, and fiction, the teachers began the enthusiastic lessons by targeting the staple food of mountain residents, cornbread. They sought to replace it with what they considered a more healthful, appropriate, and civilized alternative, the white, wheat-based biscuit and light bread. Corn was, of course, not the only characteristic ingredient used by Appalachian cooks, as we explored in the introduction; teachers could have targeted wild berries, ramps (those uniquely strong wild onions whose odor can follow eaters for days after consumption), or mountain trout, for instance. Yet corn, as chapter 1 discussed, already had a metaphoric target on its back from its association with moonshine. Hindman's teachers were simply fascinated by mountain moonshine. Daisy Dame had her adventures at a still around the Oneida Baptist School, around the corner from Hindman. Her sister Olive Dame Campbell, who visited both places, conflated "mountain" families and "moonshine" families in the photojournals she created for the Russell Sage Foundation, labeling the same photograph one or the other, depending on the journal's audience. Pettit and Stone helped with Campbell's photographs, as she visited Hindman frequently, and her fundraising efforts in turn brought attention to the school. The plots of Lucy Furman's Hindman novels, *Mothering on Perilous* and *The Quare Women*, centered around feuds fueled by moonshine. Even the women's first summer diaries recorded moonshine used as medicine, currency, and source of language creation in the mountains.[8] Targeting liquor drinking and the feuds moonshine produced, teachers were already predisposed to think of corn as a problematic ingredient. What is fascinating, however, are the ways the danger of cornbread extended beyond its shared ingredient with moonshine.

Not every association clustering around cornbread was negative. Pettit and Stone benefited from corn's complementary side, which was fortunate for them. If corn had only and entirely been negatively connected to illegal liquor production, it and its region might have been seen as too dangerous, unable to be saved, and overall too corrupting for women working alone to address.

Larger American food practices could also be evoked through corn to justify the women's continued presence in the mountains. Food historian Mark McWilliams argues that in the early colonial period corn was used to distinguish the future United States from Britain. Eating corn declared one's allegiance to the new country as effectively as throwing tea into the harbor. By the mid-1800s, in the Northeast and coastal population centers in the South, corn was no longer such a mark of national pride; it had, in fact, been largely replaced by the consumption of other grains. But after 1876 and the nation's centennial celebrations (which included much rekindled interest in colonial foodways), corn became a nostalgic and patriotic symbol of America. Thus, for fundraising purposes, and as a justification of their presence, corn proved particularly symbolically useful for the women going to the mountains to teach.

Appalachians' old-fashioned reliance on corn supported the popular configuration of them as what William Frost, president of nearby Berea College, termed "our contemporary ancestors"—quaint but safe for modern single (white) women activists to go among. Pettit, Stone, and other Progressive women in Appalachia were in fierce competition for limited philanthropic monies; they drew from the same pool of donors as contemporary projects, for instance, with African Americans, Mormons, Eskimos, and Philippinos.[9] Portraying cornbread-eating Appalachians nostalgically as living ancestors made them worthy American subjects for funding from philanthropists of both conservative and liberal political leanings—and, thus, let the Progressive women set forth with their lectures and lessons in cooking.

Pettit and Stone also benefited from corn's strangeness to their colleagues in the Progressive movement. Amy Kaplan argues in her much-cited article, "Manifest Domesticity," that "when we contrast the domestic sphere with the market or political realm, men and women inhabit a divided social terrain, but when we oppose the domestic to the foreign, men and women become national allies against the alien." Kaplan examines how women at the turn of the century supported and were active in the United States' overseas expansion, even from their home armchairs. She argues that men and women's whiteness united them much more strongly than gender divided them.[10] Perhaps in this sense it was more than poetic that the recipe Pettit and Stone recommended was made with a much whiter grain than most corn. Although the South and its mountains were part of the United States from very early in the colonial period, and although women like Pettit and Stone constantly insisted on the whiteness of residents, they also emphasized for readers the unfamiliar, foreign, and alien in Appalachian food. On some level, women like Pettit and Stone wanted to ally with men—the men running philanthropic organizations, the men shaping public educational policy, the male Progressive leaders with whom they worked. They wanted to be much more than teachers in remote places—they wanted to be national leaders, successes, well-funded experts called on to help solve American problems. Corn supported the project of constructing an "Appalachian race" and shored up the legitimacy of women who taught beaten biscuits instead.

Early in their journals, Pettit and Stone reported as a success that "Mrs. Green and two girls came and wanted to learn to make light bread, but it was so late that we taught them how to make good soda biscuit instead."[11] The Hindman women considered soda biscuit, using white wheat flour and baking soda worthy of being taught in a pinch. Light bread, using white wheat flour and yeast, was even better. My grandmother's biscuits resembled the soda biscuits Pettit and Stone described; their light breads preceded store-bought bread loaves.

More appropriate for the mountain women, judging by its appearance in Pettit and Stone's journals, was the beaten biscuit. This was the recipe they most preferred to teach and crowned as the height of domestic achievement. For a special occasion, Katherine Pettit noted she was "up earlier than usual this morning to make beaten biscuit for Miss McCartney's luncheon." She and Stone were pleased when native mountain woman "Ida Francis... walked down with a pint of flour to learn to make beaten biscuit for her sick brothers." For other families, they "promised to send them some beaten biscuit and go Wednesday to show the mother how to make them." So important was the beaten biscuit to their efforts that contemporaries looking to criticize the Hindman women derided the entire project as the "beaten biscuit crusade."[12]

Only when we examine the recipe for beaten biscuits do we begin to understand why Katherine Pettit had to get up early to prepare them. Contemporary chef Bill Neal, in his *Southern Cooking*, writes that the beaten biscuit involves flour, salt, sugar, lard, and cold water. He lists the necessary equipment as a "mixing bowl; blending fork; wooden spoon; mallet, cleaver, or rolling pin, biscuit cutter, and baking sheet." Anyone cooking this recipe needs a way to regulate the temperature for baking (such as an oven), and a board or flat table that is sturdy enough for the beating process. In 1913, journalist and cookbook author Martha McCulloch-Williams claimed that, for the perfect beaten biscuit, "householders, and especially suburban ones, should indulge in the luxury of a block or stone or marble slab—and live happy ever after." These perfect blocks, stones, or slabs were crucial because what distinguished the beaten biscuit was that not only was it mixed in a bowl and kneaded on a board (Neal suggests twenty-five strokes), but also it was beaten with the mallet on a hard surface. Neal calls for at least three hundred strokes for one's family and five hundred for company.[13] The idea was to leaven it by capturing small pockets of air in the beaten and folded dough. As my godmother suggested when I told her I was writing this chapter, the beaten biscuit was nothing like a good cat-head biscuit that we might long for today (in other words, each one as big as and as fluffy as a cat's head). The Hindman women's beaten biscuit had no leavening and thus was much more like today's crackers or an unsweetened English biscuit.

Reading Katherine Pettit and May Stone's journals today, one might think that the mountain women cooked no bread at all until Progressive activists came along to teach them. In fact, as most fiction about Appalachia (written both by women from the region and elsewhere) made clear, Appalachian women baked plenty of bread. The action in Maria Louise Pool's novel, *In Buncombe County*, centers on the visit of two white, upper-class women tourists to the mountains outside of Asheville, North Carolina. Watching two mountain girls fix dinner, one observes, "They mixed a pone and set it down in its kettle by the fire; they called it 'making bread'."[14] This was not wheat bread. Instead, these characters, and Appalachian women in general, cooked cornbread. And corn pone, hoecake, dog bread, hush puppies, corn fritters, and spoon bread. The basic ingredients of all the recipes—cornmeal, buttermilk, lard, and salt, occasionally embellished with an egg or two and additional (although not strictly necessary) leavening—needed only a bowl and spoon and a source of heat. Unlike biscuits, cornbread could be cooked in a variety of conditions—over an open fire or in an oven—and in a variety of containers—a skillet, Dutch oven, the proverbial hoe, or even just flat on a hot hearth.

Although these were just a few variations of the basic recipe, almost all of the cornbreads could be mixed in the time it took to heat a skillet. Unlike in other parts of the South and for many African American southerners, most Appalachian cornbreads did not include flour or sugar. Tommie Bass, from northeast Alabama's mountains, recalled for his memoirs his mother's basic recipe: "When mother made cornbread, she added baking soda, not always. It was about a teaspoonful to a cupful of meal. And she added a little salt and sugar and buttermilk, to make a thick batter. Then she melted a little grease (lard) in the hot skillet, and drained that into the batter. And she put a little dry cornmeal in the hot skillet, and put it back on the stove." He continued, "When the dry cornmeal was brown, she knew the skillet was hot enough to pour in the batter. She put the skillet of batter in the stove and cornbread would just swell up, you know, and become just as light as it could be."[15] It was an adaptable and forgiving recipe.

Other writing of the era gave a sense of the ubiquity and flexibility of cornbread baking in Appalachia. A short story by Tennessee author Grace MacGowan Cooke, "The Capture of Andy Proudfoot," tells the story of a northern, Irish bounty hunter searching for and then deciding to abet a fugitive mountain man. Cooke mentions meals of corn pone and fish that Andy and his potential captor eat in a mountain hideaway. At most, Andy and his captor have camp equipment; their cornbread is cooked over an open fire. If they have milk or eggs, they stole them. Theirs is probably a very simple combination of meal, water, and possibly lard. Margaret Morley described such a recipe in her 1913 naturalist text about the areas around Asheville, North Carolina, *The Carolina Mountains*. A mountain man told her, "'Stoves?... I ain't never owned a stove and I don't never aim to. I don't see no use in stoves noway. I would n't have one in the house. You can't bake bread in a stove. I don't want nar' thing but meal and water mixed together and baked in the fire. I don't want salt in the bread. I was raised on that bread and it is the best in the world.'" From her position of middle-class adventurer, Morley commented archly, "Imagine a condition where one's physical wants are reduced to corn-meal and water." On a different end of the political spectrum, Miss Matt Crim, in "The Strike at Mr. Mobley's" (an antifeminist story of women's domestic work stoppage gone wrong in a mountain community), opens with Mrs. Mobley cooking her family vegetables and cornbread in her well-appointed kitchen. When order is restored, Mrs. Mobley is right back there with the cornbread. Similarly, Amelie Rives Troubetzkoy's novel, *Tanis, the Sang-Digger*, tells the melodramatic story of a mountain woman who makes a living digging ginseng root in Virginia until she meets a northern, middle-class family and is taken in to be their maid. Mountain resident Sam chooses to eat corn pone and honey while waiting for Tanis, his girlfriend, to finish her domestic duties serving the wife of a railroad engineer. Even in Pettit and Stone's journals, we glimpse how pervasive cornbread was; they mention a "Mrs. Godsey, over seventy, [who] brought her turn of corn to the mill and then came here to learn to make bread."[16] If we could ask her, Mrs. Godsey might have said that she was not ignorant of bread making, but that she first took care of her family's everyday staple and then learned a new luxury for special occasions—wheat bread or beaten biscuits.

CLASS CONSCIOUSNESS

For turn-of-the-century mountain women, choosing whether to cook cornbread or biscuits was not simply a question of what a woman or her family preferred on any given day. Instead, as the texts and memoirs of the time revealed, the decision made a statement about class in the Appalachian mountains. The biscuit, in other words, marked middle- and upper-class status in 1900. Pettit and Stone judged the households into which they were invited by the breads they were served for dinner. For instance, they reported that "the Cornets are all clean and thrifty"; the *only* evidence of cleanliness and thriftiness that they gave readers was: "They had a good dinner, beautiful honey and whole wheat biscuit from the wheat they had raised themselves." According to the Hindman teachers, the Cornets were in contrast to most of the mountain residents, who "live on fat bacon, cornbread and a few vegetables, all cooked in the most unwholesome way. Everything is fried in as much grease as they can get." Prioritizing their cooking plan, the Hindman teachers noted, "Our efforts in the line of cooking were to teach them to make good bread, to cook the vegetables in as many ways as possible, and the meat without so much grease."[17] For Pettit and Stone, domestic practices marked the achievements of superior social classes. Moral and intellectual lessons could follow once bread making was standardized.

In the journals, mountain residents are not the only group whose class dynamics are illuminated by a focus on corn. In their resistance to, yet interaction with, the ingredient, women like Pettit and Stone could "elude classification" in the way literary scholar Amy Lang suggests female protagonists did in mid-nineteenth-century domestic novels. Lang argues, "the sign of successful membership in the middle class in domestic novels lies squarely in the capacity of the female protagonist to elude classification, to take possession of an ideal self putatively outside class—and therefore outside history—and thus able freely to negotiate the divergent social universes of the rich and the poor." In other words, the perfect middle-class female heroine in nineteenth-century novels freely interacts across all class positions; she moves easily between the very rich and the very poor. Reading with Lang's framework that "unlike the drudge or the belle, whose places in the scheme of social classification are clear, the point of the 'woman' is that she has no particular class location" makes Pettit and Stone's journals (which, after all, were deliberately crafted for a public audience) even more interesting. If needy Appalachians were drudges and potential philanthropists were belles, then Pettit and Stone, who literally split time between the two groups, were the perfect middle-class figures. Even scholars refer to them as "Hindman women," not "Hindman ladies"; they themselves discussed the freedom of being out of fashion and away from balls and gowns, and yet they still were aware of that world in which they were no longer imprisoned. It was useful for people like Pettit and Stone, who thoroughly enjoyed their mobility in Appalachia but who were equally invested in being able to move back and forth into communities outside of Appalachia. And it was especially important since committing to life in Appalachia often carried a heavy economic cost (neither Pettit nor Stone made much money of their own, and what they did gather mostly went right back into schools) but could "pay off" in social mobility, authority, and legitimacy.[18] The beaten biscuit recipe became currency or passport in this exchange as it served to buy them entrance to the Appalachian kitchens and give them safe passage back to American middle-class communities.

When she was not taking photographs of mountain families that might or might not be moonshiners, Olive Campbell edited her husband John's widely influential *The Southern Highlander and His Homeland*. In it, Campbell proposed that class and bread could be charted together to reveal social hierarchies in the South. He argued, "It is probably safe to say that the main sustenance of many a rural household a good share of the winter is fat pork, beans, potatoes, and cornbread, with the addition of sorghum or honey and strong cheap coffee. Soda biscuit of wheat flour, and 'grits' are also used extensively among families in better circumstances. 'Light bread,' or raised white bread, is very unusual." In other words, cornbread was available to almost everyone; middle-class residents added in wheat-based soda biscuits; but only the most financially and socially upper-class people could choose to eat the yeast breads regularly. In fiction, it was often passed as unremarkable that people of higher classes would avoid cornbread. While Sam, in Troubetzkoy's *Tanis, the Sang-Digger*, eats corn pone in the servant's area, Alice Gilman, the middle-class railroad engineer's wife new to the mountains, offers her guests biscuits and milk.[19] Although both corn pone and biscuits emerge from the same kitchen, the mediating figure of Tanis, an Appalachian woman hired to serve biscuits but eat cornbread, further codifies the class-bread hierarchy.

While Pool, Troubetzkoy, and even occasionally Pettit and Stone implied that all mountaineers were poor—eating cornbread, unaware of the modern world—memoirs of the time supported the Campbells' argument that there was a range of class positions in the mountains. Joe Gray Taylor in his *Eating, Drinking, and Visiting in the South: An Informal History* wrote, "the amount of wheaten bread consumed rose with wealth and social position." Anecdotally, he also remembered that "everyone of substance that I knew ate them [biscuits] for breakfast." Herbalist Tommie Bass reminisced, "Back in my days, biscuits made from wheat flour was special for the poor people." Alabama resident William Bradford Huie grew up in the southern tip of the Appalachians. In his semi-autobiographical novel, *Mud on the Stars*, he wrote, "Biscuit for breakfast is a social and economic self-measurement among croppers and hands. Those who always have biscuit for breakfast regard themselves as successful persons of dignity. They pity and look down on the unfortunate who have to go back to corn pone during hard times."[20] A friend of mine, a medical doctor, recalls her grandfather-in-law asking her upon her marriage whether she could make biscuits; when she said no, he said, "Well, can you at least make cornbread?"

Thus, we find a dividing line primarily between corn and wheat, with gradations on each side. Yeast bread and beaten biscuits occupied one end of a food-and-class hierarchy; the many varieties of cornbread occupied the other. Soda biscuits and quick breads filled the middle ground. The logic of the divisions reveals much about gender and race in the South around 1900. This logic can be seen more clearly when we examine the ingredients, equipment, leisure time, and national standards encoded in the recipes themselves.

INGREDIENTS

The most obvious difference between biscuits and cornbread was their ingredients. Biscuits usually required wheat flour, but it was difficult for mountain residents to grow wheat. Significant annual rainfall and frequent shade around Appalachian fields meant that wheat was particularly susceptible to the growth of fungi. Taylor documented the effect of rust fungus on wheat and suggested that, compared to corn, wheat with rust yielded much less usable food. A mountain family needed large, cleared, unshaded fields and the economic security to afford less efficient planting if they were to grow wheat—or they needed the financial security to purchase food not from their own gardens or farms. African American Appalachian families in both rural and urban mountain communities tended to be in worse economic shape than their white counterparts—which meant either they were less likely to afford growing or using wheat regularly or they joined the first waves of the Great Migration out of the rural South. For all families, Taylor pointed out, "Corn demanded little skill in cultivation, and it was certainly easier to gather a given amount of corn than to harvest half as much wheat. Perhaps most important of all, corn was much easier to process with the crude machinery available." Wheat, then, required a greater investment of labor at all stages of its production. Tommie Bass revealed another reason that southern farmers favored corn when he remarked, "Corn is a wonderful plant, we didn't waste any of it"; he then described the medicinal value of cornsilk tea, recipes with hominy, corn as feed for both people and stock, and even corncob toilet paper. All of these factors were behind what Pettit and Stone observed: "very little wheat is raised in the mountains."[21]

For women, the differences between wheat and corn were particularly significant. Unlike wheat, corn was a garden plant; even a woman living in a rigid patriarchal system—which some parts of Appalachia surely were—could "handle" growing corn if she had to. Frances Goodrich, in her memoir of founding a woman-based handicraft industry in the North Carolina mountains at the turn of the century, *Mountain Homespun*, portrayed Aunt Liza, who showed off her garden with pride. Liza said, "Ever since my old man died I've made enough corn to do me, and sweetening too. The boys they come and plough for me in the spring of the year; they'd be willing to do more than that, but I believe in working, then a body has something."[22] Women in mill towns, women with children or other domestic responsibilities, black women working in white women's homes or as laundrywomen (common occupations throughout this time period), and women on their own could grow a patch of corn without too much physical or social difficulty. For families without many resources, the return on the investment made planting corn by far the better decision.

CONSUMER-MARKETED EQUIPMENT

Once grown, both corn and wheat were ground into flour. Yet, race, class, and gender differences in the choice between corn and wheat were not left behind at the mill. Visitors to and writers from Appalachia at the turn of the century often commented on the mountain residents' lack of proper cooking utensils. The Campbells noticed that, in one mountain family they visited, they "found the mother baking pies. She was rolling out the crust, not on a molding board but on a piece of cloth spread on the table, her rolling-pin being a round bottle." Tennessee native Emma Bell Miles, writing in her semi-autobiographical, theoretical *The Spirit of the Mountains*, concurred with the Campbells, since, "I have seen a woman carry water, dress a fowl, mix bread, feed her cow and pick up chips all in the same big tin pan, simply because it was the only vessel she had; I have seen pies rolled out and potatoes mashed with a beer-bottle found in the road." But these were not isolated instances; Olive and John Campbell suggested that even in the country stores in Appalachia "cooking utensils are exceedingly scarce."[23] Equipment for cooking targeted women's daily lives particularly; both Miles and the Campbells implied that even if mountain women wanted to move up the class scale from cornbread to biscuits, they might have had difficulty acquiring the additional equipment that biscuit making entailed.

Pettit and Stone, reflecting the philosophies of their parallel, cooking-school, Progressive colleagues, linked moral and mental strength to domestic science's emphasis on cleanliness, purity, and standardized cooking. Even if women baked wheat-based pie crusts or bread, beer bottles were not acceptable equipment for doing so. Thus, the class-bread hierarchy was not measured simply by the end product placed on the family table. The *equipment* employed to cook was as important an element in the class-bread hierarchy as that which was being cooked. Recalling her experiences as a teacher during the early Hindman years, Furman described the proper equipment and method of cooking in her novel *The Quare Women*: a "very pretty young woman, in a crisp gingham dress and large white apron, was kneading a batch of light-bread dough, and explaining the process of bread-making as she worked." Furman emphasized the clothes one needed to cook properly, the tables, ingredients, and recipes that would help in the kitchen. But the process, for Furman, did not stop when the kneading was over. She continued, "After the dough was moulded into loaves and placed in the oven of a shining new cook-stove," the crowd moved on to another tent to learn the proper way to set tables to receive the bread.[24] This emphasis on process reminded readers that the ultimate goal of the lessons extended beyond the recipe in question.

The Hindman teachers worried about their students, saying, "Add to bad air, dirt and bad cooking, the use of tobacco by men, women and even children as soon as they can walk and talk, and how can we expect good health? And without any regard to the laws of health, how can the people be strong, mentally or morally?"[25] As their Rev. Mitchell suggested, moral and educational gains were to follow from women teaching other women how to cook. But how were the activist teachers supposed to measure their moral successes? The visible signs of new cooking equipment became a way to judge not only material success—they also stood in for the mountain residents' spiritual accomplishments. Thus, rather than quizzing the Cornet family on their morals and beliefs, Pettit and Stone treated them as a successful mountain family on the evidence of the table their women presented.

Yet, few of these writers suggested how to make the biscuit's additional equipment available to all of the mountain women. Few interrogated how the very class system into which they were placing biscuits contributed to some women having to use beer bottles and others getting to judge the moral character of women without rolling pins. The difference between equipment for biscuits and cornbread was essentially, with the exception of the pan, a matter of local versus imported goods—and that was a question of barter and handicraft versus cash money. Biscuits worked better with marble rolling boards, rolling pins, biscuit cutters, mallets or cleavers, and ovens with consistent and steady temperatures. Most of that equipment needed to be purchased either through the network of general stores with access to railroad lines or by means of mail-order catalogs such as Sears, Roebuck and Co. or Montgomery Ward, which relied heavily on the rural free delivery mail service begun in the late 1890s.[26]

Of course, in the 1890s and 1900s, when Hindman was established, many southern mountain residents were well integrated into cash economies. In the area immediately around Hindman, heavy industry, including mining and railroad construction, connected residents to large national markets. The difference between the two recipes' ingredients, however, turned on the detail that cornbread did not *require* active, successful participation in the networks. Cornbread needed only a bowl, a spoon (although fingers would do), a skillet of some kind, and a heat source. Unlike many of the biscuit items, bowls, spoons, and fires for cornbread could be created out of resources readily available in the mountains. Wooden bowls, wooden spoons, and open fires or fires in hand-built hearths and chimneys worked fine for cornbread; all could be made or traded for by the women themselves. Cooks did not need national currency to make cornbread. Even the poorest mountain woman could fashion the container, spoon, and heat source to produce cornbread for her family.

TIME FOR WORK AND LEISURE

Another significant difference between the two recipes concerned the time necessary to produce each. In her journal, Stone related an incident in which "Miss Pettit went to make beaten biscuit for the sick boys while they all looked on." She noted that the boys then "asked if it was worth while to go to so much trouble."[27] And in fact, while writing this chapter, I tried out Bill Neal's recipe for beaten biscuits; while I am sure that Pettit was more practiced than I, she could not have significantly shortened the time and direct attention it took me to make them (and I just barely made it to the three hundred strokes for family, much less the exemplary five hundred strokes he recommends).

Household economies encompassed more than the labor of an individual. I had no help in beaten biscuit making, but some turn-of-the-century women did. The leisure time to put beaten biscuits on the table often suggested hired women's time and labor; in the South, that often implied black women's time and labor. Although many of Appalachia's corps of activist teachers were from the Northeast, Katherine Pettit and May Stone came from downstate Kentucky. While it is difficult to trace the origin of the first beaten biscuit recipe, some suggest that it began in the low country South. As food historian Joseph Dabney writes in his reflection on southern mountain cooking, *Smokehouse Ham, Spoon Bread, and Scuppernong Wine*, "My first inclination . . . was to omit any mention of 'beaten biscuits,' since they appeared to be more of an upper-class tidewater status symbol dish that depended on a lot of labor." He lists recipes for them from Philadelphia, Virginia, and Kentucky. The author of one of the earliest extant African American cookbooks, Abby Fisher, began *What Mrs. Fisher Knows about Old Southern Cooking* with "Maryland Beat Biscuit," presumably a recipe she learned while cooking for white plantation families before she moved to San Francisco.[28] In other words, the recipe that was so championed by activists in Appalachia most likely developed in the race politics of the antebellum nineteenth-century South.

That beaten biscuits featured so prominently in Martha McCulloch-Williams's 1913 cookbook, *Dishes and Beverages of the Old South*, fit with the larger plantation nostalgia sweeping the United States in the early twentieth century. Southern foodways—by fetishizing both recipes (like beaten biscuits) and cooks (like Mammy)—became a centerpiece of the social movement that sought to reconcile the nation to Jim Crow segregation while romanticizing lost racial divisions. Writing in the 1930s about south Georgia and Florida in *Their Eyes Were Watching God*, Zora Neale Hurston said her character Janie "went to see [her grandmother] Nanny in Mrs. Washburn's kitchen on the day for beaten biscuits"; Nanny's task reminded readers of the time-consuming tasks the Mrs. Washburns of the world could ask of their black Nannys in order to continue hierarchies of white privilege well into the twentieth century.[29]

Teaching mountain women that they should find time—their own or someone else's—to make beaten biscuits subtly supported the racial politics associated with other parts of the South (and existing throughout the United States). In fact, in cooking and elsewhere, Pettit, Stone and other white activists replicated the politics in their writings. Although the mountains did not have so firmly entrenched a tradition of slavery and class division based on domestic workers as other parts of the South, Pettit and Stone found African American Appalachian women to hire as servants. These women, who were rarely named in Pettit and Stone's journals, primarily washed clothes; nevertheless, one white teacher "made bread this morning and showed the wash woman how to make it."[30] Cornbread, on the other hand, was something that could be easily prepared by anyone after other paid or unpaid work was completed.

This issue of available leisure time to prepare breads other than cornbread belied a mixed message in women's activism throughout the nineteenth century: where and how a woman should spend her leisure time. Upper- or middle-class white women activists worked *outside* their homes—to improve society for other women and to spread the values of feminine virtue—but the ideal they presented to working women defined success as having the leisure to spend more time *inside* the home. For activists, coming to the mountains meant escaping traditional domestic life; they enjoyed the outdoors, they hiked, sketched, and rode horses unaccompanied by fathers, husbands, or brothers.[31] But they taught local working women how to bake biscuits—and in so doing pushed them to stay inside domestic spheres. Had everyone the ability to bake biscuits, women like Pettit and Stone would become unnecessary in the mountains—so rarely did these activists publically question the economic and social reasons behind Appalachians' seeming preference for cornbreads.

Staying in Appalachia meant prolonging their own freedom and mobility; staying was an escape from domestic duties awaiting them at home. Yet, ironically, staying took away from some southern mountain women freedoms they had previously enjoyed. Emma Bell Miles suggested of mountain women that "at an age when the mothers of any but a wolf-race become lace-capped and felt-shod pets of the household, relegated to the safety of cushioned nooks in favorite rooms, she is yet able to toil almost as severely as ever." While some of us might not want to toil severely in our old age, Miles found in it a "strength and endurance... beyond imagination to women of the sheltered life," and was generally critical of making women stay indoors.[32] Although not everyone would have agreed with Miles, many cornbread-cooking women might well have wondered at the double standard proposed by activist women.

From women's leisure, it was not too far a rhetorical distance to the even more high-stakes question of women's pleasure. Pleasure in eating had a long tradition of evoking sexual pleasure, and the biscuits and cornbread struggles were not free of such undertones. Just as we saw with the simultaneously American and foreign cultural meanings of corn, sex and bread had complex associations. First, there were curious hints in the texts that the Appalachian women liked their cornbread just a little too much. For instance, after Tanis makes the cornbread for Sam, she narrates how she felt something like sparks going up a chimney through her body when she lay in bed thinking of him. The relationship between Andy and his captor in Cooke's story uses the language of their shared food to imply a more physically and emotionally intimate relationship. Cornbread, especially when it was cooked outside over open fires—was a recipe verging on being too wild, not appropriately feminine for the times. In *Perfection Salad*, analyzing the turn-of-the-century home economics pioneers, Laura Shapiro suggests that women were not supposed to enjoy eating (or reading about men eating, for that matter): "the naked act of eating was little more than unavoidable, as far as gently raised women of their era were concerned, and was not to be considered a pleasure except with great discretion." Lessons in home economics became a process of "containing and controlling food, draining it of taste and texture"—surely a description, even outside of my own particular tired arms—of the beaten biscuit, in which the taste and texture were literally hammered out of the food. Therefore, the switch away from corn served to regulate wild and unnatural Appalachian gender passions that could make women like Pettit and Stone profoundly uncomfortable.[33]

On the other hand, corn could be the less sexual, safer choice. As the blues song suggested, women made cornbread for their husbands and biscuits for their men. Although Tanis in Troubetzkoy's novel makes cornbread for her boyfriend, Sam, she falls for the more taboo Mr. Gilman (and, Troubetzkoy implies, possibly Mrs. Gilman as well); the Gilmans eat the biscuits Tanis carefully prepares, while the sexual tension continues. Troubetzkoy was always in trouble for putting sex on the surface of her novels; *Tanis* ends with a heroic sacrifice in which a kidnapped Alice is saved by Tanis agreeing to go back to Sam, the kidnapper. She returns to her mountain and its open-fire cooking, which we can extrapolate means back to cornbread, away from biscuits.[34] The danger in both biscuits and cornbread reminded readers of the worry that women might liberate themselves in the moonshine literature. Regardless of the direction in which leisure led to pleasure, the beaten biscuit recipe, in its extremes, realigned gender and place as well as class and race.

NATIONALLY STANDARDIZED CONSUMERISM

Finally, biscuits and cornbreads differed in their participation in national, as opposed to regional or local, standards; definitions of race, class, and gender in small southern communities were nationalized as a result. Stone and Pettit returned after their first summer to find one mountain woman who "told us that she had tried to cook everything like we had taught her and that she had learned from the cookbook we sent her. She had a rice pudding with blackberries around it, just as we had served it the day she was with us. She said she had taught her friends our way of cooking and that she had made beaten biscuit for many weddings."[35] Not only did this woman follow the educational lessons of the Hindman women, but she also followed a cookbook that was standard for all of the United States. This practice implied standard ingredients, equipment, and expectations, as well as definitions of proper white womanhood that could be generalized across the United States.

Imported wheat, marble slabs and rolling pins, technologically advanced and consistent cook stoves, and cookbooks were all parts of a national distribution system fueled by the buying decisions of women. Grace MacGowan Cooke said explicitly in her novel about mills in Appalachian Tennessee,

The Power and the Glory, "Illustrated magazines go everywhere these days"; the era's women's magazines especially portrayed "the 'homemaker,' a newly coined term" and her responsibilities for material consumption. In this rhetoric about women's important role in consuming wisely for one's family, female homemakers with more money (often a combination of class and race privilege during this era) were more valued. As McCulloch-Williams suggested, "happy ever after" could come from the proper kitchen equipment in a turn-of-the-century home. In the burgeoning consumer culture in 1900, things moved in to supply satisfaction to women across the United States and "value [was] inexorably linked to both elaborate embellishment and to sheer quantity."[36] More tools, more equipment, and mass-market sources for both meant that these new beaten biscuit cooks participated in the nation's consumerist culture and that the Progressive activists who helped them could claim success to their funders in the goal of "civilizing" the Appalachians. This new homemaker and her buying power had to decide between biscuits and cornbread in many mountain families.

Fiction of the period reflected the nationalization of taste and class. For instance, in Louise Baker's *Cis Martin*, a novel about a sophisticated northeastern family having to live in Appalachian Tennessee until their finances recover, a mountain woman offers to serve "fried chicken and soda biscuits for breakfast," presenting them as something special, if only the newly arrived Cis would stay and help her play a prank. The action in Cooke's *The Power and the Glory* centers around class tensions inspired by national and regional values in a Tennessee mill town as northern mill owners clash with local workers. Her heroine, who eats corn pone at the beginning, is recognized as a member of "what we are learning to call the 'leisure class'" by the end of the novel, having helped resolve the tensions largely through local ownership—but is singular for refusing to renounce her local tastes and values.[37]

When southerners, including residents of the southern mountains, did embrace baking with flour, they favored the soft winter wheat flours produced by historically regional companies such as White Lily Flour from Knoxville, Tennessee, or Nashville's Martha White Flour. Distinctions between soft winter wheat, as opposed to the hard wheat flours more often preferred by and milled in the Midwest and Northeast did not even appear in the writings of women like Pettit and Stone; reading their texts, one was left with the impression that Appalachian families were completely ignorant of the finer points of baking. It is hard to tell whether the purchase of a Tennessee flour would meet the standards of Pettit and Stone, though the nature of the beaten biscuit recipe would likely respond well to the softer flours.[38]

RESISTANCE

Despite the general adoption of biscuits as a marker of higher class by mountain residents and newcomers, some residents resisted the hierarchy. Based on the erosion of women's precious free time, controversies over health effects, and, in at least one case, an overarching social critique regarding local values, cornbread had its defenders.

Olive Campbell recorded in her travel journal from her research trips around Appalachia that she found "quite a prejudice against domestic science"—which would have included biscuits and cooking lessons—"as being merely 'dish washing' of which [the mountain women] say they have plenty at home." Such a sentiment was also expressed by the boys watching Pettit make biscuits; whether a food was worth the trouble to make was, in fact, a trenchant question. Studies such as Arlie Hochschild's *The Second Shift* or Susan Strasser's *Never Done* show that time-saving devices for women, especially ones that target housework and food preparation rarely decreased the amount of time diverse women across the United States spent on the tasks. Resisting a new recipe such as the beaten biscuit that might erode one's quality of life seemed a reasonable tactic. Or, as an anonymous mountain woman told Pettit and Stone after watching their extensive preparations for bed, "Ye all must be a lot of trouble to yerselves." Furman, in *Mothering on Perilous*, acknowledged that mountain residents were especially suspicious when they felt the biscuits were not even as filling as what they were used to: "Last night Taulbee, the eldest, who is very opinionated, took occasion to enter a general protest against innovations such as nightgowns, tooth-brushes, fine-combs, and the like, and wound up by arraigning the school methods of cooking. 'Them little small biscuits you-all have don't even make good bite,' he declared."[39] Hardworking women, often with families to feed, then, had several grounds upon which to reject the change.

Other resistance focused on the middle option of the bread hierarchy, the soda biscuit. That resistance reached opposite conclusions, but was united in the belief that soda biscuits were not a healthy food for long-term consumption. While commercial baking powders and baking sodas were on southern store shelves by the 1870s, their quality and reliability varied greatly. Some cooks used cheaper sal soda or saleratus, which could be either sodium or potassium bicarbonate, and the results could be startling.[40] Independently, Maria Louise Pool and Margaret Morley used the assumed unhealthiness of soda biscuits to justify the superiority of yeast breads. Emma Bell Miles used the same assumed unhealthiness to argue for a return to corn-based breads, therein inverting the hierarchy.

Pool's narrator in *In Buncombe County* notes, "I had apple-butter and saleratus biscuit for my repast. I know they were saleratus biscuit because frequent yellow lumps appealed both to the eye and the palate. But I am not complaining. I knew that the apple-butter would not hurt me, and I was just as sure that, at one meal, I could not eat enough sal-soda to destroy the coats of my stomach." Morley made a similar comment when she reported, "The most frequent disorder among them is dyspepsia, for which the pale-green, or saffron-yellow, brown-spotted, ring-streaked and speckled luxury known as 'soda biscuits' undoubtedly bears a heavy burden of blame. These wonders of the culinary art are freely eaten by all who can afford to buy white flour, and their odorous presence is often discernible from afar as you approach a house at mealtime." Pool, Morley, and others like them (upper-class, white women travelers) felt that the leavening used in biscuits—in particular in the newer commercial baking powders—was quite dangerous to the digestive system. Beaten biscuits, made with little or no leavening, had an advantage over the risen biscuits Pool's character encountered near Asheville, North Carolina, but they were not offered. Behind this brief comment in Pool's novel lay national concerns about cuisine, health food, and nutrition, ongoing conversations stretching back through the nineteenth century. Sisters Stowe and Beecher were concerned about breads at mid-century; they worried about the damaging effects of eating bread hot (as cornbread and soda biscuits certainly were in the southern mountains), as they claimed was especially the practice in the "South and West." Their solution was to advocate for cold, sliced yeast bread, suggesting that "lightness is the distinctive line between savage and civilized bread."[41]

Emma Bell Miles, who grew up in and lived most of her life in Appalachia, agreed with Pool and Morley about the dangers of risen soda biscuits, even as she reached a different conclusion about what to do with this knowledge. Miles worried that "civilization is not likely soon to remedy this evil" of unhealthy food in Appalachia. But she blamed industrialization outside of Appalachia for "introduc[ing] cheap baking powders and the salicylic acid which is so dangerously convenient in canning fruit."[42] She wanted mountain residents to avoid all of the store-bought food (including flour) and thus supported the continued use of corn-based bread. Later in the twentieth century, conversations about various breads in Appalachia moved into controversies over pellagra and the relative healthiness of any store-bought and commercially ground flours and meals, debates to which chapter 4 turns. Today health food experts advocate for locally produced, organic food, arguing it provides protection against allergies, as well as more vitamins and minerals. Miles would have agreed.

Miles did not stop at insisting imported ingredients could be dangerous to individual women and families. She extended her argument to make a social critique that reached beyond the individual women involved. She suggested that, while "it is easier, far, to buy city tools with city money," they came with a high long-term cost. She argued, "the old-time mountaineer never knew the taste of ice-cream in summer, he was, on the other hand, never without cornpones and side-meat in cold weather." She mourned to "see them buy meal by the half-peck to eat with the invariable white gravy" and concluded that the newcomers who had initiated this market economy in her community "would not think the pay so well proportioned to the sacrifice, after all" if they had stayed to see the effects of their changes. She found local ingredients, indigenous traditions, and a barter economy to be more ecologically, socially, and individually sustainable. Cornbread, grown at home, using handmade equipment, as a part of a self-sufficient community, was a centerpiece of her argument. And while Miles used the third-person pronoun to write, we know from her biography that she was speaking out of the individual experience of running a household of six in extreme poverty. In a diary entry from May 8, 1915, Miles noted, "I had only cornbread and wild greens, with a very little potted ham; but we used big green leaves for plates, leaving them in the hollow of our left hands, and the children enjoyed it."[43] Cooking nonlocal, more expensive, and time-consuming food was hardly an option for this social critic.

One final solution to the pressures to serve beaten biscuits was to embrace and profit from them. Some women turned the message that they should stay home in domestic spaces into successful businesses. Abby Fisher migrated to San Francisco and founded a catering and pickling business; other women, black and white, joined the Great Migration, and used their kitchen skills to open restaurants or start selling food products in their new communities. Some people invented and patented beaten biscuit machines that eliminated the need for the mallet and arm strength and that were suitable for caterers making large orders. Others invented beaten biscuit tables that featured hoods so that cooks could make the biscuits in moments broken up throughout the rest of the day without the dough drying out.[44] In other words, caterers, inventors, and working women eventually made over the recipe on their own terms.

CONCLUSION

Food memoirist Joe Taylor suggested that, like cornbreads before it, various forms of the biscuit, too, were eventually discredited and displaced. Creating standardized housewives across the country helped fuel the market for and influence of media targeted to those women, all of which resulted in the promotion and takeover of mass-produced, commercial, sliced bread for daily use. Taylor concluded, "In the 1920s small-town and country stores began to carry commercial bread, brought out from the nearest city in trucks, and soon it was presliced... as more housewives were influenced by women's magazines and home economics courses, toast rather than biscuits became breakfast fare."[45] Sliced-bread sandwiches, such as those spread with mayonnaise and sold by Duke's outside Greenville, South Carolina, became much more common in the South. The ascension of toast into southern and American kitchens may have facilitated the movement of both biscuits and cornbread into their present-day categorization as old-fashioned, down-home food, into both being sources of nostalgia. Both foods remain gendered—women are most often responsible for preparing them and are identified closely with them in our nostalgia about their symbolic meanings. Their association with soul food still nods to the labor of African American women in the South's kitchens.

Beaten biscuits and cooking lessons continued and spread to other parts of the South as the twentieth century developed. Jane S. McKimmon, one of the original tomato club organizers, began working with women about a decade after Pettit and Stone. McKimmon's work was headquartered in the Piedmont region, instead of North Carolina's mountains. But was it just more of the same attitudes about food, class, gender, and region that we saw in the moonshine literature and here in the beaten biscuit crusade?

At first, the answer seems to be yes. Taped into a large scrapbook she called her "Conceit Book," a 1923 *Farmer's Wife* clipping featuring her beaten biscuit recipe was carefully preserved by McKimmon. A nearby article also taped into the scrapbook, this one from the *Country Gentleman* of June 29, 1918, quoted McKimmon on the beginning of her work with North Carolina women and girls. About her first days, she said, "Ten years ago I was just a society woman. I always had liked gardening and human beings, and if I had any gift at all, it was that of making the most of what I had to do with. I had a friend who was in farmers' institute work, and knowing my taste for people, she took me with her on some of her trips."[46] Primarily targeting male farmers, the institutes were usually three-day gatherings that featured lectures and information for more efficient and cost-effective methods of farming. Spreading across the United States, and especially the South, farmers' institute work prefigured agricultural extension and home demonstration agencies, the eventual umbrellas under which McKimmon did most of her work. The institutes' problem, to McKimmon, was that they only addressed half the farmers, the men and boys. McKimmon was frustrated on behalf of the farm women and girls.

McKimmon described the few women she saw on those first trips as "my forgotten women, who lived in the backwoods and who didn't know how to cook or to plan, and who had almost nothing to do with. There they'd sit, listening to talks." She continued, "Well, I didn't think I could talk, but I knew there were certain things I could *do*. I had seen that very few of the women I had met knew how to make bread. So I asked the director of the institutes if I could not help a little by showing how I made bread. I didn't think then of using the word 'demonstration', but that is what I was about to do—demonstrate bread making." Saying, "I went, first of all, before the people way off the main roads. I met them in schoolhouses, churches, and Woodmen of the World halls. I've made bread on pulpits and desks and barrel heads," McKimmon described her early days of working with rural women.[47]

With her offhand dismissal of the women's other cooking skills and her pointed choice of bread baking, McKimmon certainly evoked the rhetoric of Pettit, Stone, and the beaten biscuit crusade in the mountains. But McKimmon's details quickly revealed the significant philosophical differences she had with the beaten biscuit women—and her attitudes extended into the larger tomato club movement. Even at the beginning of McKimmon's career, she used "the simplest sort of equipment—a bowl, two big pans, some little pans, a glass, two or three spoons, paper bags and some Manila paper." The final detail was her way of making do: "I would take the Manila paper, fasten it down with thumb tacks—there was my sanitary bread board." Refusing to lecture to the women and making sure her demonstration could be done without major purchases of equipment or supplies, McKimmon reached out to rural women proposing cooperation and conversation. In fact, the title of the article, "She 'Lifted' Sixty-six Counties," evoked the African American club women's motto of "Lifting as We Climb." More than that, McKimmon hinted that she viewed these as conversations among equals rather than lectures from above; saying "we lifted each other," she insisted they listened to and learned from each other. In other words, despite being from a more privileged social class and more cosmopolitan background than the women for whom she led demonstrations, McKimmon made it clear she valued them and their knowledge.[48] McKimmon's impulse to share information, talk, and learn from each other made the girls' tomato club movement, the life work of McKimmon and other women across the South, something very different from the effort to get women to stop making cornbread and start making beaten biscuits, while being judged on their morals in the process. We turn to those tomato clubs next.

Photographs documented not only the quantities girls produced, but also the scientific methods they used, as did this one of "Three members of the Pleasant Hill 4-H club in Craven County, NC," 1920s, North Carolina. Courtesy of Special Collections Research Center, North Carolina State University Libraries, Raleigh, North Carolina.

CHAPTER THREE

Canning Tomatoes

GROWING "BETTER AND MORE
PERFECT WOMEN"

> Tomato Club. Tomato Club.
> See how we can. See how we can.
> Give us tomatoes and a good sharp knife—
> This is the place to get a good wife.
> Did ever you see such girls in your life—
> As the Tomato Club?

SHORTLY AFTER Jane McKimmon began demonstrating bread making on the margins of farmers' institutes in North Carolina, Marie Samuella Cromer sat in the audience at a 1909 teachers' meeting in South Carolina. A rural schoolteacher in the western South Carolina town of Aiken, Cromer heard a speech about Dr. Seaman A. Knapp's boys' corn clubs that were transforming southern crop yields. According to her own retelling, Cromer raised her hand to ask, "But what are we doing for the farm girls?" She was not the first audience member across the South to ask such a question; but what made Cromer different was what she did next. She headed back home and, by 1910, had organized a girls' tomato club so that "girls will not learn simply how to grow better and more perfect tomatoes, but how to grow better and more perfect women."[1] Before long, more than five hundred thousand girls across the nation were in tomato clubs, mostly in the South; they wrote songs (like the one above), designed labels, adopted mottoes, created uniforms, won scholarships, traveled to conferences, and made hundreds of thousands of dollars in total profits. Although short in duration, the tomato club movement was long on potential; the South really had never before seen "such girls in your life—as the Tomato Club."

From the first, Cromer had both economic and educational goals in mind for the tomato-club girls. Writing in an undated newspaper clipping preserved in her scrapbook, Cromer suggested the clubs would give girls a course in reading, science, public speaking, and socializing; in short, they would provide "lessons economic and lessons ethical." While Cromer may have had her focus almost exclusively on the girls, Knapp, who had been debating such a plan for a while, was looking also to the women who were the girls' mothers or who the girls would become. Cromer's colleague, Susie V. Powell, who was appointed by Knapp the following year to pioneer tomato clubs in Mississippi, remembered him arguing, "Canning the tomatoes will give us entrance to the farm kitchen. Tomatoes, fresh and canned, will be a valuable supplement to the family diet. The sale of the tomatoes will provide an income for the girls."[2] McKimmon quickly joined Cromer and Powell, leaving bread behind and becoming North Carolina's tomato club organizer. The tomato clubs and the women who organized them, then, intended from the first to use food to transform social hierarchies and practices—but not from the top down. Rather, by targeting girls, arguably the most disenfranchised family members, the tomato club movement explicitly worked up from the grass—or garden—roots.

Far from being threatened by women and girls with money, far from being worried as the moonshine literature was about Lucy McElroy's independent Juletty, the canning movement made putting money in girls' hands one of its explicit goals. It did not propose girls had to leave rural communities as Sis did in Joel Chandler Harris's "At Teague Poteet's." The tomato clubs suggested communities help themselves, giving concrete form to Sal's pledge at the end of Martha Gielow's *Old Andy, the Moonshiner*: to stay in the mountains and help her own people. The tomato club movement had faith that capitalism and consumerism could work for girls from rural backgrounds; they were not worried about how money might tempt girls into underground economies as it did a couple of decades later in Sherwood Anderson's *Kit Brandon*. Even more importantly, resistance to tomato club work did not come from the girls themselves feeling judged or forced to learn things they already knew, as the girls pushing back against beaten biscuits occasionally did. Instead, the canning movement pulled girls' economic earning abilities out of the illicit background and into the center of a national conversation about southern food and gender, valuing their abilities and intelligence in the process.

From their beginnings in South Carolina in 1910, the tomato clubs had their heyday from 1911 until the eve of World War I. They were under the pioneering direction of five white, southern women: Cromer in South Carolina, McKimmon in North Carolina, Powell in Mississippi, Ella G. Agnew in Virginia, and Virginia Moore in Tennessee. In that short decade, the girls' canning club movement swept the southern United States.[3] In this chapter, Cromer, McKimmon, Powell, and the girls with whom they work take center stage as representatives of the larger movement. The tomato story takes us beyond the mountain communities at the heart of the cornbread story to places where the beaten biscuit recipe was developed; it takes us to southern communities where moonshine was no longer a grizzled stereotype but instead was part of the economic fuel of modern life. Race politics, gendered leisure and work, and class struggles are ever more on the surface of the story as we find ourselves in piedmont, delta, and coastal areas of the South. In such communities, the tomato club movement walked a fine line between an agricultural past and an industrial present.

Leading the way for the girls joining the movement was Cromer (1882–1965). Native to Abbeville, South Carolina, in Aiken County, Cromer's work was deeply connected to her South Carolina roots. In 1910, hers was a southern state coming to be dominated by its piedmont industries. Against the background of cotton factories, furniture factories, and other mill economies, a populist movement that pledged to unite agricultural and industrial workers against absentee owners and aristocrats was hijacked by race-baiting politics. Local, self-styled new populist "Pitchfork" Ben Tillman rewrote the earlier script of workers' political alliances instead to unite white South Carolinians against African American citizens. State's pride and Jim Crow violence rose as Tillman concentrated his political power in the United States Senate. Culturally, the cosmopolitan dominance that South Carolina's coastal cities like Charleston had enjoyed during the Confederacy and colonial eras had been eclipsed by the rising power of Atlanta and Georgia to the south and fast-evolving North Carolina to the north. In other words, South Carolina (and especially white South Carolinians) entered the twentieth century in the midst of a painful transition and identity crisis, and the girls' tomato club movement in South Carolina reflected the anxieties and tensions. From the very beginning, the clubs were about more than just the girls. Cromer made sure girls knew that these clubs were not simply local groups, saying, "We must work this year for the whole world is watching us. If our club succeeds this year Dr. Knapp has promised to put a woman in every country [sic] in the State to organize clubs."[4] Cromer predicted—accurately—and thereby built expectations that girls in their Aiken, South Carolina, home gardens would draw international attention. From the first, tomato clubs were public, not private, phenomena.

Jane McKimmon (1867–1957) was born and lived her whole life in Raleigh, North Carolina. She was a married, middle-class town woman who nonetheless knew well North Carolina's agricultural roots. North Carolina in 1910 had the factories and textile mills that were also reshaping South Carolina's economy. Industry was, in fact, present across the state—the mountains' extractive industry of logging reached its peak in that year; the piedmont held the wide swath of furniture and textile manufactory; and the coastal plains hosted the state's largest city in 1910, sprawling, naval-oriented, industrial Wilmington (though that would be the last year that was true, before piedmont cities like Charlotte took over). At the same time, North Carolina was strongly agricultural with tobacco, cotton, and food produced for export. Truck farming, tobacco production, and subsistence farming all coexisted in the state, with sharecropping families, tenant families, and small and large landowners all holding stakes in and shaping the rural identity of the state. Class and race differences and tensions stratified towns, cities, and even regions of the state—state political and social power concentrated in the piedmont; more of the state's African American residents lived in the coastal plains; people believed the poorest white residents lived in the mountains.[5] The tomato clubs constantly negotiated these structures.

Finally, Susie Powell (1869–1952) headquartered her tomato club work at Mississippi's Starkville, from where she could easily access both the delta and northern hill regions of her state. Mississippi in 1910 was in the midst of a sharecropping and tenant-farming system that restructured and revivified antebellum plantations in its concentration of power in the hands of owners and overseers. Although both poor black and poor white Mississippians toiled in agriculture, a large enough population of African Americans existed in the state to make them key players (though politically and economically disempowered ones) in the state's futures. The hard farming of cotton—labor intensive, vulnerable to slight changes in the market, and exhausting of soil—continued to dominate Mississippi agriculture and the state's economy. Unlike Cromer and McKimmon's Carolinas, Mississippi had few other industries and no major urban cities. The separation of races was a more extreme version of the Jim Crow policies existing in North and South Carolina as well. White Mississippians were nervous (to say the least) about the number of African American residents joining the Great Migration to Chicago and other northern cities. At the same time, Mississippi's white 4-H clubs pledged in 1925, "Land of our birth, we pledge to thee, / Our love and toil in years to be, / When we are grown and take our place, / As men and women of our race," neatly capturing the centrality of and yet separation between races in the state.[6]

Despite individual differences between the women organizers and the states in which they worked, the tomato club results were immediate and impressive in all three locations. Cromer's first state champion, Katie Gunter, produced 512 cans and $35 profit. In their first year, McKimmon's 440 girls produced 70,000 cans and realized an average profit per girl of $14.75. (In today's dollars, that is the equivalent of $330.00 they did not have when they started.) Powell's 510 girls produced 110,050 cans and an average profit of $25.76. In only the second year of the clubs, North Carolina had grown to include 1,500 girls; there were 2,914 in the third year, by which time the girls were averaging

$39.90 in profit and producing a total state profit of $75,256.43. According to Mary Creswell, who began as Georgia's state agent but who was later appointed to oversee Home Demonstration at the Department of Agriculture, already by the 1915 season, 32,613 girls were enrolled from across the South. They produced "5,023,305 pounds of tomatoes [and] 1,262,953 pounds of other vegetables and fruits." By 1917, the North Carolina girls processed an astounding 8,778,262 containers, not counting the amount of dried and brined food they put away. That same year in Mississippi, 4,503 girls produced a total of 2,313,284 containers with a total value of $248,006.76. By 1918 in North Carolina, an additional 2,225 African American girls were officially enrolled. In Mississippi, though numbers are harder to come by, 2,773 black girls were involved in 1923, five years after the first "Negro Home Demonstration Agent," Alice Carter Oliver, had been hired. By 1920, although the transition was well under way to 4-H and home demonstration, club girls reached five hundred thousand. Girls' club work took up columns of media inches in magazines and newspapers across the nation; it was celebrated and documented in federal Department of Agriculture reports; and it brought worldwide attention to the stories of farm girls. As an Oklahoma paper asked rhetorically in 1915, "If somebody were to tell you that a group of little country girls who never have been near a big city have built up a business so large and important that papers all over the country are telling about it, you would think it was a new kind of fairy tale, now wouldn't you?"[7]

Unlike the historical record surrounding the moonshine literature and the beaten biscuit crusade, in which we had to search for actual women and girls under the rhetoric and representations, the record around the tomato club movement holds a treasure trove of women's and girls' voices. McKimmon, Powell, and Cromer all left papers, with clippings, scrapbooks, and some personal letters; in addition, the state and federal government documents they helped create contain handwritten reports of their work, as well as the words of the women and girls they served.

More than that, though, we have the opportunity to listen to girls themselves. Cromer's scrapbook quoted her prizewinners; Powell's archive included handwritten reports from local club presidents. Most vividly, nestled in the collections of the North Carolina Division of Archives were dozens of brightly painted, beribboned, and bound tomato club reports. Sent to "Mrs. McKimmon" from rural girls all across North Carolina, the earliest ones dating from the 1911–1912 season, each report documented the experiences of a ten- to twenty-year-old girl and her one-tenth acre of tomato plants. Some were poetic, like the one that began "I once was a little seed and I was in an envelope and some one carried me to Maggie Ray" and the one from Katie Poovey that read "Plant a little seed / Very small indeed. / Put it in the ground / In a little mound. / And wait to see what / It will be." Others were practical; some used nineteenth-century scrapbook techniques of cutting and pasting bright images into a whole, and others employed striking watercolors to illustrate the story within. One even existed in two versions: the first with a story of boys seeing Ethel Baggett's bare ankles after a mishap with a kettle of hot water and the second with that story excised in favor of a more formal recitation of her final canned results, evidence of the gap between what girls found funny and what teachers found appropriate.[8] It was a rare intervention, however; for the most part the reports give an unedited glimpse into early twentieth-century farm girls' cultures.

Each of the following sections of this chapter focuses on one of these girl-authored reports or women-penned records in order to see into the worlds of southern farm girls as they encountered and negotiated technology, consumer culture, career choices, and changing race and class politics on the one hand, and home, tradition, and family on the other. However little known it is today, the newspaper's so-called fairy tale of girls' economic success in canning launched significant career paths and connections across social classes for thousands of women and girls. It fostered interracial cooperation and professions at a time when Jim Crow segregation was entrenched. It allowed the articulation of critiques of the gender politics of rural life. Tomato clubs and the writing they generated reveal the continuous blurring between categories as food—in this case, tomatoes—became the language around which race, class, gender, and regional politics played out in their gendered lives in the South.

WHAT WAS A TOMATO CLUB?

My dear Little Girls: Time is flying and you haven't joined the "Tomato Club" yet. Of course, you intend to later—but now is the time. I must have your names before I can have bulletins sent to you, and you must have the bulletins before you can know how to grow tomatoes... Don't delay, but send your name at once to the woman who is deeply interested in you, and she is, Yours most sincerely, Marie Samuella Cromer

From the first season announced by Cromer in South Carolina's newspapers (and then carefully clipped for her scrapbook), to be a tomato club member, each girl had to map out a one-tenth acre plot of ground on her family land and plant it in tomatoes.[9] Participating girls sprouted seeds and prepared for their crops; bulletins with hints about how to propagate, water, and prepare the land were distributed free to the girls. Tomato clubs welcomed girls from roughly twelve to eighteen years old. In the early years, virtually all of the girls were white; although some African American girls participated in similar clubs in their schools or communities, it was not until closer to World War I that Powell, McKimmon, and others officially hired and collaborated with African American women for canning club work. Because of the land requirements, the poorest girls in a community were also unlikely to be involved; families that were tenants and sharecroppers or working in small mill towns and unable to freely decide how to use the land around their homes were cut out of the early canning club work.

In her first yearly report, McKimmon described the steps subsequent to seed preparation: "A club member is expected to do all of her planting, cultivating, staking and gathering of the fruit, but she can have the ploughing, harrowing and heavy work done for her." A long summer of weeding, watching for insects, and tracking rain or carrying water followed. After the harvest began, the girls were "divided into squads—sterilizers, peelers, packers, cappers, and those doing the actual cooking and attending to fires." McKimmon noted, "These positions are changed frequently so that every girl learns every part of the process, and is then allowed to can at home when she desires."[10] With this arrangement, girls each learned sanitary canning methods and processes, and they also gained standardized recipes and processing tips.

For many of the clubs, as soon as the technical skills had been mastered, the girls themselves began giving public demonstrations to other community members. Estelle Mauney described in her report of 12 October 1915 how her western North Carolina club "gave a public demonstration in Murphy. The woman's club entertained us and served a nice lunch. From 1 o'clock until four we demonstrated." Other clubs focused on creating displays for fairs and state and (by 1912) national competitions. Along the way, tomato club girls developed uniforms, songs (such as the one at the beginning of the chapter), pins, and mottoes. Using a picture of a tomato, the motto "To Make the Best Better," and a symbol of a clover, they developed labels for their products and reputations for marketing savvy.[11]

The five pioneering women soon found they could not supervise every club that formed. With enrollment in North Carolina, for instance, almost tripling in the clubs' first year of existence, Cromer, McKimmon, Powell, Agnew, and Moore looked for help. They created a network of adult women to oversee the clubs. According to McKimmon, "In each county a woman of good business ability as well as education is selected to supervise the girls. She selects three communities near together and organizes a club in each, going to the schools and trying to enthuse both teachers and girls in the work." From her earliest lists, we can see that the majority of these women were single and ranged in age from their twenties to their fifties; most were teachers, some were businesswomen, and a few were daughters or wives of prominent farmers.[12] In marked difference from the newly arrived beaten biscuit crusaders, women guiding tomato clubs had long lived in the communities in which they worked.

Powell's records agreed, showing that the earliest Mississippi club directors were teachers and college graduates she found through the state network of boards of education, the Mississippi Federation of Women's Clubs, and various business groups. Powell's tomato club report of 1914–1915, under the heading "Cooperation," asserted: "The Mississippi Federation of Women's

Clubs also has been a consistent and earnest supporter of the club work of the women and girls. The Federation has given financial aid, offered prizes, used its influence to secure appropriations, bought club products and given a prominent place on its programs to Home Economics." More specifically, Powell remembered the help of clubwomen for the first Mississippi girls who won national awards for the canning work: "Not one of these girls had ever been outside the state or seen inside a Pullman car. Local clubwomen honored the girls with a 'shower' on the eve of their departure. A traveling bag was provided for each girl fitted with dainty garments and toilet articles for the week's trip." Powell returned to work for the state women's club after resigning from extension work, bringing the connection full circle.[13] Over time, leadership ranks were filled by former canning club girls. In addition, the positions moved into agricultural schools and even federal government offices, making the tomato clubs the beginning of a path to national careers for a group of women in the United States.

SALLIE JONES'S FAVORITE MECHANICAL CANNER

While today the prospect of lessons in canning could seem quintessentially domestic rather than public or career oriented, girls' reports showed that in the early 1900s, tomato clubs represented the newest modern and public science and technology. That promise led to one report cover featuring a looming gray machine. Carefully detailed model numbers, brand name, and coloring gave the equipment weight on the page. Sallie Jones of Alamance County in North Carolina's piedmont—"Club No. 3, Member No. 7," as she called herself—illustrated her tomato booklet with neither her crop nor her finished cans, but instead with a rendering of her club's mechanical canner. With its sealed metal casing and impressive venting smokestack, the Standard Cannery she pictured emphasized the soldering, high temperatures, and chemistry mastered by tomato club girls. Jones lingered on the technology of the tomato canning—and her role as the scientist or engineer in charge. She precisely detailed the process, from lining up tomatoes in scalding trays to dropping "the tomatoes in the boiling water" and allowing them to "remain for one minute after which we put them in cold water to make them firm." She reported the exact time to leave them in the canner after sealing (twenty-two minutes) and recommended turning the cans "up side down for twenty-four hours to prevent them from bulging." Jones even imparted lessons on affixing labels, suggested recipes (with precise measurements), and calculated her personal yield: "Considering the drought this summer, my $1/10$ acre of tomatoes has done remarkably well; the yield being 780 the total number of pounds 2340. There were five dozen tomatoes used at home, and ten dozen and a half sent to market."[14]

Around 1910, corn clubs, poultry clubs, pig clubs, and sewing or general homemaking clubs began occasionally opening their membership to girls. But tomato clubs were the ones that really took off in terms of membership, success, and enthusiasm of participants, supporters, and reporters. Some of the successes should be attributed to the tomato itself. Tomatoes grew well in the soil and climate of the South, where the agricultural work was focused. In the Carolinas, relatively few acres were planted in tomatoes when the clubs began. As a result, Cromer and McKimmon argued (and convincingly documented) that more profit could be made from systematically canning tomatoes than from other crops currently being grown. Mississippi, on the other hand, was already growing a surplus of tomatoes, but farmers there did not have the habit of canning so fruit lay rotting in the fields. Powell and her supporters could argue that tomato clubs reaped profit by turning those losses into easy gains. Further, tomatoes were acidic enough to be forgiving items to can; even under less than ideal circumstances (such as outside with wood fires and makeshift tables), tomato canning produced less spoilage than, for instance, sugary fruits or fresh meats. Tomatoes held up well for canning, and the end product tasted quite good, which meant that people were willing to purchase and use canned tomatoes. Finally, tomatoes were easy garden plants for young girls to handle. They did not require heavy machinery to plant or harvest (unlike, say, grains); therefore tomatoes did not necessarily challenge people's ideas about appropriate gender roles on the farm.[15] Ironically, by seeming so perfectly suited to girls, the tomato cleared plenty of space for radical challenges to gender, race, class, and science on the farm through girls' club work.

Today, if we think of home canning, we likely picture rows of glass jars that make that satisfying pop when their lids are opened. But in 1910, canning in glass presented challenges for the tomato girls. Powell wrote of Virgie Cogdell, who carefully scavenged glass containers such as ink bottles and Vaseline jars for her first exhibit since she had no money to purchase containers. Cogdell spent her five-dollar prize to purchase standard containers for the following year. Most of the tomato clubs concentrated on canning in tin or steel, using equipment like Jones's carefully rendered Standard Cannery. Doing so was faster and allowed for more volume with less weight. As James Tanner, documenting the Mississippi work in 1945, remembered, "The early marketing was practically all done in tin because of the less loss in shipment and handling." More than the possibility of breakage, choosing to can in tin also responded to the expectations of consumers, or, as Franklin M. Reck, in his history of 4-H work, argues: "The powers-that-be had decided to teach canning in tin because girls were going to sell their surplus, and housewives were used to buying tins rather than glass jars." In addition, widespread sanitary canning in glass needed the easy availability of pressure cookers, which were not available in the first years of the canning clubs.[16]

Central to Cromer's initial argument for the girls' tomato clubs was the statistic that every year South Carolina sent eleven million dollars out of the state to purchase canned goods. A local newspaper added, "In the homes in that vicinity the tables are no longer furnished with tomatoes 'canned in Baltimore,' but with the inscription, 'Canned by the girls' tomato club of Aiken, S. C.' ... the lords of the tomato canning industry will have much ado. How could one pass by a can of tomatoes prepared by a club of South Carolina girls—with the autograph of the particular maiden who did the work?" Despite fetishizing the innocence and attraction of young girls, the paper nevertheless put its finger on the tension into which the girls' clubs stepped. As a state close to the industrial canning capital of the United States, South Carolina knew its girls would have to match technological skills with their Yankee neighbor, Maryland.[17]

Well before California's Cannery Row became the symbol of that state's dominance of the United States canned goods industry, the symbolic heart of commercial canning was an East Coast city: Baltimore, Maryland. First achieving its dominance by the 1870s, Baltimore was selling more than $71 million in canned goods in the 1890s, and Maryland as a whole had 25 percent of the nation's canneries. The city's operations processed food grown throughout the United States, seafood (and especially oysters) harvested along the Atlantic coast, and international products, such as Bahamian pineapples. Baltimore factories were large, combined skilled and unskilled labor, struggled through the economic and union upheavals of the early twentieth century, and seemed far removed from the individual farmer or consumer elsewhere in the United States.[18]

Yet American consumers were purchasing more and more canned goods. In part, canned food succeeded because consumers viewed their products as hygienic and sanitary, two buzzwords of the early twentieth century. Katherine Pettit and May Stone used the same concepts to propose what in their view were hygienic and sanitary biscuits over unclean or suspicious cornbread, but they were less successful in convincing people that their biscuits were necessarily better. A decade later, when the tomato clubs were starting, unclean conditions in large food operations famously exposed by Upton Sinclair in *The Jungle* and periodic sweeps of food carts and small producers led to federal involvement in food regulation, which encouraged consumers to look for standardization and certification in their foods. These were balanced by displays of canned goods at world's fairs and by advertising campaigns that attached ideas of modernity, progress, and consumer desire to new presentations of foods.[19] Tomato clubs used their uniforms and uniformity of product as well as their bright packaging to good advantage in the crowded marketplace.

Canned goods also were a viable solution to feed the family as more and more Americans moved into cities and away from home gardens. In South Carolina and other southern states, as tenancy and sharecropping increased, and as factory, mill, and coal towns grew, pressure rose to spend money or credit at company or landlord-controlled stores. Economic pressures forced people to plant fields in monoculture money crops, such as cotton or tobacco, and not to garden. Time pressures and crowded housing caused by industrial jobs constrained families' abilities to even plant kitchen gardens. Canned goods became options as families tried to counter the South's meat, meal, and molasses diet, listening to medical advice that advocated for more fruits and vegetables in the American diet. Booker T. Washington, for instance, would stop black farmers taking empty wagons to town in order to fill them with canned goods bought on credit. Washington wanted them to load the wagons with home-produced items to sell, but he was fighting an uphill battle. Food companies encouraged the practice of consuming canned goods—then, as now, more profit could be made on processed food than unprocessed.[20]

The early tomato club organizers had to tread carefully as they stepped into the market for canned goods. Would they be able to produce consistently strong product when small groups were standing in fields learning new skills? Would they be viewed as cutting-edge entries in the market? Would they be too successful, thus inviting the "lords of industry" to oppose them? In South Carolina, Cromer quietly borrowed from the organizational methods of large industry, for instance, writing letters to the president of the Southern Railway, asking for free passes for herself and girls in tomato club work, and planning a statewide "tomato expo" to feature products and promote expansion of tomato cultivation. Cromer, or perhaps the girls themselves, adopted uniforms and promoted their hygienic and sanitary practices in canning—something that spread quickly to tomato club girls in all the states. And yet, early reports told stories of tension with both merchants and producers. McKimmon, in setting up North Carolina's tomato clubs, first explored the possibility of shipping the girls' products to New York, overseas, and into other major markets. As the program developed, she increasingly focused on selling in the home county, often through local storekeepers, and sometimes directly to local consumers. Nonetheless, given the value of the goods, the girls' products encroached on the territory of industrial canning. As Julia F. Burwell, one of the early North Carolina tomato club girls, suggested, "I thought that the tin cans bought from the store were canned in large factorys [*sic*] and that no one could can like that. But I have learned better now, how to can in tin and glass also." In Mississippi, organizers noted, "Later day club girls were not as keen as the early ones to work at canning on a commercial scale because they must compete with the factory product at a comparable price and that supplied a slender margin of profit." At the same time, the girls learned from large factories important lessons in standardization of product (they policed the weight of their packs), quality control (they certified sanitary methods and consistently ripe goods), and branding (they carefully built the tomato club and 4-H brand).[21] Their cooperative efforts went a long way toward putting profit in the individual girls' hands.

Perhaps the lessons in technology and chemistry that canning in tin involved explain why southern girls were so enthusiastic about the tomato clubs' domestic lessons, when they were so dismissive about the beaten biscuit crusade's earlier home training (the so-called dish washing that they already knew how to do). Learning to can in a tomato club really was a challenging and new lesson in the machinery and markets of the public world. Sallie Jones's Standard Cannery continues to bear witness to the knowledge of chemistry and technology the tomato clubs allowed her to gather.

CHARLOTTE YODER'S CHECKBOOK

Charlotte Yoder took a different benefit from her tomato club experiences and documented it in her report. She tied her cover with a fuchsia ribbon and drew a large tomato on it with colored pencils. Yoder was only twelve years old when she became a tomato club girl, and she wrote like a girl whose thoughts moved faster than her pen: run-on sentences, underlined words, and sporadic punctuation. She was consistent, though, in her overall message: tomatoes equaled money—a new concept for this farm girl outside Hickory in the western North Carolina foothills. Money, in fact, was the subject of her opening sentence: "I joined the tomato club because I had never had any money except what my mother gave me and I did not feel like that was mine." She continued on the same note: "When the tomato club agent came to our schoolhouse and told us about club girls making money I wanted to join." Tomatoes were an attractive option for Yoder, because she was limited in what she could do to raise money: "I have lots of work to do at home helping mama and I have an invalid brother that I wait on most of the time." Her report detailed her crop, the weather, and her battles with bugs. Nonetheless, that first year she produced "<u>88</u> cans of tomatoes for sale," her enthusiastic underlining indicating her sense of achievement.[22]

From the beginning, the women pioneering the tomato clubs wanted girls to realize a profit from their work. Although some of their harvest was destined for home use, which technically freed up family money that would otherwise have been spent over winter in local stores for processed food, most of their harvest was marketed and sold by the girls so they would end the season with cash in hand. To do this successfully, girls had to learn entrepreneurship, to price their goods, to research their markets, and to emphasize branding and standardizing their products. One historian of the Mississippi work noted, "The commercial canned products prior to 1914 were not available to many who like tomatoes so the agents under Miss Powell's direction began almost immediately to standardize the canned tomatoes... The work of the early canning specialist was as much a grading and marketing one as a job of teaching how to can." McKimmon carefully documented her and her girls' attempts to find markets in the state and beyond. Most striking was her commitment to helping girls develop the skills for themselves. McKimmon really wanted the girls to be independent and self-sufficient. For instance, she remembered a girl who, upon approaching a merchant and being told he was overstocked, "insisted on showing what she had, cutting the can and exposing the ripe, red fruit and solid pack, and straightway made a customer of that merchant." Secondarily, all of the early clubs competed for prizes with their wares, their reports, and their yields. Many of the prizes were monetary.[23]

The explicit goal of getting money into girls' hands may have been the most provocative aim of the first tomato clubs. Feminist labor historians have shown how solid was the expectation that working girls' wages belonged first to their fathers and then to their husbands (assuming they were even allowed to keep their jobs after marriage). Female wages were set low to provide only enough money to augment a larger family income. In addition, scholars document middle-class outrage when working girls dared to support themselves and make their own decisions for leisure activities, fashion purchases, or self-sufficiency. Progressive activists often had very firm opinions about how girls should spend their precious money and would withhold help from "uncooperative" cases. A fellow audience member at the South Carolina meeting during which Cromer developed the tomato club idea seemed to agree that girls should not make practical money and should use their leisure time in dainty pursuits. She proposed that girls' work be safely leisurely and gender appropriate. Cromer disagreed and "put aside as unfitting the suggestion of another of the teachers that she organize a 'chrysanthemum club,' realizing that what was needed was something which would be of vital usefulness." In other words, growing flowers was not going to accomplish the economic transformation the tomato club organizers had in mind. Knapp himself suggested that the ultimate reason for choosing the one-tenth acre requirement for the girls was that planting a 40-by-100-foot plot that was too large for any one family to use forced the girls to market their product—it explicitly moved beyond home and domestic space and consumption and into public, economic production.[24]

Making a nod to more traditional rhetoric, McKimmon in an interview "agreed that the ultimate object of demonstration work was the uplift of rural life." However, she continued, "the first step in the uplift was to get a few dollars into the girl's purse so that she could buy a dress, a bit of finery, and a few school books." Embedded in McKimmon's discussion was the freedom of girls to *choose* what to do with their earnings, a point the *New York Times* grasped as well: "It is understood with the parents that the children shall have and spend in any way they may desire all the money earned from their ventures." Putting money in the hands of people generally disempowered by society and trusting them to make decisions about spending it gave the girls a powerful sense of agency and freedom. The girls themselves recognized the possibilities. Margaret Brown, from outside of Charlotte, North Carolina, said the clubs "give the farm girls an opportunity to make some money, to use as they need it, and make it so they do not have to ask their parents for money every time they want it." Yoder's brother urged her to become a full economic actor with her tomatoes, telling her "when I sold them [I should] put my money in the bank and get me a check book." Yoder concluded by saying firmly, "I think I shall."[25] We do not know whether Yoder chose McKimmon's options of buying a dress or finery; perhaps she set up a savings account and earned interest on her tomatoes. Regardless, the tomato club organizers put the power of economic decision making into the girls' hands.

Powell also argued that girls should have the option to spend their money on pure luxury items—McKimmon's dresses and finery—if they wanted. Powell told the story of a "little Cajun girl" who rowed her tomatoes in a skiff across a bayou and walked several miles to reach the canning contest. When she won, "she was asked to choose the prize from the stock of the department store which offered the award. After careful looking she pointed with a finger and said, 'I want that pink silk parasol, I've wanted one all my life'." Powell's conclusion supported the girl's decision and further suggested that poor girls had as much right to aesthetic taste as anyone else. Powell wrote, "So her yearning for delicate beauty was gratified and she left the store twirling the open parasol over her left shoulder. Who can measure the joy and pride in the heart of the little girl from a one room cabin with its dirt floor."[26] Tomato club organizers never wavered in their assertion that the girls owned the money they earned, profoundly challenging many social and gender hierarchies of the early twentieth century in one of the most striking features of the movement.

Although nowhere in their writings that I have found did McKimmon, Powell, or Cromer describe themselves as feminist, prominent feminist thinkers in the United States at that time were also making the argument that women should earn their own money and make decisions about what to do with it. The tomato club organizers took an additional step toward turn-of-the-century feminism. The *New York Times* described the program as saying a girl "must charge ten cents an hour for her labor against the crop." In her "History of My Tomatoes," Betty Vann Tapscott confirmed the figure, writing, "Mama helps me and I pay her 10 cts an hour. When she cans I help her and make my money back." Writing in 1898 in her treatise *Women and Economics*, feminist scholar Charlotte Perkins Gilman argued, "To take this ground and hold it honestly, wives, as earners through domestic service, are entitled to the wages of cooks, housemaids, nursemaids, seamstresses, or housekeepers." Giving women's house or farm work concrete economic value had the ability to revise the division of power within many households by equalizing the contribution of men and women, boys and girls. Scholars of rural women point out that the stakes were raised on farmwomen's entrance into cash economies. As more agricultural business was conducted with cash, women worried they were losing status within the farm family if they only contributed to subsistence rather than to income generation. By counting women's farm labor as wages in practical, not theoretical, ways, the tomato clubs marked a concrete expansion of women's roles.[27]

For southern girls, economic resources from tomatoes came directly from southern soil and their local communities. Because joining the tomato club did not mean trading self-sufficiency (or the belief in it) for cash, tomato clubs were radically different from the other economic options available to them: going to work in a nearby factory or a culturally distant urban work force. Tomatoes generated value within individuals, and by extension, their communities, counties, and states. Rows of canned tomatoes did not symbolize breaking laws to buy self-sufficiency—as moonshine did—nor were they examples of what local girls were doing wrong—as cornbread was. Instead, tomatoes were food items that lent part of their value to the very girls who produced them, enabling the girls and their families to celebrate rather than worry over the girls' work and leisure.

MARGARET BROWN'S
TOMATOES-FOR-TUITION SCHEME

The third element in McKimmon's list about what tomatoes offered, money in girls' purses for "a few school books," was potentially the most life changing. Margaret Brown took the possibility to heart. McKimmon said, "when she wished to go to college," Brown approached the university's president and successfully proposed exchanging canned goods for tuition. She was not the only girl to recognize the power of education. Charlotte Yoder had her eye on it, as she thought about getting her bank account. She finished her report by saying, "And sometime I shall want to go to college and I'll try for the Scholar-ship." Cromer's first tomato club had as its grand prize a four-year scholarship to Winthrop College in South Carolina, which Katie Gunter won. The tomato reports from every state were full of statistics of girls winning scholarships or devoting their profits and prize purses to their own educations. McKimmon's report of 1915–1916 cited 27 tomato club girls going to school on scholarship and an additional 110 girls paying their own way in school from the profits of their tomatoes.[28]

Not only scholarships and savings contributed to the education of girls like Brown, but participation in the clubs themselves prepared the girls for future learning. No tomato club or individual girl was finished until they had written their formal report of the season and submitted it to Cromer, McKimmon, or Powell. Within the pages of their reports, the girls detailed and reflected on the chemical, botanical, and technological lessons learned. Much more went on in those pages, though. Looking back on her decades of work in her 1945 memoir *When We're Green We Grow*, McKimmon commented, "Someone has called home demonstration work 'The Country Woman's College,' and I think it is a good name."[29] We might view the earlier tomato club reports as the girls' preparatory study for that college.

Cromer outlined the report format that would be adopted across the South: "Make a cover design which will, in a neat and attractive manner indicate just what can be found within the book ... Use water-color paints, if possible ... Bind the book at the top with red or green satin baby ribbon or card ... Whenever possible illustrate your story as you proceed." Cromer outlined four topics to cover in the report: "the life history of the tomato," the history of the individual girl's club, the "object of Girls' Tomato Club," and "why you enrolled." She allowed that the rest of the booklet could cover "tomato facts" and anything "that will help a tomato grower." But it was McKimmon who really had a vision for the reports. Along with filling out what quickly became a standardized United States Department of Agriculture form (as did girls in Mississippi, for instance), each North Carolina report also included a detailed narrative description of the crop: when it was planted, what kind of fertilizer was used, whether the girl staked her plants, what the weather was like, and what she would do differently in the future. McKimmon's girls calculated precisely the amounts they harvested and canned, the expenses they absorbed (including what they paid others to help them), and the profit they made. Reports were judged not only on details included but also on clarity and creativity of the narrative.[30] By way of canning a garden plant, tomato clubs leveraged these written reports to teach girls lessons in math, narrative, creativity, business, and science.

Certainly some of these educations were put into use back on the farm, as the *New York Times* hoped, but many were constructed to help girls become professionals, shift class positions, and develop careers for themselves. Powell wrote of a club girl who "put herself through High School and Teachers College by her club work during the next five years. She is now a trained librarian." McKimmon reported on one North Carolina county in 1915 in which 22 percent of the tomato club girls were "going to school in part or wholly through their profits in canning." Virginia Jones wrote, "I want to spend my money for an education. I think that would be as nice away [sic] as I could spend it." Sadie Limer, in Warren County, North Carolina, expanded on Jones's statement, saying, "As my ambition is to be a school teacher, (and knowing that to be a good one, one must be educated[)], I wanted to get a fairly good education, that is to say, go off to a good high school or college. I also knew it would cost considerable to do so, and I wanted to pay my own tuition, or the greater part, if possible." A newspaper clipping from Mississippi celebrated the fact that thirty-six African American girls were "paying expenses at school from money earned in their club work." Sometimes the girls themselves set up innovative entrepreneurial systems to finance their education, as did Brown with her tomatoes-for-tuition scheme. Looking back on the early tomato club work, Powell concluded, "Today these pioneer club girls are teachers in High

School and Colleges, secretaries to business and professional firms, proprietors of tea rooms and other business ventures; librarians and journalists. They are active in church, in women's clubs and on school boards."[31] At a time when most girls were attending rural one-room schools, the dream of college and higher education received solid financing by a humble garden plant.

CITIZENSHIP, RACE, AND RESISTANCE

> Always the mother's permission was asked to make changes in the kitchen arrangement to conform with the instructions for demonstration. These instructions were read and placed for ready reference by the workers, and in sight of all the participants. When a question arose, often the mother was asked to read the specific instruction aloud. Then the leader explained the importance of following instructions exactly so the club member could qualify for the prize contest and her canned goods meet requirements for marketing under the club label. When the demonstration was over and tables and utensils cleaned the agent would offer to put things back as she found them. But the mother would say indifferently, "Oh, let it stay there is no hurry about it."
>
> JAMES TANNER, "County Extension Workers"

Often, the first challenge tomato club organizers faced concerned getting inside the houses. According to James Tanner, Powell found that "A natural difficulty in getting county aid for the women's work was the almost universal attitude that it would be an intrusion of the privacy and paucity of the home for an agent to go into the home and infer that the housewife needed any instruction." This attitude came from rural households, but it was not confined to them. Powell continued, "Even the members of the Federation of Women's Club[s] which gave support to the Extension Staff in selling the idea, had to be convinced." Tanner expanded on Powell's point, saying, "Women are more sensitive about the affairs of the home than men are about those of the farm. The home is a sacred place not to be invaded by a critic or reformer. Suggested changes must be very diplomatically presented."[32] Powell's careful solution to the problem, quoted in full above, points out that creating a cooperative situation in which both agent and mother united for the good of the girl was a supremely tricky situation the tomato club organizers managed gracefully.

Once the home's doors were open, some of the radical potential of the tomato clubs could be explored. More ephemeral than concrete economic and educational benefits, the potential for political and social change was no less profound. A newspaper in Jane McKimmon's Conceit Book dated 4 June 1915 described a "Unique Entertainment Given at the Normal." The events of the evening were perhaps a silly example of the social function tomato clubs served for women and girls as they "appeared on the stage as huge tomatoes and as the curtain rolled back they sang a tribute and performed a movement thoroughly in keeping with the spirit of their club. Then one of these human tomatoes climbed to the top of a step ladder by the side of a can six feet high and announced she was ready to be canned." The article continued, "A group of mountaineers, ladies who came from the far off hills as far [away as] Cherokee, filled the hole in the top of a can."³³ Bringing together girls and women from different parts of the state, sharing public performances, and generally having fun in a large group could open horizons for both rural and urban people. It is easy to overstate rural isolation, but it is equally easy to forget the liberation and freedom that could come from social gatherings. Tomato clubs could be crucibles for issues of citizenship, interracial dialogue, and multi-class alliances, as well as for racism, patriarchal control, and class conflict in the early twentieth-century South.

Media of the day were bringing more consumer desire of the type that the moonshine literature explored to rural farm families. Historian of 4-H Franklin Reck argues that from 1900 to 1910, "Farmers were not only making more money, they were emerging from frontier isolation." The introduction of new technologies—such as rural free mail delivery, telephones, and automobiles— "aroused in farm people a growing discontent" precisely because they had such ability to compare themselves to other Americans. Others worried that rural schools were training media-savvy youth to leave home rather than stay in local communities. Tomato clubs walked a middle line here—girls did not *have* to leave to earn money, but many *did* leave with the money they earned for college or careers. At the same time, unlike factory or city work, the kinds of careers many of the tomato girls contemplated brought them back to their rural communities. Alma Tromberger of Bessemer City, North Carolina, began her tomato report with the story of how no one stayed for the first club meeting. But, she said, "We had read of it in the 'Progressive Farmer.' When I got home and was telling mama about it she said 'O Alma why didn't you stay? That is the very thing that I want you to join. I'm so glad that they are getting that up in this county'."[34] Southern girls like Tromberger were supported by their politically aware families to emerge from inside their homes or from inside the family circle to be more fully visible Americans of the early twentieth century.

What did it mean to be a visible American, though? Underneath the rhetoric of the tomato clubs lay a deep concern about citizenship. For Cromer, the clubs were a way to "elevate labor" and "keep girls away from the streets and make their bodies stronger," but she did not explore what could happen politically if the girls were to see themselves as "labor." In other cases, the language of citizenship rose to the surface, such as in this from a Department of Agriculture letter: "The tomato signifies the relation of the garden products to a happy and contented citizenship." Writing a decade later, at the cusp of the Depression and in the midst of the Great Migration of African Americans out of his state, Mississippi's James Tanner, State Boys Club agent, echoed the argument, when he said, "The whole point is that the very safety of our nation itself depends upon a contented, prosperous rural people. It is largely because of economic ills that such a condition does not exist today."[35] The tomato club rhetoric seemed more concerned with bringing citizens into the national polity from their position on various borders (regional isolation or modernity, for instance), than with predicting what might happen once they were included.

Program organizers within the states and at the federal level worked to make the government feel like an ally or friend; such efforts went forward in terms of both race and gender simultaneously. "Negro Agent" Emma McDougald, writing to McKimmon in 1922, said, "Our colored people seem delighted that the government should think enough of them to send some one to help them. Before this happened, the government was just a name to most Negro farm folk; now they feel that it is a real friend." An Arkansas county agent agreed, writing, "Country women seem to be more hesitant about asking for help wanted than are the men. They have not fully overcome the feeling that the right of government belongs mostly to the men." The same cluster of beliefs was likely behind the 1924 yearbook of girls' work in Mississippi that diverted from recipes and plant guidance to explain parliamentary law—and then suggested exercises encouraging girls to practice using the language of government.[36] The story of girls' tomato clubs was a chapter in the nation's history in which women and girls of different classes and races at least were poised to build a cooperative social movement less riddled by schisms of hierarchy and power, organized around a quintessentially southern garden plant.

Tomato clubs found innovative ways to bridge the gulf between races in the South, approaching an interracial cooperation similar to the interclass cooperation they were also achieving. Knapp had paved the way for this when he traveled to Booker T. Washington's Tuskegee Institute as early as 1906 to hire Tom Campbell as the first Negro demonstration agent. Campbell had already been working with African American farmers in a privately funded effort, but Knapp found a way for government to support the work. Links between white and African American workers were strong. When Ella Agnew in Virginia took on the canning work, she knew she needed more knowledge about tomatoes. Agnew accepted an invitation from the principal of African American Hampton Institute, Dr. Hollis B. Frissell, to take a course in tomato culture. African American communities, in fact, pioneered strategies for teaching canning and forming girls' clubs. A program privately funded by a white Quaker heiress, Anna Jeanes, placed rotating master teachers in counties, demonstrating vocational and classical education strategies. Jeanes teachers worked to improve African American education in the South by hands-on work with students and teachers. Many of their lessons and strategies were adopted by Knapp and his workers; some specifically responded to the needs of African American rural communities and greatly benefited the African Americans who were later hired to do the "Negro Work."[37]

In North Carolina, it was not until 1919, under federal pressure from World War I to teach food conservation to all citizens, that forty-one African American women were officially hired as emergency home demonstration agents. Before that, O. B. Martin and the Negro Rural Schools agent, N. C. Newbold, had quietly hired African American workers, many of whom were Jeanes teachers; because they could not use government funds, they paid the workers from the same Rockefeller General Education Board money that Knapp used to pay Cromer and Agnew, the first white women workers. Once black workers were hired for the war work, McKimmon launched a fight to keep them on staff and integrate the demonstration work. She used her yearly reports as chances to speak out for the work. In 1917, she noted, "The Council of the State Federation of Women's Clubs voted approval of the plans to introduce conservation programs into the clubs, and voted their support of the city home demonstration agents appointed to push the emergency program." In other words, McKimmon used her connections with the state women's club to get them onboard with supporting the work of the African American female agents—because most of those city agents were African American. By 1920, McKimmon took an even more explicit stand and wrote, "There is not a home agent in demonstration work who is not eager to see work for negro women and girls continued. The results in each county organized were so marked, and the desire for instruction so manifest, that the Home Demonstration Division feels no better expenditure of funds could be made than that for the payment of the negro assistants." McKimmon won the battle and hired African American women as full-time agents for six North Carolina counties. One of those women, Dazelle Lowe, went on to become state agent for the Negro Home Demonstration work; her yearly reports combined a detailed accounting of the extra work that black agents had to take on with strong calls for more equal pay and resources—statements McKimmon supported by including them in her own accounting.[38]

South Carolina's African American home demonstration workers, in the words of scholar Carmen Harris, "managed to empower themselves" despite "a system of oppression under which white South Carolinians attempted to use black home agents as part of their social control mechanisms." Unlike the North Carolina system, the divisions between white and black female agents in South Carolina were so strongly enforced that black agents had to shape their programs while simultaneously resisting the imposition of lessons from parallel white agents sure of their own superiority. In her careful study of black and white clubwomen in South Carolina, Joan Marie Johnson could find no evidence of the two most prominent women even meeting.[39] What happened in South Carolina occurred across the South (and in North Carolina, too); we should not overstate the connections tomato clubs could foster. Nonetheless, moments in which women used a garden plant to reach across racial divides tell us about the potential, however fraught, for change and connection.

In her study of women and white supremacy in North Carolina, *Gender and Jim Crow*, historian Glenda Elizabeth Gilmore calls McKimmon's and Lowe's early club work an example of interracial cooperation that formed "alliances... that held strong enough for black and white women to choose to continue to drive together down rutted roads, chatting about their work and their hopes for the future." McKimmon's reports were full of examples of white and black agents sharing information, working closely together, and teaching each other lessons that they would then pass on to their constituencies. For instance, McKimmon discussed how they started with segregated training programs, but by 1933 both white and black agents sat together, and "a mutual feeling of respect and appreciation was engendered when each had an opportunity to hear reports of the other's good work." She then almost slyly noted that "the results of the plan proved to be so satisfactory that Director Schaub decided to arrange the next year and in years thereafter for a joint conference of all the extension groups of white and Negro men and women agents." Thus, in some counties even as social and legal Jim Crow segregation was the practice of the time, demonstrations were opened to both black and white women, creating striking moments of integrated space in the segregated South.[40]

Reading McKimmon's papers, it becomes clear how much both the interracial alliance and interclass cooperation were works in progress, having to be rebuilt and renegotiated each year as new workers and new outside pressures came into the club work. Thus, the tomato club organizers repeatedly articulated what interclass cooperation looked like, called it into being, and celebrated its successes. Speaking in front of the annual state meeting of women's clubs in 1924, McKimmon reiterated "how she had looked forward to the day when the forces of the county and city women might be co-ordinated that they might work together to the best interest of the state." Following McKimmon, Rosalind Redfearn of Wadesboro, one of McKimmon's most dedicated workers, reminded the crowd, "Country folks we once were called, but now they call us rural women." The article paraphrased Redfearn as saying, "The city club women may know all about menus but the rural club women can tell you how the food is produced and prepared."[41] Moving from "country" to "rural" meant rejecting a more derogatory term in favor of a more neutral one, exhibiting a spirit of cooperation and equality; Redfearn hinted at conversations both long begun and necessary for the future, ones explored in more depth in chapter 5.

Because personal letters between Lowe and McKimmon have, for the most part, not been preserved, it is hard to say if, how, and in what ways their friendship developed. Being women of their times, Lowe and the other "Negro agents" may have followed the codes and practices historian Darlene Clark Hine calls the culture of dissemblance, which black women employed to hide their true selves and families from the white people with whom they had to interact so as not to make themselves vulnerable to later racism. As Gilmore puts it, white women like McKimmon "wanted to work with black women on social problems." But, she continues, "This does not mean that white women questioned or rejected the ideology of white supremacy." Instead, the tomato club women "were left with the more confusing business of sorting out their thoughts and developing a racial ideology that allowed room for continued racial interaction." Gilmore provides a helpful reminder of the continuing challenges; we also should mark the achievement here, though. From hints in the historical record, including one letter from another African American worker, Lucy Wade, to McKimmon in which she lingered over her travel, a cold she had, and the work in front of her, the warmth of genuine friendship was certainly possible.[42] As much as the early tomato clubs focused on this interclass cooperation, they had to revisit and rebridge the gap in the turn-of-the-century South between white and African American women, even as they did the same activist work.

Powell's professional attitude toward interracial work is more difficult to discern than McKimmon's. Her experiences and those of her staff, both white and African American, showed that resistance to tomato club work could also simultaneously involve race and class. Even after African American women were hired to do the war work, they had to proceed carefully. All work with black sharecroppers or tenant farmers needed approval from white landowners or overseers first—and this applied to demonstrations within the home as well. In his study of the extension work in Mississippi, historian Danny Moore details one agent who was fired for simply talking with a homemaker whose landlord had not given permission. Powell wisely hired Mississippi resident Alice Carter Oliver, a former Jeanes teacher, graduate of the University of Illinois, and astutely politically savvy African American woman, to head the "Negro Work" for women in the state. Oliver "paid her own travel expense, bought equipment and did the same pioneer work as was done by white agents employed before 1912," according to a history of the work written by James Tanner. One of the reasons it is hard to tease out the working relationship between Oliver and Powell at our historical distance is that they both worked for R. S. Wilson, a complicated man who managed to sound thoroughly racist even while (tepidly) making Progressive arguments and who eventually forced the resignation of Powell over gender politics at the agency. Wilson rarely included any details on the work with black Mississippians in his report, saying only that it copied the white work.[43] The professional, educated Oliver and her counterparts in North and South Carolina worked against the background of organized racism. Nonetheless, they took the materials and support offered by

McKimmon, Powell, and others and created a responsive and flexible program for southern African Americans. Girls canning again proved the catalyst to restructure economic and political power in the farm family—whatever the race of that family.

Early home workers in all the states had to work harder than their male counterparts to document changes brought about by the programs. Making women visible proved complicated. As T. Roy Reid, writing of the Arkansas home demonstration work, explained, "Once worked out [home improvements] are not as evident as are similar changes on the farms. The growing crops, good livestock, terraces in the field may be seen by all who pass, if the road is not too conducive to speed. Signs may be put on the roadside to attract attention to these. This is not true of demonstrations in the homes." At the same time, danger lay in being visible in the wrong ways. Organizers who necessarily had to speak in public could be targeted as inappropriate. Powell described a Natchez club trying to secure funds from their county board for the tomato clubs. She said, "When I told them we would have to go before the Board to make our request, the little white haired aristocrat who was president said 'Why Miss Susie, not one of us ever set foot on the Court house grounds. No respectable woman would be seen going into the Court House.'" In this case, Powell did not have to solve the problem herself, as one of the other clubwomen stepped in: "After discussion, the president of the club, whose husband was the President of the Board said she would go and it ended by all members of the club accompanying me. The appropriation was made." In Virginia, Agnew faced similar responses: "As Miss Agnew drove a horse and buggy through four selected counties, trying to get the work started, she was handicapped by the feeling of the country people that no Virginia lady should make speeches in public. In one town, as she jumped down from a wagon after talking to a group, she overheard one woman say: 'No self-respecting woman would talk in public that way.'" The stakes could be even higher. Arkansan agent Hudson was seriously burned when a group of husbands insisted on prematurely opening the lid of a new pressure cooker she was demonstrating.[44] The general professionalism and competence of Powell, McKimmon, Agnew,

Hudson, and others—and likely the changing mores of the United States as suffrage was ratified and more women entered government and education jobs—helped such criticism and threats die down over time.

CONCLUSION

Tomato clubs themselves soon evolved into more general canning clubs as girls planted their acres with other vegetables and fruits. The federal Smith-Lever Act passed in 1914 paved the way for extension agencies in every state; home demonstration agencies were simultaneously established, and the workers who previously oversaw the tomato clubs began to work even more with adult women. Work with girls moved ever more under the new umbrella of 4-H, which served boys as well. The focus shifted away from the profit-making potential of tomatoes to other home skills, statewide conferences and gatherings, and extra-curricular activities. Agents established offices in the network of land grant colleges across the South, and the reporting and support of the work became ever more centralized. Food conservation measures federally mandated by the war allowed (in the case of Powell and McKimmon) and forced (in the case of some Mississippi and Arkansas counties, for instance) the work to expand among African Americans. By the 1920s, many of the first tomato club girls were graduating from college with newly minted home economics degrees; many took positions as demonstration agents themselves.[45] In contrast to the earliest club messages of empowerment and social change, the movement changed over the century to be more traditional in its vision of home, family, gender, and economics. But the early clubs pushed at the limits of possibility for rural women and girls in the South.

In the end, despite her predictions of the national character of the tomato club work, Cromer staked her claim as a South Carolinian. Reading her scrapbook is an illuminating experience; unlike the papers of McKimmon and Powell, Cromer's were more ego-driven. She traveled north for vacation right at the first tomato harvesting season, for instance, getting a certificate from the American School of Home Economics and attending the Green Acre

Conferences in Maine for personal growth and restoration.[46] Still, I cannot help but admire Marie Samuella Cromer—she defended her reputation and stake in beginning the work, never ceding to the national story, despite pressure from federal coworkers and later generations of historians; her scrapbook is a very human collection of personal mementos, ambitions, and documents of good work. For all her gestures to the national scene, Cromer remained very local, very South Carolinian—she kept working for schools and towns in her neighborhood; she got married; and the rest of her scrapbook is made up of the ephemera of her personal life. It was left to other tomato club girls and organizers to flesh out the bigger potential of the movement.

The tomato clubs' interclass and interracial cooperation meant to McKimmon that, "I know more than they do about home demonstration, but there are many things they could teach me. It's getting together; it's having the right point of contact with them; it's an exchange; it's lifting each other—." Rhetorically matching the black women's metaphor of a jointly climbed ladder, McKimmon emphasized a radical equality in her final words of the *Country Gentleman* article discussed at the end of chapter 2: "all over the state," McKimmon said, "is that great circle of women, lifting, lifting."[47] Even McKimmon's memoir avoided the personal "I" for the collective "we": her dedication to cooperative and collaborative learning through food continued throughout her life. McKimmon's dedication to a wide vision of North Carolina's women and girls may be why she is the best remembered of the tomato club pioneers. After a long career in extension, she retired to acclaim. Her memoir sold well; she continued to be active in North Carolina education. As a result, North Carolina still honors her, naming buildings, centers, and the extension programs at North Carolina State University after her. McKimmon's legacy is quite different from that of her fellow worker, Susie Powell, in Mississippi.

Powell's legacy is more conflicted. Resistance to the Mississippi tomato club work and its successes resulted in 1924 in what Susie Powell called "my forced resignation" as the "culmination of a series of unreasonable disturbances made in my department by the Director of Extension, with the evident purpose of forcing me to resign . . . [which] grew in frequency and violence until the situation became intolerable and made it impossible for me to go further with my work under Mr. Wilson as Director." The documents testifying to Powell's end days with tomatoes were far from the vision of economic freedom, career opportunities, and power for girls and women the first tomato clubs explored, as mutual accusations of physical abuse and conspiracies flew. The Mississippi Federation recognized the implication of Powell's firing for all women and girls in the state, saying, "The women of the Federation cannot afford to allow their own organization to be dealt such a blow. The interests of all Mississippi woman [sic] are identical, and what tends to injure and disturb extension work for rural Mississippi, injures and disturbs extension work for the Federation," but they were unsuccessful in getting her reinstated. The work survived, though without, perhaps, its initial revolutionary enthusiasm; Powell went to work for the Federation and later for the federal government during the floods of the late 1920s, which were devastating especially to black Mississippians, and she continued to help fellow Mississippi women.[48] Such profound gender-based resistance to tomato clubs, though, proved the potential they held to transform life in the South by beginning with what food women and girls had to hand.

At a time when activist work (especially government-sponsored work) did not have to feature *any* interracial contact—much less interracial cooperation—the tomato club work and its progeny of home demonstration programs brought black and white women together to can food, preserve cooperative knowledge, and grow economic opportunities for women and girls. Farm girls in South Carolina, North Carolina, and Mississippi faced different challenges in the first decades of the twentieth century. South Carolina girls had to negotiate emerging textile and small factory economies against a background of faded national prominence. North Carolina's farming girls were already surrounded by those mills and factories, but also faced rising stereotypes about living along Tobacco Road or as ignorant mountaineers or beaten-down tenant farmers. Mississippi girls felt pressure from the state's monoculture farming and starkly drawn racial divisions. Individual communities and families differed as well, with some embracing girls' efforts to bridge the private farm experience and public markets with their tomato canning, and others being nervous or suspicious of the changing racial or class environments such bridges might bring. Girls met each other—at national exhibits and competitions, wearing their badges and trading songs and pledges. Organizers met from across the states, sometimes for the first time sitting down with women of different races and classes from their own, talking about their shared challenges and expressing their individual perspectives. For a moment, rows and rows of shiny cans of tomatoes promised a union of science, technology, self-sufficiency, education, freedom, and possibility. The retreat of 4-H work through the rest of the century into the nostalgic and traditional forms of domesticity it often takes today testifies in its pendulum swing to the radical possibilities of the earlier tomato clubs.

When fictional Kit Brandon used the freedom of her automobile to drive as fast as possible away from the rural farms of the South toward the nation's cities, she could have met an actual tomato club organizer going the opposite direction in her own Ford. As an article from 1922 by Charlotte Hilton Green celebrating North Carolina's "emancipation of the rural housewife" proposed: "mayhap some great-great-granddaughter of some powdered belle of long ago who trod a stately minuet in celebration of that first independence is today gliding over the same county in a Ford, teaching women and girls to can fruits and vegetables." Those women, with their vision of economic freedom, the power of education, and an interclass and interracial method of "lifting, lifting" each other, helped girls like Annie Laura Peterson to "feel like I was some good in the world, while I now [sic] we should have some pleasure, I also know we should know how to work and be ready for business where we are needed."[49]

Some girls, many of whom, by virtue of their race or poverty, did not benefit from the tomato club work, found their way into the business Peterson described through employment at textile mills and factories, the subject of the following chapter. It turns out that canned tomatoes and vegetables are a way to understand their lives as well. For many girls, disease, starvation, and a failure of consumerism's promises awaited—and the vitamin-deficient pellagra victim takes center stage in the next moment of the southern food and gender story. Nonetheless, if we forget the legacy of the tomato club girls, we lose the lessons we might take from a wide-ranging social movement that harnessed the power of a humble vegetable to give a measure of freedom to thousands of girls like Annie Laura Peterson.

Girls recognized the presence of technology increasingly in their daily lives; some celebrated its possibilities. Sallie Jones, "Girls Canning Club" book cover, ca. 1915. Jane S. McKinnon papers, PC 234. Courtesy of the North Carolina Office of Archives and History, Raleigh, North Carolina.

CHAPTER FOUR

Will Work for Food

MILL WORK, PELLAGRA, AND

GENDERED CONSUMPTION

> Beneath the label "Oysters," "Shrimps,"
> Or "Beans," or "Peas," or "Corn"
> Is canned a pound of frolic missed
> Upon a summer morn:—
>
> ....
>
> A pound of health, a pound of strength
> From cradles snatched, we find:
> A pound of young intelligence
> Robbed from a childish mind.
> Packed here together, snugly fit
> Teresa's eyesight, Tony's wit.
>
> ....
>
> Come buy sweet childhood by the can.
>
> SARAH N. CLEGHORN, "Canned Childhood"

WHEN MARIE CROMER raised her hand to propose founding a tomato club for girls in 1909, she made the suggestion to counter putting girls in a chrysanthemum club. To Cromer, flowers represented mere domesticity, daintiness, and leisure time—something fun and distracting for whiling away the hours—but not something helpful to the disempowered rural girls she was targeting. Cromer looked for a task that would help girls become productive members of their societies; something that might train them in leadership, responsibility, and economic self-sufficiency. Later, in retelling the story, Cromer revealed one of her inspirations for choosing the tomato and the process of canning to help girls in South Carolina. A magazine article titled "South Carolina's Tomato Lady and How She Jarred the Mossbacks" included in her scrapbook reported, "Miss Cromer, remembering a kid ambition to manage a cannery, suggested tomatoes." It is a striking detail. One might have to work pretty hard to find a girl in the South with such a "kid ambition" today. Traces of factory and mill girls, however, pop up in select southern stories from the early century. Actual girls' labor helped power southern mills and southern labor movements. Scholars have noticed how girls' culture affected labor movements in the South. For example, historian Jacquelyn Dowd Hall investigates how girls in a strike in Elizabethton, Tennessee, used fashion and fun, teen culture to disrupt the government forces against them.[1] Cromer was not alone in being aware of and even striving for a place in a perfect cannery.

At the same time, Cromer's phrasing serves as a useful cautionary moment for us as we try to look back and tease out the messages of gender and region in the stories of food from the early twentieth century. Cromer was talking about a romanticized cannery, not the type poet Sarah Cleghorn watched stealing the childhood of child laborers in the service of profit and hard work. Cromer was not thinking of photographer and researcher Lewis Hine's images of girls and child labor in migrant camps, canneries, textile mills, and other factories, whose bent bodies testified to the difficult working conditions. Cromer's dream cannery, instead, allowed a woman to be in charge of a safe but exciting workplace, where the messiness of the actual labor, physical danger, hardship, and complicated economic realities could be glossed over. (Remember, even Cromer hoped tomato clubs would keep girls from being lost to hard factory work.) Contrast Cromer's girlhood dream of managing a cannery with letters sent in 1917 from E. Val Philips to her friend Blanche Hanks Elliott in Arkansas. Philips wrote from Oklahoma; her family had recently moved from

Arkansas to Kansas to Sapulpa, Oklahoma, seeking work. Perhaps Philips was in the same canning club as Elliott the previous year; in any case, she longed for it in her letter. As she said, "I hope that you get the prise [*sic*] this year on your fruit. When does the fair begin, I would like to be there during the fair or for a few days any how."[2] Instead, she worked in a glass factory and was sad that she no longer attended school.

More worrisome, Philips revealed she was losing weight fast, losing Cleghorn's "pound of health" and "pound of strength." Philips blamed the water in Sapulpa, but one suspects the difficulty of the work she performed and the economic precipice on which her family balanced had something to do with how "Oklahoma don't go as well with me as Ks did I have lost 9 pounds since I left Ks." Perhaps even more to the point, Philips was silent on the matter of her diet; we do not know what food was available to her around and in the glass factory. We do not know how long her lunch breaks were, whether she had time to help her (likely) female family members cook, or if she could afford anything other than cornbread, fatback, and sorghum when she did eat. Nonetheless, Philips had a new perspective on her own "kid ambitions," and she gave advice to her friend Elliott. Philips wrote, "I am getting $2.75 per day and don't have to work as hard as some that pick appels [*sic*] for $2.00 there. You can get $2.00 per hundred for picking cotton here but I don't want any of that in my mine well I hope that you get to work in the appels if that is what you want to do . . . and speaking of your fruit or vegetables I am glad to see you girls get the prizes more especialy [*sic*] you. Ha ha." She found glass-factory work better than harvesting fruit; both were easier than work in cotton. None of it, however, was nourishing. Philips's and Cleghorn's "canned childhood" realities countered Cromer's (and perhaps Elliott's) optimistic dreams.[3]

Cromer and the girls she targeted, or Elliott and her fellow tomato club members—these girls could use the image of the factory or cannery to build dreams of sufficiency and wealth. Girls like Philips, or girls whose families did not control their own land or whose families needed their factory wages to survive—these girls were the other side of the fantasy. Philips and girls like her were vulnerable to pellagra. Triggered by a deficiency of niacin (vitamin B-3), pellagra caused extreme weight loss, skin lesions, severe diarrhea, insanity, and death.[4] The disease occurred in people who were starving or eating only a limited range of foods. Like the more famous scurvy or rickets, pellagra could be present even in those who consumed sufficient calories for survival. It swept the South in the early twentieth century, deeply puzzling doctors and social activists, as it occurred simultaneously with an influx of southerners joining a cash economy and in a region that was one of the country's agricultural powerhouses. With money and food around, why was pellagra appearing in epidemic numbers?

If the tomato clubs were one vision of food as cash, the canneries, factories, and mills in the South that employed working-class girls' labor were another. Our story of southern food and southern gender must tackle head-on the issues of lack, absence, and desire in food. This chapter investigates three disturbing paradoxes of southern food: How, in a region still producing a substantial portion of the nation's agricultural crops, could its people be suffering from starvation, malnutrition, and their resultant diseases? How did changing relations to time among southerners who finally participated fully in a consumer, capitalist culture long promised as American salvation cause them to be so punished by that consumption? And how could the foods celebrated as quintessentially southern—biscuits, cornbread, moonshine, and canned goods—be tied to a monstrous body, the grotesque starved pellagrin (as sufferers of pellagra were termed) that worried the body politic? At the heart of these paradoxes and thus at the heart of this chapter lie stories of food and gender haunted by pellagra—the pellagrin in literature made visible the difficult costs of modernity and industry and the otherwise invisible social hierarchies troubling the southern dinner table—all of which get lost in a romanticized narrative of southern food.

FOOD MATH: HOW THREE *MS* EQUAL FOUR *DS*

It must not be understood that these people live sparingly. The contrary is true, generally speaking, though the food is not always well chosen. Fried pork, swimming in grease, and huge yellow soda biscuits are staple articles. Fried eggs and sausage and fried chicken are also common. Choice steaks are bought, but soup is rarely seen... Almost before the mill-owner feels that he can afford to have strawberries, tomatoes, peaches or pineapples, the operatives have them, though they may put the strawberries into a pie. Usually, pie of some sort is on the table every day, often for every meal. These people are large consumers of canned goods, knowing and demanding good quality always. They will use nothing but the finest flour, though they may tinge it yellow with soda. Pickles come to the stores in barrels, and the assortment of tobacco and snuff is always large. This extravagance in food is probably induced by the revolt of the stomach against the unappetizing staples.

HOLLAND THOMPSON, "Life in a Southern Mill Town," 1900

Around the same time Cromer inaugurated her tomato club, scholar and North Carolinian Holland Thompson researched the fast-growing mill town of Concord, North Carolina. Both Thompson and Cromer believed strongly in the South; both felt that benevolent industry could help the region catch up to its northern neighbors. Complicating their views, though, a new disease was making headlines across the southern states. Cromer's home state of South Carolina would soon take the lead in fighting the disease, pellagra, and its political fallout, pellagraphobia. It was not the only illness sweeping the South; hookworm, tuberculosis, pneumonia, malaria, smallpox, and the following decade's major influenza epidemic all affected many of the region's citizens. Family after family had at least one member who was said to have more generally "broken down"—in the mills, in the mines, in the fields. Their stories haunted the novels, short stories, and scholarship from the first third of the twentieth century. These were the images: sallow complexions, lazy demeanors, distended bellies, stunted height, and glazed expressions. Sometimes described as the "mill type," other times as "white trash" and the "typical southern Negro," whether on Erskine Caldwell's Piedmont Tobacco Road, on the Deep South's cotton plantations, or in Appalachia's mountain communities, from this historical distance it is almost impossible to know just how many of the people in photographs or descriptions were actually victims of disease.[5] Behind the stereotypes hid a hungry, tired, and ill version of the South that even today is difficult to see or understand. Thompson certainly missed it in his catalog of abundance.

Looking sunburned, feeling fatigued, moving with a pained and jerky gait, and unable to keep down food, early stage pellagrins were often mistakenly labeled lazy or indolent or misdiagnosed with colds or rheumatism. Only when skin, especially on their faces, peeled and hardened, leaving visible butterfly-shaped lesions, and marking them much like the victims of leprosy, was pellagra undeniable. Sometimes called "the butterfly caste," sufferers of pellagra faced comparisons to and similar quarantining as leprosy victims. Fear of the disease, pellagraphobia, led friends and family (not to mention southern states' political apparatuses) to shun victims. Turning pellagrins out of homes and villages, and often locking them behind the doors of poorly funded institutions, raised the death rate of the disease even higher. Described as the disease of four D's—dermatitis, diarrhea, dementia, and death—pellagra made many of its sufferers suicidal or dangerous to others. Doctors could not predict which victims would develop acute cases leading quickly to death and which would experience chronic, yearly outbreaks that debilitated but did not kill. Looking back from today's perspective, scholars suspect many more southerners suffered from milder, undiagnosed cases of the disease, but exact numbers are lost to time. Nor could doctors around 1900 explain why certain months saw spikes in pellagra cases, why the South seemed so vulnerable to the disease, and what role the typical poor southerners' diets of three M's—meat, meal, and molasses—played.[6]

For New South boosters like Thompson, middle-class observers who pinned the recovery of the South from its post-Reconstruction slump on industry and the extraction and processing of the region's raw materials, pellagra's rise in cotton mill villages was both inexplicable and unsettling. Mill villages brought high-quality canned food, imported national ingredients, and stocked store shelves with much more than typical pork, cornmeal, and sorghum molasses. Seeing in mill stores and on some mill tables pickles likely from Pennsylvania factories, strawberries from Florida, pineapples from the Bahamas by way of Baltimore, steaks from the Chicago meat packers, and the whitest of flour from the Great Plains, observers, such as Thompson, concluded that the mill villages had plenty of food. Surely, they protested, new employees must be coming to the mills already infected (more reason to abandon past ways); as a character in Mary Vorse's *Strike!* says, "We sell milk, vegetables, everything to the workers at cost. Sometimes we run at a loss . . . If any one has pellagra they would have had it before coming here." As that explanation failed scientific tests, boosters suggested that the new employees' unfamiliarity with town sanitation procedures could be blamed (more reasons to force unhealthy families out of their homes). In Myra Page's *Gathering Storm*, mill worker Marge critiques the reality of the mill housing, pointing out that houses have windows but the mill refuses to fix the window screens, which does nothing for sanitation. Similarly, she continues, outhouses have been removed and toilets installed inside the houses. However, without running water, the toilets merely bring pests and insects into living and cooking spaces. Residents are forced to board them up and make do outside, now without even the benefit of the outhouse. Yet mill boosters continue to blame the workers. Surely the mills themselves could not be incubating pellagra; surely modern science and industry would find a vaccination or cure rather than be indicted as a cause.[7]

Cracking the code of pellagra proved a triumph of early epidemiology, but not in the way Thompson and other boosters hoped. Given the South's political insecurities in the post-Reconstruction era, it was especially galling that the disease seemed to target the South, where the vast majority of victims resided and deaths occurred. Researchers expected pellagra to parallel recently solved insect or sanitation diseases such as hookworm, dengue fever, and malaria. Yet careful studies of sanitation and insect vectors conducted by federal public health officer Dr. Joseph Goldberger and his team of national and local researchers, including Edgar Sydenstricker, turned up no such germ or insect. When scientists then turned to food-based explanations, they took their cue from Italy, where pellagra was first identified, and tried unsuccessfully to show that the problem lay in the quality of the "meal" of the southern diet. Because in the South more and more agricultural acres were being planted in money-making monoculture like cotton and tobacco, corn was increasingly imported rather than grown. Looking for danger in spoiled (moist, infected, or improperly milled) corn allowed nativist southerners to blame the disease on northern or midwestern business interests that might be storing corn for too long, shipping inferior product south, or skimping on sanitation in their mills—all to keep the South down.[8] While the political uses were effective, the scientific evidence proved insufficient; eventually insects, sanitation, and bad corn were rejected as explanations.

Researchers under Goldberger turned back to the diet of victims and the race, class, geographic location, gender, and age distribution of pellagrins. Going much beyond Thompson's list of items on store shelves, Sydenstricker led a team to detailed, repeated, and long-term questioning behind the doors of mill family life. The resulting detailed maps and surveys suggested wide distance between actual eating habits and theoretically available food on shelves. They documented the sharp downturn in many families' food over winter when gardens lay fallow and wild food could not be gathered, which, in turn, allowed researchers to understand why so many got sicker or died in early spring as meager rations completely ran out. Their research prodded them to suspect a missing nutrient. In experiments to induce the disease by withholding foods suspected to have that nutrient, Goldberger homed in on a missing vitamin.[9] Although the exact vitamin, niacin, would not be identified until decades later (vitamins in general were poorly understood until the midpoint of the century), effective, if temporary, treatments were developed.

Treatments, not cures. Those southerners in the early twentieth century who ate their wild greens, had fresh eggs, milk, fish, and meat regularly (which meant being close to a farm healthy enough to support its animals, as starving cows do not deliver sufficient milk, for instance), and varied their intake of fresh and canned goods and beans along with cornbread, molasses, and cured pork would not contract pellagra. They needed to be aware that the corn from the store was less likely to come from local farms and instead was more likely to have fewer nutrients because of greater processing. Similarly, store-bought pork after the turn of the century was frequently imported and more likely to be fatback rather than their parents' staple of bacon.[10] Curing pellagra in a society took education on how foods worked together to provide a necessary range of vitamins, calories, and nutrients. It required enough economic stability and security to weather setbacks—the temporary loss of a family member's income, the death of a cow or loss of a crop, unexpected health or housing expenses, or other personal emergency. Curing pellagra benefited from a community's ability to grow or import a range of healthy foods and its agricultural diversity rather than its pervasive monoculture. Individuals needed either time to prepare diverse foods or high enough quality equipment and convenient ingredients to cook good food quickly. Societies that cured pellagra dislodged their internal racism and sexism enough to privilege feeding adequate amounts to the most vulnerable as well as the most privileged.

With public distribution of niacin-rich foods, such as brewer's yeast, canned salmon, beef, and even tomatoes such as the girls' canning clubs were producing, and with fortuitous upturns in the southern economy, Goldberger and his allies put pellagra on the run by the early 1920s. However, as soon as federal and private funds for vitamin-B-rich rations ran out or, as repeatedly happened, social hierarchies reemerged to dictate who ate what on a family's or institution's table, and as soon as mills cut hours without raising pay, individuals were forced to rely again on the cheapest, least diverse foods available. The foods Thompson witnessed sat on the shelves and gathered dust. With rations of only poorer quality meat, meal, and molasses, and precious little of them, pellagra came roaring back. It took well into the middle of the century for epidemic pellagra no longer to threaten the South.[11]

In 1929, when a violent strike broke out in Gastonia, North Carolina, only forty-five miles from Thompson's Concord, years of illness and malnutrition within hardworking families came to the surface.[12] Food for families, health care, and an economic safety net all were demands of the strike, which was notable for the participation (and assassination) of women, involvement of the radical left, brutal violence and a corrupt justice system that sanctioned it, and a proliferation of novels and songs produced about it. Although pellagra was not the only life-changing disease of the era, and not all of the "broken down" folks had the same disease, in pellagra could be seen most clearly the equation of food, gender, social power, and region. In pellagra resided the darker math, the Ms and Ds of southern food and gender.

WHAT LIES BEHIND: TRACKING SILENCE AND LACK

> [M]odern life has grown so complex that it is harder today than ever before to get the feeling, in terms of actual human beings, of what lies behind news of strikes, riots, closing down of mills and the spread of pellagra.
>
> SOUTHERN SUMMER SCHOOL PAMPHLET, CA. 1931

By 1927, when the Southern Summer School for Women Workers in Industry, a group dedicated to helping female mill workers through education and support, was founded, pellagra was again sickening more than two hundred thousand southerners a year. The problems of poverty, starvation, disease, and agricultural instability in the South seemed ever more intractable. The Progressive movement was in disarray as well: while poems like Cleghorn's "Canned Childhood" helped pass child labor laws, lax enforcement and collusion meant that children still worked in southern mills; the maximum length of a work day was regulated, but mills responded with physically brutal stretch-out and overtime systems that were anything but voluntary; women and African Americans ostensibly had the vote, but equal rights were a long way off. Club work was mainstream enough to be an official part of mills, but the tradeoff was the erasure of any revolutionary potential of the clubwomen, as it became instead a propaganda boon for mill owners.[13]

Two years later, in 1929, Ella May Wiggins, a balladeer and union organizer central to the Gastonia textile strikes, was assassinated, joining in death four of her nine children, at least one of whom had died of pellagra when only sixteen months old.[14] Writing in the early 1930s, in a pamphlet containing some of the few extant essays by mill women themselves, the Southern Summer School organizers found "modern life" so complicated that perhaps it is no wonder that they were ready to turn the responsibility for speaking over to women workers. Pellagra was complicated, too; the foods that cured it and the strategies that proved effective were dishes and recipes that rarely appeared in cookbooks because they were so commonplace. Yet curing it required balancing menus over time, a task not at all common or easy in mill society. Thus, this chapter makes a significant departure from the rest of *A Mess of Greens* in that its focus is not on a specific food or a specific recipe. Rather, the focus here is on what was missing, on the lack of food, the absence of healthy eating, the vanished pieces. We are so quick today to romanticize southern food as nourishing, hearty, and comforting that if nothing else it is worth remembering a major portion of the southern food story was one of decidedly unromantic, painful loss.

In the early stages of the crisis, in the decades around the turn of the century, while confusing theories and incomplete science swirled around southern states, pellagra raised uncomfortable political, social, and regional questions. For our purposes, epidemiological breakthroughs, though fascinating, are less interesting than how pellagra became a symbol for food and gender's most troubling intersections. In the era's novels and stories, pellagra was partly historical but mostly symbolic. In the historical record, thousands, if not tens of thousands, of pellagrins were institutionalized when their disease flared. Mental institutions and penitentiaries hid the pellagrin away from society, out of official view. In the novels, however, the pellagrin was a family member, mother, child, or neighbor, and was not removed from the community. He or she died at home. A character in Olive Tilford Dargan's *Call Home the Heart* faces the decision: "Having to choose between going on to the county and dying at home, she chose home and the further starvation the choice entailed."[15] Therefore, it is reasonable to conclude that the pellagrin served a symbolic and critical purpose in the novels—our task becomes teasing out what that purpose was.

A novel published in 1904, Marie Van Vorst's *Amanda of the Mill*, opens up the experience of mill life; we turn first to it. Van Vorst wrote in the middle of Goldberger's investigations. Pellagra was neither named nor understood—but it was clear something was very wrong at the southern table. Finding the problem required going beyond the dinner hour to the sights, sounds, tastes, and bodily experiences of the southern mill world; Van Vorst began exactly there.

Finding the answer to pellagra also required looking deeper than the surface of food on the table to see where it came from, what its ideological weight was, and how the mythologies of American consumption turned into food to consume on these southern tables. Novels highlighted conflicting theories and feelings of despair around the practices of who ate, when, and in what quantities—decisions that had everything to do with how race, class, gender, and age were distributed in the people at any given table. The Gastonia strike novels of the early 1930s, especially Grace Lumpkin's *To Make My Bread*, Myra Page's *Gathering Storm*, and Olive Tilford Dargan's *Call Home the Heart*, all feature characters suffering from pellagra. Their pellagrins persistently haunt the novels' southern landscapes. They function as figures of failure for the New South, monsters troubling the radical potential of class alliance, and horrible reminders of food that did not nourish. Pellagrins embody consumption consuming itself.

MARIE VAN VORST'S AMANDA: MILL TIME, SOUND, AND TASTE

The iconic photographs of Lewis Hine and others, the vivid portrait of Upton Sinclair's *The Jungle*, the legacy of deadly violence (including the Loray Mill Strike that killed Wiggins), and the necessity of major public health suits (such as brown lung) installed mills and early century industry in general as epitomes of danger and harm. We picture confined quarters, long hours, brutalized bodies, polluted water, and ravaged land. Today the appeal of mill life can be hard to fathom.

Yet in the first decades of the twentieth century, subsistence farms across the South were in serious transition. Whether they ever were fully self-supporting is debatable, but by 1900, more and more farm expenses needed to be paid for in cash. With agricultural prices swinging wildly, barter economies and neighborhood support were insufficient for farms to avoid sinking into debt. Across the South, business people representing extractive industries such as logging and mining were buying land and mineral rights out from under some of the same longtime settlers facing biscuits, cornbread, moonshine, and tomato club decisions. In the piedmont and cotton belt regions, more and more families were facing pressures to become tenant farmers or sharecroppers as they lost hold or failed to acquire lands of their own.[16] For many, then, the lure of mill life was powerful and rational. Escaping a cycle of farming that seemed to spiral ever downward, finding a way into cash economies that seemed increasingly inescapable, even representing last ditch efforts to hold onto family land by paying store debts, families from around the region were drawn into mill work.

Mills, fed by the ready influx of workers, grew astoundingly in the early century. For instance, in 1899, North Carolina already had 177 mills; by 1909, that number was up to 281. South Carolina boasted 80 and 147, in the same time period, though compared to North Carolina, South Carolina's mills tended to be larger facilities. The money was similarly impressive: mills in North Carolina grew from yearly profits of $28.4 to $72.7 million in the decade. In North Carolina, thirty thousand mill jobs existed in 1900; there were forty-seven thousand by 1910. Another forty-five thousand mill workers labored in South Carolina by the later date. One scholar has calculated that by 1905 in South Carolina at least "one of every six white persons lived in a mill village."[17] The villages varied widely in quality of life, but the common denominator was that most mill workers lived in housing that belonged not to them but instead to the company for whom they worked.

As a result, housing could be taken away as quickly as a layoff or firing could be ordered, and thus, decades-long employees could lose everything in a day. Loan sharks—offering furniture, better stoves, beds, even family pictures—preyed on employees, setting up weekly payment plans that almost guaranteed goods would be repossessed. By the turn of the century, almost all of the textile mills were equipped for electric power, but only some of the mill housing offered residential electricity. Mill villages with running water for indoor plumbing systems were rare as well. Goldberger and Sydenstricker looked carefully at available green space or garden space in mill villages; again, only a small number of model mill villages boasted of yards or gardens for employees.[18] Just as we learned from Holland Thompson's catalog of available food, however, even when facilities like water, garden space, or electricity were theoretically available, employees were not necessarily able to take advantage of the innovations. Nonetheless, from the outside, mills were new, promising, and modern for workers ground down by older systems of farming for subsistence.

Mill work, even the harsh southern form of it, also promised pleasures. Emerging consumer culture could be powerfully attractive. Chewing gum, ginger ale, movies, books, electricity, toilets, cookstoves, window glass and screens, new dresses, items from the newly arriving mail-order catalogs, restaurants, even just a paycheck, all enticed potential workers.[19] Additionally, as we saw in the debates in the moonshine literature over women and girls, the newly invented teen girl was by definition a consumer of goods. How she had the money to fulfill her role was hotly contested with wage-earning labor one of the practical options. Even the tomato clubs recognized the lure of the factory—girls who bought their first pretty dress or parasol with money from their tomatoes might have wished to purchase more. They might have turned to mill wages to do so.

Writers during the time tried to understand the lure of the mill and the embodied experiences of it. Marie Van Vorst was one such woman. Raised in a socially prominent New York family, she spent most of her adult life in Europe, marrying an Italian count late in life. On the face of it, she seemed an unlikely spokesperson for disenfranchised southern mill women. However, on December 18, 1901, she carefully undressed from the $447 worth of clothes she wore. Laying aside her $40 hat and $200 sealskin coat and even disposing of her $30 underwear, she redressed in the clothes of a working girl. A felt hat, woolen gloves, flannel shirt-waist, and cheap $1 underwear were part of her $9.45 outfit. So costumed, she traveled first to work in a shoe factory in Massachusetts and then to cotton mills near Columbia, South Carolina—where she became a spinner in the "pest-ridden, epidemic-filled, filthy settlement where in this part of the country the mill-hand lives." Her sister Bessie worked in a pickle factory and in sewing. Part of a flurry of such efforts around the turn of the century, the Van Vorst sisters collaborated to write 1903's *The Woman Who Toils*, an exposé of working life. Marie Van Vorst then wrote a novel inspired by her time in South Carolina, *Amanda of the Mill* (1904). While Bessie had a hard time not blaming the women she met for their own difficulties (seeing them as frivolous and selfish for working or wanting nice hats), Marie found them resourceful and intelligent, suffering under an economic system unlikely to be corrected by anything other than collective action. At first, Marie backed away from all-out social revolution and instead called for incremental change. *The Woman Who Toils* embraced a Georgia mill owner who appeared more reasonable; by *Amanda of the Mill*, however, Van Vorst had moved closer toward revolution. She brought in a flood to wash away the old order and raise the possibility of a worker-led, new one. On the one hand, Van Vorst fit into a long line of stunt reporters titillating readers with "exotic" experiences; on the other, because of her detailed attention to and tolerance of the stories of the people she met, Van Vorst's work has been described as early oral history and ethnography.[20] Regardless, her novel achieved visceral connections to mill sights and sounds.

Amanda of the Mill opens with Amanda skinny-dipping innocently in a Blue Ridge mountain pool. Unaware of time or her surroundings, Amanda is interrupted by Henry Euston, a northeastern city man with a mysterious past trying to drown himself to escape his alcoholism. Amanda and Henry's lives are entwined from that moment on, though before they get together, Henry mistakenly marries Amanda's sister. All three land in a South Carolina mill village that a recruiter came to the region advertising. Henry eventually sobers up and becomes spokesperson for the new labor union. Amanda's sister cheats on him, leaves him, and eventually dies; in the meantime, the mill owner's independently wealthy wife adopts Amanda and takes her to Europe. Amanda's benefactor learns that her husband abandoned a pregnant first wife to falsely marry her (that child, as befitting a good melodrama, turns out to be Henry). With money and polish, Amanda returns to the mill town to fulfill a deathbed promise to deliver the wife's forgiveness to her mill-owner husband. Amanda tries to reform the mill from within the system; when that fails, she allies herself with Henry to bring about a workers' revolution. In the end, only Henry, heir to the mill fortune, and Amanda, rich in her own right, are left to begin again after the flood. Poetically, the novel ends with Amanda and Henry on the edge of another pool of water, about to found "new industries operating for the mutual benefit of employer and employed."[21] Throughout, Van Vorst lightly fictionalized stories from *The Woman Who Toils* for a new audience—child labor; sexual harassment and other gender discrimination in the mills; poor food, sanitation, and resulting diseases; and consumer seductions paired with economic setbacks.

While they are still in the mountains, Amanda's life is organized around the natural world—she swims when the weather is warm; she feeds Henry when he awakens; she watches the moon cast shadows. This stands in sharp contrast to life in the mills and even to the fantasy life described by the mill recruiter who passes through. He spins a tale of the "heaps of stores; elegant hotels and all sorts of conveniences" in the mill town. Although the narrator comments that much of the recruiter's details were only plans at this point, he also lists the "six- and eight-room dwellings" with paint, windowpanes, and "St. George ranges" available to mill workers. Only Henry knows to ask how time is controlled in the mill village. The recruiter's answer proves telling: "'Well,' hesitated Bachman, too clever to tell the truth to these free children of the woods, 'Mr. Grismore ain't scheduled out his time just yet.'"[22] In other words, time would be handed over to the mill owner and no longer belong to the workers.

The mill recruiter and his fantasy tales recurred in almost all of the novels. In Myra Page's *Gathering Storm*, longtime mill worker Ole Marge recalls the recruiter's "soft hands, what'd never plowed or hoed in their life ... He wore clothes the like we'd never seen afore—a black coat 'n trousers, 'n a white bossom short, 'n across his chest was a big silver chain, 'n on the end of it, the first watch we ever see." The recruiter tells of two-room cabins, with wooden, not dirt floors; water pumps on every block; and good pay for everyone, including women and children who "kin work too."[23] Marge had yet to learn that women and children were *required* to work for the housing; his watch symbolizes constraints, not freedoms.

In Grace Lumpkin's *To Make My Bread*, a peddler comes through recruiting for mills. He talks up the cheap and plentiful mill store and promises "you get a house with windows and cook on a real stove." He also claims, "whoever goes down to work there is going to be rich like [the mill owner]—for he started out as poor as the next one. They say out there the rivers flow with milk and honey and money grows on trees." Lumpkin gave a particularly poignant extension to the fantasy when two of her characters, Emma and Ora, practice on an ancient loom their grandmothers used. Emma thinks "of herself sitting in a factory beside a quiet machine working it easily, talking to the other women who would be working at the machines beside her. It would be a very neighborly arrangement, as if neighbors had gathered to sit around and talk at a quilting. And she would get money for her work." She is sure that, "if she worked hard, bright, shining dollars would pour into her lap, and with the money she could buy new clothes for the young ones, and books for school, a fiddle for Granpap, and perhaps for herself a new waist, or a scarf for her head."[24] The scene is affecting not only because the money does not pour into her lap once she is in the mill but also because she and the other workers cannot choose to work at their own pace or on their own (or even humane) hours. They lose control of time itself.

Today, watches can be had for pennies. Learning to tell time is a developmental marker in children. Our cell phones, computers, ovens, even our cars blink the time at us. But time is not natural or preordained. We made a conscious decision as a society to standardize time around the globe, to value a mechanical division of the day, and to prioritize hours over seasons, cycles, or moon phases. That decision happened in fits and starts, but it was formalized in the United States in the late nineteenth century with railroads, science, and communication technologies playing roles. Also, and significantly, factories shaped our present-day definitions of time. For mill workers, often their first encounter with strictly standardized time was the mill recruiter who entered their farms, villages, and homes, wearing the watch prominently across his chest. Time profoundly affected their new lives, food, and health. Families had clocks. But they were routinely stopped to mark death. They were set to an agreed-upon local time, not to mean standard time, and minutes could be more like suggestions than absolute imperatives.[25] The mill time, and the watch that represented it, was, whether subtly or overtly, a symbol of ownership. It symbolized a lack of freedom in mill life.

In fact, as Amanda quickly learns, in the mill village time belongs to the mill owner and the factory clock. In his first speech in the novel, Mr. Grismore says, "you are to give me your time and work conscientiously." Van Vorst calculated in detail the different effect an allegiance to time had on various classes in the United States: mill workers worked six hours by noon, "to these six hours add two, and you have the full day's work fixed by humane State laws in twenty-six States of the Union." She continued, "Subtract from the first six one, and you have the agreeable day's work of the man of business. Subtract all, and you have the day of the leisure woman and man who represent consumers and purchasers of commodities." She concluded by adding "seven hours to the original six" to get to the thirteen-hour days mill women, men, and children worked at minimum.[26] Lost in this relentless math was the agency of individual workers to control their own days.

When workers tried to intervene, often their only choice was to give more of their days to the mill—in a brutal cycle, to have more freedom, workers like Amanda asked for overtime or extra shifts to change their conditions (or, in her case, to forget the pain of her fractured family when Henry is with her sister and she has to support herself). Alternatively, workers could internalize the system of mill time to prove themselves good workers, worthy of special treatment. In Lumpkin's *To Make My Bread*, among the first things the family acquires is an alarm clock and the lessons they need to read it. A clock symbolizes one brother's material successes, purchased at the cost of rejecting his family entirely. John visits Basil, who looked "at the alarm clock on the mantel and moved restlessly in his chair." Yet Lumpkin was most explicit that time was the one thing workers did not have. In fact, efficiency experts coming into the mill and installing "hank clocks" on each machine spurred the strike.[27] Clocks ushered in the so-called stretch-out, which made fewer workers produce more goods for less pay. Even the name, "stretch-out," evoked the malleability of mill time for everyone but the workers.

Time could be stretched, standardized, manipulated, and withheld; but it could not nourish. Lest this seem too far from pellagra, newspaper columns of the day blamed the summer of strikes, including that at Loray, on the introduction of clocks, saying "operatives resented the presence of the efficiency experts . . . with stop-watches who timed every movement." In the demands made in the initial days of the Loray Mill Strike, "changes in methods of work" appeared next to "improved sanitary conditions" in importance. In the novels, discussions of clocks nestle up to discussion of pellagra too frequently for us not to notice. In Lumpkin's novel, next-door neighbors, the Mulkeys, house the story's most significant pellagrin, Mrs. Mulkey, as well as a boarder, Alma, who teaches the main character, Bonnie, "how to find time on the alarm clock." The Mulkeys' son, Statesrights, assassinates Bonnie at the novel's end in a struggle between management and labor. In a tight radius, the main characters, changes in methods of work, the results of unimproved sanitary (or so it was thought) conditions, and the violent consequences all collide. For Dargan's characters, a paragraph explaining the "rationalization" and stretch-out time systems directly follows a paragraph listing spring deaths and illnesses.[28] In none of these examples did time allow rest or restoration, health or energy.

As Amanda slowly starves in her mill life, time keeps her from health and nourishment as well. At her first boarding house meal, Amanda is assaulted by smells: "odours of grease frying, bad fish, and the unmistakable odours of warm and unwashed human bodies." No vegetables grace the meal, which consists of tin plates bearing "fish-skin, bones, head and tail all cooked and served together with naïve indiscrimination; another was stacked high with cold hominy; one bowl contained fat drippings. There was a pitcher of molasses and one of coffee." People gulp down what is in front of them. This establishment had a reputation of feeding "lavishly." Soon, Amanda loses even more time as she assumes responsibility for cooking for others.[29]

Boarding with Amanda and her sister is one of the first children readers witness suffering from the work and poor food. The child, Milly, works the night shift and is wracked with chills, "skin and bones enveloped in shocking, filthy rags." Milly's mother cannot keep food down either and is so ill she no longer works, which forces Milly into taking a shift. Lunch for many like her, including Amanda, is unwrapped from a "piece of newspaper containing a bit of bread and pork." For Amanda, "it cost her all she earned to live on pork and beans and coffee, and to sleep on straw." The novel discusses disease in metaphor: "spring—as far as it is able—will bring its gifts of liveliness; and how fain it will be to lay a flowery hand, a gentle touch, on the mill villages! But as there is nothing there to respond, it withdraws abashed, and advent of the new season is only ill languor, sapping the last force from the weary spinner whom winter has left shivering."[30] Although Van Vorst wrote the novel before pellagra had been widely named by experts, she documented the fatigue, digestive problems, and disease pathway. Without a name, though, the pellagra-suffering characters fade into the background of the novel.

What Van Vorst emphasized instead was the threat that could be named to Amanda and the mill workers: the mills themselves. They were not just alive; they were dangerous monsters. Here, food got turned on its head, and the people no longer consumed but instead were eaten by their workplaces. The anthropomorphizing, which was common to almost all of the mill novelists, began on first sight. On her first night in the mill town, Amanda lies awake listening. She first thinks she is hearing wind "a-rustling and a-whispering"; to her horror, she finds the sound "burring, humming, and whizzing" with none of the "beauty of modulation" of actual wind. Instead, when she goes to her window she discovers "a giant building with argus eyes alight. Each window shone wickedly forth out of the brick face, mocking the night and grinning at sleep. Alive, active, enemy of rest and repose, it hummed, buzzed, whirred and sung its epic of Labour and Toil at the cost of brain and body and soul." Even for Grismore's wife (the woman who would be Amanda's rescuer), a northeastern woman used to modern conveniences, the mill is a "nightmare," a place "so deafening... that I am only conscious of the sense of hearing... *I can't see* anything!"[31]

For Emma and Ora in Lumpkin's *To Make My Bread,* their first sight of the mill is a far cry from the neighborly vision of women spinning peacefully: "Up from the brick structure rose two huge chimneys, towering into the sky, like two towers of Babel. Smoke poured out of them into the wide open heavens." They feel the ground shaking like "people were dancing a long way off"; both try to make the impression as positive as they can, noting, "You remember that church song that says, 'There's power in the blood.' Well, that sound seems t' say, 'There's power in the factory, there's power in the factory.'" But upon hearing the whistle for the first time, "a terrible earsplitting shriek, as if many people cried out in sorrow, just once," they see the monster in the mill: "The late afternoon sun shone right on the factory and made out of its windows fiery eyeballs that watched the home-goers steadily." By the time Emma works for a few months, she can only compare the mill to "a story the teacher told the young ones at school" about an ogre who grinds bones to make bread. Emma thinks, "At first the throb of the mill had been like the throb of a big heart beating for the good of those who worked under the roof, for it gave hope of desires to be fulfilled." The narrator continues, "A woman, one of the weavers, said to Ora and Emma one lunch hour during the summer, 'the weave room has a sound different from the other rooms. It's like the sound of sinners' teeth grinding in hell.' Now to Emma the throb of a heart had changed. She was feeling the grind of teeth. The mill crunched up and down—'I'll grind your bones to make my bread.'" Myra Page in *Gathering Storm* echoed the same theme, as one of her characters says, "The boss-men'll feed them machines the gold outta your hair, the shine outta your eye, the quickness outta your fingers."[32] Over and over, mills that promised to set employees up as consumers in their own right turned the promises around to consume the employees instead.

In Lumpkin's *To Make My Bread*, Emma, who dies of pellagra, combines the criticism of hours in daylight with one of South Carolina's monoculture surrounding the mill districts. Not only is she unable to get the garden planted before darkness falls, but Granpap needs every single inch of land possible for cotton in order to break even. One of Goldberger's most intriguing studies showed that two otherwise identical mill villages differed on pellagra based only on one having access to a single vegetable farm and a single slaughterhouse—and the time for residents to shop from them.[33]

When Mrs. Grismore finds Amanda, she has not eaten for days and is in a dead faint from a twenty-four-hour shift. She is fending off threats to her bodily integrity as her manager sexually harasses her daily; her mind is dulled by the repetition; and her spirit is bent under the buzzing, humming, and whirring. The monster has enslaved the freeborn Amanda, who has almost completely lost her will to live.[34] Only the timely intervention of milk and food and a quick exit to Europe for rest and healing bring Amanda back from that brink. The corruption is so profound that even years later, with the benefit of education and money, Amanda cannot improve the mill with reforms. It has to be slain to save the employees from fates similar to the one Amanda narrowly avoided.

What began as descriptions of new and exciting modern workplaces—places where hard work would be rewarded by the ability to choose and acquire consumer goods—ends in a terrifying portrait of lost time, self, and dreams. Characters lose control of their own bodies as the mills come alive. Personifying and making monstrous the buildings and, by extension, economic systems of mill life were shared, pointed metaphors of consumption turning in on itself. Van Vorst's Argus-eyed monster could, perhaps, only be defeated by something as biblical and profound as a flood. With the giants destroyed, the mill buildings swept away, Henry and Amanda, freeborn that they were, stood ready to begin again with the dream of a nourishing and healthy worker/owner relationship that provided consumer participation for all involved. The full-blown specter pellagrin was still to come.

ELLA MAY WIGGINS OF THE MILL: THE GHOST PELLAGRIN

> How it grieves the heart of a mother
> You everyone must know,
> But we can't buy for our children,
> Our wages are too low.
>
> ELLA MAY WIGGINS, "Mill Mother's Lament"

Van Vorst's portrayals of mill workers were joined two decades later by an explosion of six novels written directly from the relatively short but nationally prominent Loray Mill Strike in Gastonia, North Carolina. The novels, and the singer that inspired them, form the final window into the confusing lack of food and explanations for disease in the southern food and gender story. Mary Heaton Vorse's *Strike!* (1930), Olive Tilford Dargan's *Call Home the Heart* (1932), Grace Lumpkin's *To Make My Bread* (1932), Myra Page's *Gathering Storm* (1932), Sherwood Anderson's *Beyond Desire* (1932), and William Rollins Jr.'s *The Shadow Before* (1935) joined "The Mill Mother's Lament" by textile worker Ella May Wiggins in documenting the culmination of pellagra in the South. Dargan's biographer, Kathy Cantley Ackerman, argues that, "Unlike the male writers inspired by the same events, the women were able to recognize the special oppression of women mill workers and their children." One way that Dargan, Lumpkin, Vorse, and Page called out women's oppression was by documenting pellagra; according to Ackerman's research, pellagra's death rate in Gastonia rose by "fifty percent in the six months ending in September 1929, according to the North Carolina State Bureau of Health"—and each of the female novelists took notice.[35] We follow Ackerman's lead, focusing for the remainder of the chapter on Wiggins and the four female writers. Unlike Ackerman, we especially examine the figure of the pellagrin that haunted the women's pages, embodying nightmares of consumption—a diseased body lost to the empty promises of consumer desire.

Wiggins (1900–1929) moved with her family from their eastern Tennessee farm to logging camps throughout the Tennessee and North Carolina mountains. Soon after the deaths of both of her parents when she was only nineteen, she met John Wiggins and married him despite his reputation as a wanderer. She and John listened to the promises of a mill recruiter and headed down to the South Carolina mills. They soon had eight children, four of whom died quickly. At least one died of pellagra, but scholars speculate that pellagra and other diseases of malnourishment played a role in all of the deaths. John abandoned Ella and the children, who had settled in Gaston County, North Carolina, by the late 1920s. Wiggins had a ninth child with a cousin with whom she lived. Unique among many white mill hands, Wiggins's commitment to owning her own home or renting from someone other than mill owners was strong enough that at the end of her life she was living in the black district of a mill village. Although some of the novels and much of the coverage of her life were at pains to present her as a naïf balladeer who stepped forward to sing about mill life, Wiggins actually worked as an organizer, union bookkeeper, and delegate to testify in Washington, D.C., about labor practices. She crossed racial lines to march with black workers, testifying to her complex grasp of southern class and labor politics. Nonetheless, she captivated large audiences of fellow mill hands with her songs based on her personal experiences of grief, hard work, and suffering. Her most famous, "Mill Mother's Lament," included a verse proclaiming, "How it grieves the heart of a mother / You every one must know, / But we can't buy for our children, / Our wages are too low." Other lyrics talked about hunger, lack of clothes, and illness for both workers and children. One scholar suggests that Wiggins was forced during her time in Gastonia to forage for her food, even trapping and cooking opossums from the woods surrounding the mill. On the final day of her life, an armed mob turned away the truck in which she was riding, keeping her from reaching a rally. A group of men with guns then chased Wiggins's vehicle, shooting the unarmed truck to pieces and hitting Wiggins fatally in the chest. No one was found guilty for the murders. A postscript that almost all the novelists included in their dramatization of her life was that family members were not allowed to keep Wiggins's children after her death—the children were forced into an orphanage to be wards of the state because her blacklisted family could not secure mill jobs and thus could not demonstrate to the mill-funded enforcement officials that they had steady income to raise the children. This final irony meant that Wiggins's children became wards of the very people who either killed her or who looked away while she died.[36]

Members of the radical left, all six writers used their novels to keep Ella May Wiggins's story alive. In addition, they celebrated and called into greater prominence the alliance between labor and communist organizing internationally. Grace Lumpkin (1891–1980) was born in Georgia and raised in South Carolina, a member of a family that produced more than one strong woman (her sister Katherine Dupre Lumpkin also published about race and the South). Lumpkin spent summers in the North Carolina mountains, giving her personal experiences circling the mill districts. She had direct experiences with strikes, both on the protest lines and providing support for workers. Her novel, *To Make My Bread*, dramatizes the struggle of the McClure family, especially brother and sister John and Bonnie. Bonnie is loosely based on Ella May Wiggins and is, like the historical figure, assassinated at the end of the book. Bonnie's mother, Emma, is also a central character; before her death from pellagra, she struggles to support extended family after her husband died and her father was sentenced to the penitentiary for moonshining. *To Make My Bread* wrestles with why a family would make the decision to leave the mountains for the mills. Lumpkin's portrait of hunger is poignant, both in the mountains (when, out of bullets, John and his brothers try to catch a rabbit but are too exhausted from days of fasting to give chase) and in the villages (when Bonnie's heartbreak is palpable as she drops out of school to try to earn enough money to feed her mother fresh foods only to see her descend into the dementia of pellagra). Lumpkin carefully quoted the lyrics of Wiggins's ballads, putting them into Bonnie's voice; like Wiggins, Lumpkin carefully charted the cost of mill life on a family—by novel's end, not only Bonnie but also Emma and Granpap have died early deaths; the eldest brother, Kirk, dies in a gunfight over a girl who later becomes a prostitute; another brother, Basil, survives but only by rejecting his family and choosing a loveless marriage to a wealthier woman; and only John is left. Lumpkin held out hope that one failed strike could spark international labor movements to build and grow. Her personal denunciation of radicalism late in life was perhaps prefigured by the one page of hopefulness at the end of a novel full of painful scenes.[37] It was a testament to her skill as a writer that *To Make My Bread* has such a haunting beauty in the midst of its tragedies.

Olive Tilford Dargan (1869–1968) was born in western Kentucky but lived most of her adult life in and around Asheville, North Carolina, only one hundred miles away from Gastonia and in the mountains from which so many mill workers originated. Her farm sheltered many prominent organizers during the strike years, and she was personally involved as well. *Call Home the Heart* is the story of Ishmalee, one of the most fully realized and complicated characters of the strike novels. Ishma, as she is most often called, tries to pull her family out of poverty by improving their farm practices, avoiding having children, and weaning the family from their dependence on the local general store. After years of grinding work, crop losses, and difficult pregnancies, however, Ishma leaves her husband, Brit, to go down to the mill. Of the six novels, *Call Home the Heart* spends the most time examining why an individual would be drawn into mill work. Looking back, Ishma describes her decision as turning on how Brit "had a heart like a song, and I was not helping keep it sweet." She further admits that Rad, the man she rejected when she instead married Brit and the person who later takes her to the mills, merely "was a way" to get out of the mountains. Though she tries sincerely not to hurt him, Ishma never marries Rad, even though Brit divorces her (trying to give Ishma what she most needs and mistakenly thinking a divorce is it). Once in the mill town, she becomes involved with union and strike work. A final man falls in love with her, Derry Unthank, a union organizer who gives her books and intellectual conversation and who wants her to dedicate her life to the union. But at the close of the novel, Ishma's heart leads her back to the mountains. Dargan's descriptions of the beauty and spiritual power of the mountains pull Ishma and the reader away from the mills. Because Ishma is so human, *Call*

Home the Heart was criticized for turning back on its revolutionary promise. More recently, though, scholars such as Ackerman have argued that Dargan's achievement lies in creating a character who truly wrestles with the hard decisions social revolution requires. Ackerman claims, and I agree, that Dargan's novel avoids pure didacticism in favor of thoughtful meditation about the human costs of societal changes.[38]

Dorothy Myra Page (1897–1993) was born in Newport News, Virginia. She was essentially the same age as Ella May Wiggins, but her comfortable childhood and education separated her from the southern mill workers. Nonetheless, Page spent years working with mill women through the YWCA and as a shop clerk and machine worker while employed as a union organizer. In the early 1920s, she finished her doctorate in sociology at the University of Minnesota with a dissertation on *Southern Cotton Mills and Labor*, published in 1929 by a branch of Workers International Relief. Later, Page traveled to and lived in Soviet Russia; her novel was the most optimistic about the Soviet Union's social engineering. The gathering storm to which the novel's title refers was a positive storm of workers overturning the leisure class and reinventing the world's social systems, despite the setbacks of the North Carolina strike. Mountain siblings Tom and Marge are on parallel paths; Tom leaves for the Northeast and a career in factories and biracial organizing soon after the family moves to work in southern factories where Marge stays. After Tom returns, he and Marge partner to lead the strikes of southern workers. One of those workers is a character named Ella May Wiggins; Page included the historical figure's lyrics as well. While African American characters appear in all of the novels, Page's work was most notable for exploring how white men and women from the South could be cured of the "Dixie ailment" and form lasting friendships with black men and women—but also how difficult and dangerous these changing racial politics proved. At the same time, hers was possibly the most didactic of the novels, with long passages dedicated to correcting history, criticizing less radical unions or political movements, and listing theories or ideas acceptable to the party.[39]

The final three authors, Vorse (1874–1966), Anderson (1876–1941), and

Rollins (1898–1950), were perhaps best known for works other than their strike novels. Vorse was a prominent journalist, feminist, and peace activist. She was instrumental in the founding of the Women's Peace Party with Jane Addams, Pettit and Stone's settlement house partner, in 1915. She participated in strikes in Gastonia, Harlan County, Kentucky, and elsewhere—so much so that she won the first Social Justice Award from the UAW with Eleanor Roosevelt and Upton Sinclair in attendance. Her novel *Strike!* is told from the perspective of a visiting journalist and features a character named Mamie Lewes as the fictionalized Ella May Wiggins. Vorse's work was notable for her thoughtful portrayal of townspeople's attitudes toward the strikers, local mill workers, and outside organizers; she wanted to understand from whence the hatred and fear of mob violence arose. However, Vorse's northeastern roots showed in her reliance on stereotypes about mountain residents (for instance, she wrote, "They were living all of them in the eighteenth century ... The place of man in the universe had been untroubled by the age of reason") and insistence that outside help was needed since the mill workers were too dumb and beaten down to help themselves. Anderson, though not from the South, lived significant portions of his life in Virginia. In addition, his third wife, with whom he fell in love during the writing of *Beyond Desire*, was the organizer Eleanor Copenhaver from Virginia. Copenhaver also served on the board of the Southern Summer School for Women Workers in Industry (the group behind the pamphlet of women mill workers quoted earlier in this chapter), and her influence on Anderson showed. A disjointed and sprawling work, *Beyond Desire* gets distracted by the sexual politics between male and female organizers. While only the final section of the novel takes place in Gastonia ("Birchfield," in the novel), other sections compare Georgia factories and explore friendships between mill girls. In some ways, *Kit Brandon*, published four years later, could be seen as a second draft of Anderson's mill girl section of *Beyond Desire*. Finally, William Rollins's family life in the Northeast and as a soldier in World War I, combined with his other career as a pulp crime fiction writer, made his novel the least connected to the southern mill workers. Rollins's novel takes events from the Gastonia strike and moves them to a New England setting.[40] *The Shadow Before* brings other ethnicities to the pages—French Canadian workers, explicitly Jewish organizers, and Irish hands. It also experiments with imagistic, fractured narrative structures, but it has fewer fully realized female characters and less southern food in its pages. Lumpkin, Page, and Dargan put women and food right at the center of their novels; in so doing they mounted a critique of the new southern economic systems that screamed in its horrors.

GRACE LUMPKIN'S BREAD: GHOSTS IN THE MACHINE

In her radical revisioning of southern literature, Patricia Yaeger puts together black and white southern women writers to listen (often for the first time) to the political critiques they share across their writings. The time period she considers is later than ours here, so she is silent on the mill novels (which, while notable for their analysis of race in labor struggles, also were all penned by white writers). Yet Yaeger's directive to pay attention to the deformed, grotesque, or diseased bodies lurking on the edges of southern women's writing could have been written for the pellagra victims in southern strike novels. Yaeger argues, "southern women writers use the grotesque to map an array of social crises; the open, wounded, bleeding, excessive, corpulent, maimed, idiotic, or gargantuan body becomes the sign of a permanent emergency within the body politic."[41] In other words, she finds direct lines between the broken bodies in women's novels and the social crises like rape, segregation, or class upheaval in the southern settings. Grace Lumpkin created two female pellagra sufferers, bookending the experiences of her two main characters in the southern mill villages. Mrs. Mulkey and Emma are ghosts, both in life and in death, who guide Bonnie and John to the political consciousness Lumpkin felt they needed to take on the injustices of the mill system.

When the McClure family first moves down from the mountains to the mill village, they live next door to Mrs. Mulkey. At first, all the McClures know is that Mrs. Mulkey has pellagra "and sometimes she had spells." Her children are dirty and run wild because she cannot take care of them. For a long while,

Bonnie (who is staying home, taking care of the rest of the family while her mother, Emma, works) only hears of Mrs. Mulkey; invisible to Bonnie's eyes, the sick woman occasionally seems to call to Bonnie.[42] Only later does Bonnie receive Mrs. Mulkey's message.

That message is wrapped in one of the few explicit appearances of religion in the novel, a passage from Matthew that Mrs. Mulkey quotes obsessively. During one of her spells, she refuses to get into bed, causing her children to run for Bonnie's help. When Bonnie arrives, Mrs. Mulkey says, "I was naked, and ye clothed me." Mrs. Mulkey continues, "talking very sensibly to Bonnie, as she would talk to a friend. 'I was hungered and ye fed me. I was thirsty and ye gave me to drink.'" It *is* a sensible critique, even if Lumpkin put it in the mouth of a character out of her head from disease: Mrs. Mulkey would not have pellagra if she only had a minimum of clothing, food, and drink. Even more pointedly, Mrs. Mulkey emphasizes, " 'People say I look like a ghost,' she said, and laughed a tinkling sort of laughter. 'I reckon I do look like a ghost.'" Mrs. Mulkey functions as a ghost for the rest of the novel; readers hear no further words from her. And yet her presence remains. When Bonnie learns her own mother, Emma, officially has the disease, she is left to "ponder on the dreadful word." By this time, Bonnie knows many more children and adults with the disease. But Mrs. Mulkey is her touchstone. Bonnie immediately continues, "Only recently Mrs. Mulkey had become insane. She drove her young ones out of the house. It was said she heard voices talking to her and answered them, and imagined that horrible animals and devils were running around the walls. People said she behaved like a man who is crazy with drink."[43] For still-young Bonnie, of course these are her direct fears for her mother and herself. For Lumpkin's readers, Mrs. Mulkey voices the injustice of the broken promises that brought her family to the mills in the first place. The walls with which the recruiter had built such consumer fantasies did not shelter families; they did not nourish mothers.

Lumpkin, in her extended portrait of the McClure family, also explored how well-meaning families could fall victim to pellagra. Granpap, unhappy with the mill's offer only to give him low-paying work as a security guard, rents a farm on the outskirts of the mill village. Unfortunately, the family is unable to harvest vegetables in its first growing season. As Emma explains, "Her regret was that she had no garden of fresh vegetables. Granpap had plowed the ground and she had planted. Then they had all neglected the garden, for cotton was everything. The garden fence was almost gone, and there was no money with which to buy new fencing, so the chickens ate up most of the vegetables that came up, and then laid only a few eggs in return."[44] This family understands how important fresh food is to health. But that does not mean that the economies of mill life—even for people who take extraordinary efforts such as farming in addition to mill shifts—can yield enough supplies to avoid pellagra.

Emma's sickness means that Bonnie and John have to drop out of school and enter the mills. Although the recruiter promised free education for all the children, much like Emma's dream of peacefully sitting with other women weaving, the dream of nonworking children also proves a fantasy. The doctor who diagnoses Emma expresses the frustration of the problem. When he prescribes "plenty of lean meat, milk, and other nourishing food," Granpap answers, "I'm having a hard row to hoe right now. I don't know how I can well do it." Pellagrins such as Emma haunt even the most liberal member of the community; this doctor is fired from his job on the board of health and with the mills because he disagrees with profiting from malnutrition. Lumpkin continues, "The doctor became very angry, angry enough to frighten Bonnie who was in the corner behind the stove, listening. 'Don't ask me how,' the doctor said. 'A doctor can't produce decent food for the many that need it. What can I do? Don't ask me.' He went out of the back door hurriedly as if he wanted to shake the dust of the house from his feet."[45] Lumpkin, too, left her novel's readers with this particular dust (as the dust, death, and ghostly imagery continue) on our feet. The doctor's firing, she asserts, also came from his not being religious, a detail signaling his union sympathies and spreading Lumpkin's critique beyond the audience receptive to Mrs. Mulkey's Christian quotations. *To Make My Bread* ends with Bonnie assassinated and only the hope of John as he recommits to the fight for labor; one cannot help but wonder if Mrs. Mulkey and Emma find this answer enough to their ghostly indictments.

Consequences of Emma's disease send John into the mill through the collusion of a mill-sanctioned preacher who signs documents testifying that John is old enough to be hired. Emma languishes in bed, her face "with the cheeks sunk in" and her hands "yellow and scrawny like the claws of chickens." Her deformed body, with its fingers "bent as if in working they had grown that way," reminds the family that hard work is not enough. To assuage their guilt, the McClure family enters into more debt to see a company doctor, who replaced the more ethical doctor who diagnosed Emma. The new doctor owns the village drug store as well, and even though the family knows on some level that it will not help, "they found it the only thing to do. For they needed confidence that they were doing the right thing by Emma, everything possible that might make her well. The doctor was kind enough to let them run up a bill for drugs at his store, so the bottles on the chair beside Emma's bed were kept replenished."[46] Lumpkin's sarcasm is brutal here, since the bottles cannot hold pellagra's cure; instead, purchasing them puts the rest of the family at greater risk of contracting the disease themselves.

Meanwhile, John flirts with "a young lady [who] had come to organize clubs for girls and women in the village. She was brought there by the mill management." She is no kin to the tomato club women who looked to put money in the pockets of disempowered people. While John is interested in their conversations about books and imagines proposing marriage to her as an equal, she tries to get him to spy on fellow disempowered workers on behalf of the company. Even before John wises up (and refuses a promotion so as not to betray fellow workers), his sister, Bonnie, exposes the woman's dangerous naïveté. Bonnie reports to her brother, "She says, 'You must never have fried food,' as if hurrying home from the mill at dinner time a woman or little gal can do anything but throw together something in the frying pan, and at night with the men and the young ones so hungry and you tired, what can you do but the same? She tells us, 'You must feed your children milk every day and plenty of eggs, for otherwise young ones will get pellagra.'" John replies, "That is true." Bonnie counters, "Of course it's true." Lumpkin then slows the scene down, allowing her ellipses to remind us of the ghost pellagrins Bonnie knows: "Bonnie stopped speaking. She took one hand from the baby. 'Of course it's true,' she repeated. There was a silence, and John knew his sister was crying. 'I'd like the best food,' she said. 'And everything for my young one... but how to get them... I don't know.'"⁴⁷

Van Vorst nodded to similar dynamics within mill families (and within mill boarding houses, which functioned as extended families). Amanda adds to her mill hours extra chores in the home, saying, "Ih do chores fer him when Ih gets in from th' mill, 'n' Ih gits up 'n' cooks the' vittles fer th' bo'ders." The "him" in her case is the boarding house owner who is described by Van Vorst as sitting on the porch, profiting from women's labor and sacrifices.⁴⁸ In each case, workingwomen faced doubled burdens in mill societies, and nutrition and health were sacrificed as a result.

John and the labor unionists speak the last words on pellagra after Emma passes away. John visits a labor organizer friend who asks, "Didn't you say she had pellagra?" When John answers yes, Lumpkin walks her readers through a Socratic exchange of questions: to the query "Do the rich have pellagra?" John answers, "I never heard." In reply, his friend says, "It's a poor man's disease. Haven't you heard that?" John admits, "Yes, I've heard that." His friend concludes the lesson: "If she had the right nourishment, she needn't have died. You see the mill owners killed her."⁴⁹ Lumpkin's ghosts walk across the pages of her novel, testifying to the murders caused by willfully poor pay, greed, and exploitation that resulted in a few owners profiting and many workers facing lack and starvation.

Mary Heaton Vorse drew similarly quiet yet powerful figures. The first is an unnamed older man. Vorse said, "In one corner sat a listless man with his face the peculiar yellow by which in wartime one recognizes prisoners. He sat emaciated and staring at nothing almost with a certain expression of idiocy." His pain inspires an exchange of questions and answers similar to Lumpkin's as a male reporter asks the female labor organizer who worked most closely with families in the mills, "What's the matter with him?" She replies, "Pellagra," and continues, "It's all through the mills here. It's caused by their diet." He counters, "Why don't they eat more cabbage and green things?... Can't they get them?" She concludes, "Give them more money... and they'll eat better. All they have money for now is fatback and flour and grits." When later this victim of "pellegry" reappears, he is in even worse shape: "There he sets now and he sets lak thet most of the time. Jest sets and his han's ahangin'. Sometimes he won't answer en I think maybe he's a goin' outen his min'— en his mouth—it bleeds awful." By the end of the novel, this man—significantly now identified through the woman whose responsibility he is, "Mis' Winstead's husband"—becomes what Yaeger would call a deformed, practically epic figure, the blood spewing from his mouth grotesquely testifying to the truth of starvation. Vorse said, "His face made a yellow spot against the fields; his big earth-colored hands hung down slackly and he looked at nothing. The pellagra was bad."[50] Women writers about these southern mill villages created epic figures, scripture quoting, mutely suffering, actively bleeding and dying, to keep the broken promises of food that did not nourish, societies that did not prosper, in front of our eyes.

STARVATION'S CHILD: MYRA PAGE'S PELLAGRA FOR PROFIT

Some people in the novels are actively profiting from pellagra. Myra Page kept her eye on the money as she created pellagrins haunting *Gathering Storm*. Page's novel features a scene skewering the hangers-on to mill culture, the less obvious proponents of consumer culture. A patent medicine man comes to town, claiming he is the "poor people's friend." He launches into his pitch, saying, "This hyar's guaranteed, positively guaranteed to cure lung ailments, rheumatism, coughs 'n colds, 'n pleurisy, back ache, piles, 'n in fact it's a general all-round medicine." Someone asks specifically: "Ain't you got nuthin' fer the pellagry?" and continues, "that's what mill hands need, a cure fer it." The patent medicine man confidently claims the same cure-all would fix it. Page dryly comments, "The famous medicine was also merely water, 'seasoned 'n sweetened to taste,'" as the medicine man takes his profits and disappears from the novel.[51] Submerged in the discussion is the dilemma of feeding self and family, but authors explored both sides of the double entendre: consumption was literal food but it was also consumer goods.

In the early decades of the twentieth century, patent medicine shows toured the South, combining freak shows, live music, and theater-worthy performances with pitches for cheap, often alcoholic, certainly sugary and caffeinated products. Early food regulations targeted patent medicines along with butter and moonshine. Children were both in the audiences and a part of the shows. Yaeger warns us to pay attention to children in southern women's novels, saying "we also find childish characters deformed by the South's dreamy dreams, kids who are physically traumatized, bent out of shape by racist and sexist southern ideologies: ancient children, old before their time." In Page's novel, the two streams come together. The mill recruiter, a showman himself, is the first to draw attention to children and pellagra, saying, "All over this hill thar's babies gittin' pellagry fer want of food the well-to-do give to their hogs."[52] He implies that the mills fixed the problem, but, of course, the disparities only increase in the mill villages. Diseased and deformed children continue to testify about the absence and lack of food. Combined with Page's portraits of useless consumer goods, like the patent medicine, the children in *Gathering Storm* point ever more to something rotten in the whole consumer system the mills represent.

Page pulled no punches, saying, for instance, "There were a few more toddlers around the doors—part of the yearly spring crop which sprang up like dandelions only to be struck down by the grim reaper almost as ruthlessly as the gale tosses the bloom of wild flowers across the fields." The main character, Marge, faces just such ruthlessness as her son Bobby has "bowlegs 'n head too big for his body," which causes other characters to warn "he's gona get the pellargy if you ain't careful." Marge is already in trouble with her boss for talking back to a mill nurse who condescendingly told her "she needed to drink more milk, eat fresh eggs and oranges" for her own and her son's health—an impossible prescription without higher wages from the mill. So the tragedy is not unexpected when Marge says, "Pellagry took my baby. It got so bad that—you know what it does." Again, interrupted speech signals the silences, the unspeakable horrors. The person with whom Marge is struggling to speak picks up on her train of thought: "Yes, Jem did know. He had seen many hundreds of mill children in the past two decades taken off, crippled for life, or made hopeless idiots by the dread pellagra. Starvation's child—the scourge of mill hills, that was pellagra."[53] Although children with pellagra rarely speak in the novels, their silence does not dull their power to testify. They lurk in the corners, and their disease becomes a symbolic sibling, starvation's child ever present in the mill families.

When the strike finally begins, Marge yells, "Come on, women, we're walkin' out for more food for our chillen." For women readers and characters, the cry to save children from the ruthless disease is powerful symbolism indeed. In one of the worst moments of the strike, mill forces recognize the power of the deformed and dying bodies. They raid the union stores and specifically destroy all the food intended for children, hoping to demoralize workers into giving up the fight: "Cans of milk, planned to nourish sick babies had been ripped open. The ground outside was still wet with pools of white liquid."[54] Starvation's child, whose deformed body profited mill owners, consumers of the textiles, and hangers-on hawking useless products to the already desperate, stood as a poignant, pained reminder of the stakes involved.

OLIVE TILFORD DARGAN'S MOTHER SICKNESS

The most thoughtful portrait of the intersection of food, pellagra, and consumerism's broken promises came in Olive Tilford Dargan's *Call Home the Heart*. When the Loray Mill introduced the stretch-out in 1927, one result that affected women was the rise in pellagra, a disease to which Dargan referred in *A Stone Came Rolling* as "mother sickness."[55] Dargan picked up the themes explored in the other women's novels—ghost women's indictment, the epically deformed bodies, and the children's mute testimony—and extended them with a lengthier examination of food in the past, present, and future of mill families.

Dargan was not romantic about life in the mountains before the mills. For the Starkweather family, things have already changed as the novel opens. Most symbolically, Granny Starkweather has passed away. Not only was she the emotional anchor for the family, but she also provided the practical nourishment for the family to thrive. According to the narrator, "no more was her voice heard in the big kitchen where she had so long and capably presided over the filling of cans, kraut-tubs and bean-barrels. More and more the family became dependent on Gaffney's store in Beebread at the foot of the mountain." Granny served as Ishma's personal tomato club organizer, teaching prized recipes such as the one she used to can tomatoes, remembered fondly by her husband: "She boiled the sun in them, he said. Long before the Mexican culinary invasion, Granny would cook her tomatoes down to a crimson puree and add a sprinkling of fresh chipped peppers before applying the tin covers and sealing-wax." Life on the mountain had never been easy, but under Granny's guidance it had been self-sufficient. Now, with her dead, the family only "had Jim, whose idea of providing was limited to fat-back, corn-pone and coffee."[56]

Ishma is a transitional figure in the novel; the plot itself is less concerned with the external events of the Loray Mill Strike and more interested in Ishma's education in labor issues and awakening of her particular political consciousness. Ishma is sister to tomato club girls, yet dangerously sexual and ambitious like Kit Brandon or other moonshine women. She has recipes from Granny Starkweather, and internalizes many of Granny's lessons in resourcefulness in cooking. Dargan illustrates this in a scene in which Ishma decides in the midst of hard times for the family to create and cook a supremely local meal in the mountains. It features dried apple turnovers and foraged cymlings (small pumpkins), cooked with molasses and basil. It is practically a textbook example of how to avoid pellagra, even with few monetary resources. At the same time, Ishma learns from teachers and health bulletins. A kind teacher sends her a subscription to *Woman at Home*, which has pictures for Ishma to study of beautiful, comfortable homes, about which she thinks, "But the most miraculous of all were the laden eating-tables." Ishma also learns "from the Health and Food bulletins which the children brought from school, that the corn-product and milk made a wholesome meal." She and Brit read *Progressive Farmer* and Farm bulletins. They consult with a farm agent to institute a crop rotation, fertilizer scheme, and better cattle for their farm. They dream together of attending summer school, much like the Farmer's Institutes with which Jane McKimmon began her career. (Late in the novel, Ishma criticizes demonstrators and agricultural experts, but only after she realizes workers need to help themselves and not rely on outside welfare.)[57] Unfortunately for Ishma, her extended family lives so close to the edge of economic failure (and, Dargan shows dispassionately, are so unwilling to work, looking always for easy money and simple ways out) that small setbacks, such as a storm or failed fence, destroy their efforts to stay alive economically.

As much as Ishma wishes to rise above her mountain family's complacency, early on she demonstrates that she will hold onto her own opinions forged in the same mountains. Ishma refuses to fall into lockstep with mainstream consumer desires. When a teacher tries to show Ishma's sister how to set a table (and sounds a lot like Pettit and Stone giving lessons in dish washing and bread making that the girls around Hindman rejected), "Ishma thought that the set-out must have been a very drab affair." Instead, she makes her own ideal table-setting "as was in her heart" in the woods: "With a stick she would trace an oval on a bit of mossy ground and mark the line carefully with tiny fern-leaves. Her service set would be of galax. Flattened, the leaves were plates, and she could have them in any size; but she could twist them and pin them with their own stems into cups, bowls, dishes of whatever kind she wished." Ishma makes "food" out of "wild-flower petals and the tender rosy and red-hued baby oaks and maples that had pushed a few inches above the ground." After a rabbit and bird come and eat at her table while she watches, Ishma never plays the game again, because she believes she has experienced perfection.[58] This desire to merge nature and local food with the newest, modern life foreshadows Ishma's final plans to counter pellagra and the haunting figures of pellagrins in literature.

Facing a crisis in which she believes she is keeping her husband from his dreams and happiness, Ishma leaves with Rad for life in the mill villages. She also worries that she is missing out on life itself as the mountains drag her down with too many babies, too many hungry family members, and too many tragic blows to her plans. Quickly, though, she sees the flaws in the village system. Ishma starts taking care of sick people who cannot afford any other help. For Grandma Huffmore, a neighbor, Ishma "took away the cold corn-bread and forlorn piece of bacon on the chair by the bedside," the typical meat, meal, and molasses dinner. Ishma replaces the "untempting morsels" with a range of foods Grandma had been denied: "toasted rolls, buttered and delicately spread with honey." Ishma serves them with "a little pitcher of milk, cold and sweet from her unfailing box [an ice-box that Rad rigged up for her], and this was poured into a glass which she first washed and rubbed until it sparkled."[59] This is a meal designed for balance and interest. Cornbread and bacon are only part of the problem, Dargan suggests.

In the process of mapping exactly who had pellagra and what their living situations were, Goldberger's researchers in many ways tried to get beyond mill-funded Progressives' empty talk. They certainly found some surprising details. Women, especially those of childbearing age, were much more likely to have undiagnosed but serious cases of pellagra than they had been led to believe. And pellagra devastated children in the mills, also an unexpected finding. African Americans, thought to be immune from such diseases, had extraordinary rates of pellagra (though the focus on mill communities limited the data, given how predominantly white their residents were). Even more mysteriously, as researchers homed in on diversity in diet, families that appeared to purchase a diverse range of foods—in theory, doing exactly what was needed to prevent the disease—still had members falling victim.[60] What could be the explanation?

Scholar Harry Marks, in an article otherwise critical of Goldberger and his primary researcher Edgar Sydenstricker, uses census reports to calculate that "African-Americans, despite their lesser numbers, accounted for half of all pellagra deaths, and that women of all colors accounted for 69 percent of all such deaths." The scholars in the classic study of cotton mill life, *Like a Family*, calculate that children "between two and fifteen suffered two-thirds of all cases." Goldberger and Sydenstricker briefly speculated that, "when protein-rich foods were in short supply, men received 'more favorable consideration at the... table,' while their wives and children warded off hunger with bread, potatoes, and molasses." However, Marks points out that while Goldberger and Sydenstricker could acknowledge this unfair distribution, their methodology could not document it with any precision. Rather, researchers "treated the family as a black box."[61] Novelists like Dargan, by comparison, most certainly opened up the cover on that box and looked inside.

Dargan showed a similarly realistic understanding of how pellagra developed; she discussed what the epidemiologists were slow to learn, how pellagra could strike the women in a family when their husbands and relatives stayed free of it. With Mame Wallace, an "advanced 'case'" of pellagra, Dargan used a conversation between Ishma, her mentor Derry Unthank, and the pellagrin to talk through the disease pathway. Unthank analyzes the situation, asking Wallace, "Just starved yourself into bed, eh, Mrs. Wallace? Forgot what I told you two years ago?" When Wallace replies, "Don't be too hard on me, doctor. There's so many of us." Unthank continues, "And of course when the biscuits won't go round, mother will hunt up that piece of day-before-yesterday's cornbread and be perfectly satisfied with it." Wallace acknowledges the truth in the doctor's statement but claims it quickly became what she prefers: "I got so I'd ruther have it. I'd just ruther have it, doctor. I got so used to it because brother Jim always sent me a bushel o' meal from his farm ever' two or three months. I don't know how we'd got through without that. I'd always bake a big pone for supper an' give the children milk with it." Again, Dargan is at pains, through Unthank in this case, not to demonize the cornbread itself. At issue is the balance in diet, as well as the gender disparity that caused the children to benefit from what range the family could muster but punished the mother at the same time. He says, "That was fine, but mother didn't take any milk, and there was always enough of the pone left over for her to nibble a bit for breakfast and dinner next day." More than that, Wallace reveals that she subsisted on cornbread and cold water. She said a neighbor "let me go over to her house ever' day an' get some cold water out of her 'frigerator to drink with it. That made it good. She kept a bottle o' water just for me, knowin' I liked it with my bread. It was better 'n milk that got as warm as dishwater in the coolest place I could find."[62] Here, the pellagrin herself moves the disease beyond ignorance or neglect and into cultural terrain, as differences in taste (preferring anything cold over something nutritious), prevailing gender roles (wanting to sacrifice for her children), and a desire to cope (without asking for help from anyone other than family) all lead to Wallace's case.

We run the risk here of judging the novels on their historical accuracy or, worse, taking details in the novel as simple historical documentation. But what I want to emphasize is how the cold drinks in Dargan's portrait were bridges much like Ishma herself between old and new—and they were nonintuitive, out-of-the-box explanations of the difficult disease in mill society. Along with Wallace preferring water, Grandma Huffmore rejects the "coky" that was newly available (probably Coca-Cola itself, but perhaps another carbonated drink). A similar detail appears in Sherwood Anderson's *Beyond Desire*. In it, the mill workers understand that this new consumer good is a source of fast, cheap calories, bad for them in the long run but representative of new, fun consumer culture. Anderson's workers say, "there was a man came through the spinning-room in the middle of the morning and in the middle of the afternoon selling things. They let him. He sold a big chunk of soft candy, called 'Milky Way,' and he sold Coca Cola. They let him. You blew in ten cents. It hurt to blow it in but you did. You got the habit and you did. It braced you."[63] Even if more foods were available in the mill village, as Holland Thompson pointed out in his recitation of stocked company stores, it did not follow that they were desired or, when wanted, that the goods were at all nourishing. It would be easier if one—the old ways or the new—were evil; pellagra was so evocative and painful because it was never so simple.

Thus, Dargan turned to the consumerism destroying its newest members. She did it through a pellagrin, Cindy, who deliberately sacrifices herself for things. Cindy is very sick when Ishma goes to her, but she refuses to take a break from her shifts. She has a long list of reasons:

"Stop work?" cried Cindy, amazed. "Why, I'm payin' on a sewin'-machine, a 'frigerator, an' a bed-room set! I've wanted a sewin'-machine since I was twelve years old, an' I'm gettin' it now. An' I had to have a 'frigerator. A mountain person can't drink the water down here in the summer time without coolin' it off. Can't do it an' live. I had to have a bed too. Up in the mountains it didn't make any difference if I slept on a pallet, I could *sleep*. But down here I come out o' the mill feelin' like a squeezed dish-rag, an' if I don't get my sleep I'm done fer. I had to have a bed I could rest on. Then I had to buy two more fer the boys. I couldn't take the best, an' leave my younguns to the cobs."

Cindy, it seems, *is* her sewing machine, refrigerator, furniture, and mattresses. Yaeger suggests logic like Cindy's reflects the changes in the midcentury South. In Yaeger's words, "Even while the South lingered on the threshold of a fully commercial, mercantile economy, the ideological bonds defining personhood were already in place, defining selfhood in terms of the right to be nurtured by things that proved one's status (and offered more than a modicum of comfort) within the precincts of possessive individualism." In other words, not only were consumer goods increasingly available, but also definitions of self shifted to necessitate an engagement with those goods; status was already defined by purchasing material objects.[64] Once the strikes began, then, mills turning workers out of houses and destroying goods caused double pain—not only were workers back to where they began, but also the mills ripped away pieces of their identity in their personal items. Cindy is caught in this gruesome change—she believes that only through the objects can she have an identity in the mill village, yet acquiring those objects is the very thing killing her body.

Dargan's was the only women's strike novel in which the main character leaves before the deaths, before the ballad singers are shot, before the women marching for their children are gunned down. It was also the only novel that made space for a concrete solution and a follow-up volume. Ishma returns home to Brit and the farm he held onto for her, or as Ishma calls him, "the last farmer in history, safe on his rock ledge with its fertile spots and patches, feeding his family out of his hand." In their reconciliation, she remembers a song sung by Granny Starkweather, the last true nurturer of her family. From the Grange (an earlier political organization dedicated to uniting workers, especially agricultural ones), the ditty celebrates the virtues of the simple plow. Though Ishma is not certain that the plow would be enough to save her people, and though Dargan's message got a bit muddled between faith in technology and Soviet-style collective farming, Ishma makes a plan that relies on a new relationship between people, place, and food. Her plan deliberately turns away from money and consumerism. Ishma says, "I wasn't thinking about making money. I was thinking about a lot of little kids that I'd like to bring up here in the summer—every summer. I'd like to give them plenty to eat and turn them loose on the mountain to get strong." Ishma argues that the mill people could make the changes for themselves. She turns away from the devastating practices of monoculture that forced so many into the mills in the first place, saying, "We could build bark shelters for them, or use your old tobacco sheds, since you're not going to worry with tobacco any more. It will take a lot of milk and eggs." She wants to expand the farm so that "some of the mothers can come up and help me with the hens and cows. And I know men that the mills have scrapped who'd be made over by one summer up here."[65] However utopian, *Call Home the Heart* proposed a way for pellagrins and their society to heal.

CONCLUSION

By the end, Dargan outlined a plan at least to reclaim the disposed bodies, minimize starvation's children, and heal mother sicknesses. Pellagrins needed the nourishment and healing on top of the mountains; the society they haunt in the novels needs the same nourishment of reconnected people, places, food, and health. Perhaps the pellagrin appears in mill literature to move "background information into the foreground of a novel or story" and to reproduce "official terrorism that is both surrealistic and all too real," as Yaeger would have it.[66] He or she haunts middle-class white southerners in the stories and in their readers, provoking change or damning inaction. In the radical or social activist mill stories, the grotesque pellagrin triggers a class awakening for working-class characters and readers who identify with them. He or she inspires the working-class hero or heroine to give over his or her own life for the union, for the cause. Every one of the main characters does this: Van Vorst's Amanda, Lumpkin's Bonnie and John, Page's Marge, and Dargan's Ishma.

The brief optimism of many of the novelists did not last, however. A worker-led revolution did not materialize, and writers like Lumpkin, Dargan, and Anderson turned away from the socialism or communism of *To Make My Bread*, *Call Home the Heart*, and *Beyond Desire*. Wartime prosperity combined with the breakup of concerted union activism in most of the South ushered in the development of the postwar Sunbelt South. White bread, now fortified with B-vitamins and sold in modern southern grocery stores, helped diminish the reach of pellagra, as did government food programs. At the same time, the South's reliance on processed sugar, fat, and salt grew as large stretches of southern landscapes came to resemble homogenized America.

None of that is to say that everyone signed up for the new foods and food sources. Often subterranean, resistance persisted in gardens, recipes, and local markets. Something linked moonshine home-brewers to biscuit-resisting cornbread adherents to independent, decision-making tomato girls to Ishma standing on her mountain, repurposing her tobacco sheds for milk and eggs. And those southerners, historical and fictional, are in turn linked to today's farmers' market shoppers, local chefs, and devotees of southern cuisine connected to specific places. We can only see the links in sideways glances, but that does not mean we should not try to unearth them. That is our goal in the final chapter as we turn to cookbooks and curb markets, and immerse ourselves fully in the mess that is this mess of greens.

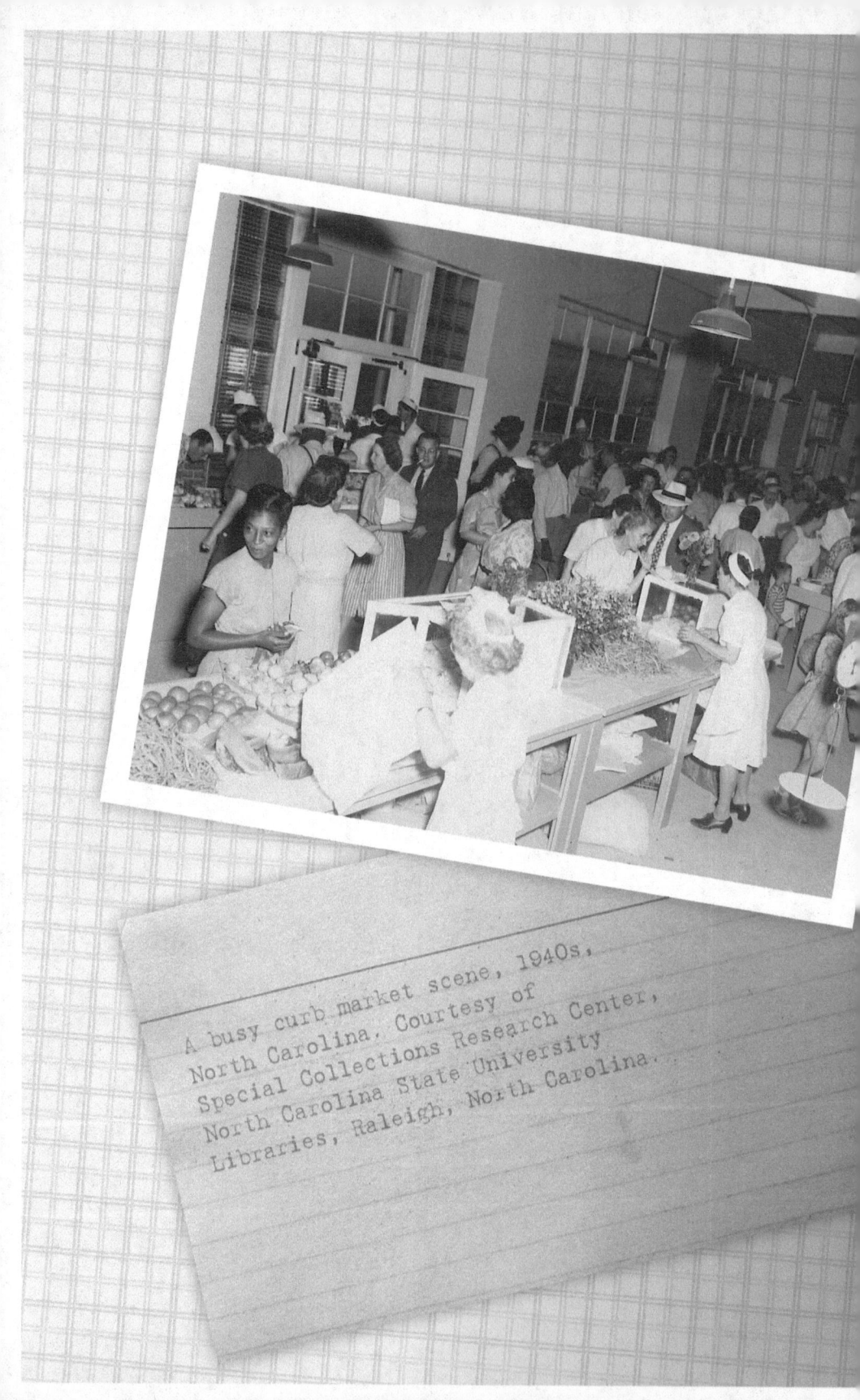

A busy curb market scene, 1940s, North Carolina. Courtesy of Special Collections Research Center, North Carolina State University Libraries, Raleigh, North Carolina.

CHAPTER FIVE

Cookbooks and Curb Markets

WILD MESSES OF SOUTHERN FOOD AND GENDER

> Besides these treasures there was a collection of recipes,
> which Granny could not read but which she had carefully preserved in
> the handwriting of numerous and long dead friends.
>
> OLIVE TILFORD DARGAN, *Call Home the Heart*

> The exchange of produce for money is one thing of value but the exchange of ideas
> and news is something else again and real friendship and understanding have grown
> up between town and country until they realize that they are all one community
> and that neither their prosperity nor their human interests can be separated.
>
> BLANCHE HANKS ELLIOTT, "Women in Different Sections"

WE HAVE FINALLY ARRIVED at the mess of greens in the southern food and gender story—and I propose we meet it on its own terms rather than force it into order.[1] It takes on Granny Starkweather's recipe collection and other cookbooks and adds in Elliott's curb market memories, each of which will be supremely messy.

The phrase "a mess of," meaning a serving of food, a portion of a dish, especially of vegetables, is surprisingly ancient. The *Oxford English Dictionary* dates its origins as a phrase to the 1300s, even while acknowledging that its use today is increasingly "US regional"—*OED*-speak for southern. In the South in which the women of this project used the term, calling a serving "a mess" worked particularly well for foods that reveled in their disorderliness—leaves of greens going in every direction with their potlikker in the bottom of a big black pot, servings of beans that did not need to be precisely measured or sorted before being cooked up all together, dishes of cabbage and potatoes thrown together without the assistance of a cookbook or a guide. In addition, "a mess" described well foods that were inherently collective—not one "bean" or a single "green" but many—many of the same kind in a pot of half-runners cooking, for instance, or many of similar but separate kinds, in a pot of turnip, mustard, and creasy greens simmering.

Returning to the dictionary and other uses of the word "mess," we find it could describe "a company of people eating together." That sense remains in the military's "mess halls," for instance, which also evoke another archaic use of the word: "a communal meal."[2] Metaphorically, this chapter and the conclusion of this book embrace all of these messes: the disorderliness of the southern food story; the collaborative, collective moments of the southern gender story within the recipes; and the communal meanings held in the moment of sharing and exchanging.

Shared food moments can be inherently elusive, though—difficult to preserve, capture, or re-create. As many have argued, including literary critic Roland Barthes, anthropologist Mary Douglas, and gastronome Brillat-Savarin, to name only a few, food constantly resists and escapes the written page. Experiencing it involves multiple senses simultaneously—taste, smell, sight, sound, and touch, not to mention the synesthesia of their combination. Our best food writers capture a moment, and we sigh because they take us to a set of food emotions parallel to our own lives. Their words, however, rarely capture the whole experience precisely. Food's symbolisms spiral outward and back, collecting memory, culture, history, and imagined communities. Its primitiveness delights in welcoming sex, indulgence, taboos, and death right along with it.[3] As we have seen with cornbread and biscuits, moonshine, canned tomatoes, and pellagra, struggles over food were never about only the food, or more precisely were always about more than just the food. Therefore, food resists neat control and simple endings.

One final obsolete compound word can be culled from our turn through the dictionary: the "mess-writer." Although its original sense indicated one who wrote about the mess, often in the nautical sense of keeping the account books around food expenditures, I propose to redefine it for our final explorations of southern food and gender.[4] Rather than tell a single story, rather than draw a final conclusion, the mess writing here explores the disorderly, collective, and communal spaces of cookbooks and curb markets. We let them be wild, be what they were or what they might have been; this chapter dwells less on proof and more on possibility, acknowledging that messes are more than their individual parts.

COMPLICATIONS IN THE SOUTHERN FOOD STORY

We began our turn through the southern food and gender story with three sets of anxieties tangling the pages of the South's moonshine literature. Using moonshine, women and girls embraced the independence, careers, and sexual and social liberation of the South's New Womanhood. Wild girls tamed by education bought with moonshine profits promised to resolve larger questions of immigration, race, and citizenship in a second set of moonshine stories. And larger-than-life female moonshiners and bootleggers jumped into their automobiles and drove roughshod over genteel expectations and domestic promises of new consumer culture. Taboo and illegal, moonshine allowed southern and American culture to explore the boundaries and borders of acceptable combinations of gender, class, and race at the beginning of the twentieth century.

Biscuit-versus-cornbread battles then proved a cultural struggle to define morality, modernity, and cleanliness in southern womanhood. Well-traveled, college-educated, career-minded, middle-class, southern New Women tried to convince local mountain women assumed to be less affluent that they should stop baking the cornbread their families enjoyed. Substituting the beaten biscuit meant endorsing purchased equipment, imported ingredients, indoor domestic practices, and embedded codes of race and leisure. Framing the debate required navigating conflicting messages about everything from sex to freedom to health. Emerging from the battles, gender and food were ever more tightly connected, but groups of women remained in tense relationship to each other over the region's breadbaskets.

The tomato club movement followed, and pioneering women around the South helped five hundred thousand girls empower themselves through harnessing the economic possibility in southern foodways. Lessons in science and technology joined new opportunities for self-financed luxury, education, and career training through a humble garden plant. An almost erased history of racial cooperation (and, in moments, integration) as well as a repairing of the bonds between rural and city, working- and middle-class adult women also emerged from one-tenth acres of a quintessential southern food. Yet the optimism about social change through capitalist consumerism was severely challenged by restrictive, traditional patriarchal forces on the organizers, imminent labor unrest in the communities, and unresolved issues of disease, starvation, racism, and poverty in the southern food story.

The tragedies of absence and lack haunted communities alongside the tomato club girls. Despite the often romanticized stories told about southern food and southern gender, women's strike novels countered the earlier century's optimism with grotesque representations of the diseased pellagrin. Starved, bleeding, sometimes voiceless, occasionally profoundly vocal, the pellagrins and the mill culture that created them exposed cracks in the southern food and gender story. Calling for class awakening, healing of racial divides, and more equitable distribution of food, labor, and social power, ghostly pellagrins brought us chronologically up to the Great Depression.

For many parts of the South, the Depression of the 1930s was a continuation of an economic downturn, especially in agricultural terms, that had begun decades earlier.[5] From the middle of the twentieth century onward, food in the South remained complicated and tangled. You still may not have enough food; you may have too much of unhealthy types of food; you may say the wrong things through what you eat; you may reinforce politics damaging to yourself and others with the food you put on your table. Depending on your class, race, and location in the South, your access to food remained limited. Depending on your investment in ideas of middle-class southern identity, your use of food to exclude other people from your construction of ideal southern life continued apace. Depending on your class and race, the same biscuits and cornbread you always fixed for your family may now be labeled soul food, white-trash cooking, or old-fashioned. Now you may serve presliced white bread from the store to be modern and hygienic, though it too has become more déclassé as the decades passed. Depending on your responses to all of the above as well as the South's general politics and job opportunities, you may well have left altogether, joining friends and family in the Great Migration to places like Chicago, Detroit, or New York.[6]

SOUTHERN FLAVORED FOOD UTOPIAS AND DYSTOPIAS

A teleological progress narrative of southern food often gets constructed in popular culture of the twentieth century. In other words, increasing mass production and mass marketing of food marched in an upward-pointing straight line toward today's abundant southern table. In such a view, more consumerism by more southerners solved the challenges put forth by the pellagrin, neutralized the radical potential of the tomato clubs, answered the resistance of the cornbread eaters, and soothed the anxieties of the moonshine literature.

For instance, progress-narrative proponents make much of how enriched bread, such as grocery store white breads, largely solved pellagra and other vitamin deficiency diseases. Once epidemiologists took advantage of government war rationing to get vitamins added to staples (flour, rice, salt, etc.) across the United States, cases of nutritionally based diseases plummeted. The success was helped by the spread of the modern American grocery chain, in which the South played a major role. From the 1916 debut in Memphis of Piggly Wiggly as the first truly self-service grocery store, to the growth and spread through the 1920s and 1930s of A&P and their competitors, grocery stores grew and introduced business innovations across the region. Jane McKimmon pointed to the speed of such change. As early as the 1930s, she reported a rural county agent working in North Carolina worrying about the feasibility of a curb market in her territory. The agent was not concerned about food scarcity or women's abilities to manage. Instead, she said, "I know they wish to have a market... but, Mrs. McKimmon, we can't have one in our town; there are too many people selling there now. The Piggly Wigglies, several A. & P. stores, other groceries, and a big city market are all doing a brisk business, and I do not think there is room for us."[7] American abundance, aisle after aisle of packaged food, entered the towns and cities of the South. Embraced by many, especially black and white women seeking relief from kitchen-based labor or wishing to stake a modern identity on consumerism's newest products, more and more of the food consumed in the South came from national and international sources.

Across the twentieth century, scientific breakthroughs aided those multiplying options. Fewer acres yielded more and more food. As the post–World War II Sunbelt development ramped up, the region saw growing profits for food companies and a thriving restaurant culture beyond previously established urban areas. As a result, celebrations of southern food as a cuisine expanded beyond the whites-only plantation nostalgia of Martha McCulloch-Williams and her beaten biscuits leading to "happy ever after." Regional newspapers hired food columnists; writers and critics from the area promoted chefs and specialty foods, and soon southern cuisine was well on its way to being established as such. With Craig Claiborne, Atlanta columnist Henrietta Stanley Dull, restaurateurs of New Orleans and other cities, and the establishment of magazines such as *Southern Living*, southern food became big business. Across the century, even through the painful upheavals of the long Civil Rights era, food still occasionally functioned as a connector and positive landmark of diverse southern cultures.[8] Analysts promoting this progress narrative emphasized the plenty and the modernity in the southern food story of the late twentieth century.

The dystopian in the southern food narrative also had proponents. For evidence, they traced an arc that began with the collapse of strikes after Gastonia and the speed up of war contracts. Both signaled a death knell to organized southern labor. Despite the dreams of people like Myra Page, no international coalition of labor developed out of the southern strikes. Instead North Carolina and others adopted their "right to work" identities that actively discouraged unions and worker protection. Such increased industrialization, urbanization, and suburbanization resulted in homogenizing and displacing homegrown food, as more and more families had to eat quickly, moved away from their gardens, and generally adopted store-bought lifestyles.

At the same time, romanticizing an ideal of the family farm or southern small town masked how much actual farmland was developed as suburbs and cities grew rapidly. From *The Waltons* to *The Andy Griffith Show*, and even in some ways to *The Beverly Hillbillies* or the later *Dukes of Hazzard*, television acted as if vast areas of the South were safely undeveloped. The cost of using fewer acres to produce food was a massive increase in the amounts of fertilizers and pesticides used. Migrant workers stepped into southern agriculture in a big way after mid-century, with few health or work protections in place. As interstates and suburbs grew, more of the restaurants in the South became the same chain and fast food establishments as in the rest of the United States.[9]

The politics of race, class, and gender never left. As Psyche Williams-Forson points out, the story of race in southern food did not move quickly in a straight line toward equality. In 1904, Minnie Fox, the sister of novelist John Fox Jr., wrote a best-selling cookbook of bluegrass Kentucky recipes. Fox at least listed the names of the black women and men who developed the recipes, but none of them received anything from the cookbook. They also had to endure typically racist portraits and titles ("uncle" and "mammy," for instance). Not much had changed in 1943 when Marjorie Kinnan Rawlings based her successful Florida cookbook, *Cross Creek Cookery*, on recipes she developed with Idella Parker, a woman employed as her maid. Parker later claimed she had an oral agreement with Rawlings to give her credit for her recipes, but Rawlings put only her own name on the book.[10]

Sit-ins took place at the South's restaurants for a reason, as sharing food between people of different races remained taboo and politically charged even as overtly racist chains like the Coon Chicken Inn prospered nationally. Hunger and lack of adequate food continued. As late as the 1960s, in the midst of the War on Poverty rededicated by Robert Kennedy's trip to Hazard, Kentucky, the U. S. South still struggled with economic disparities leaving people unfed.[11] Promoters of the dystopian interpretation bemoan the loss of self-sufficiency and of heterogeneous food communities; they worry especially about the environmental and cultural impact of growth and development.

Embedded in this dystopian narrative is profound nostalgia for times past. Such sentimentality should send up helpful scholarly alarms. We already saw how a turn to traditional domesticity confined the innovations of tomato clubs to a long forgotten and hard to unearth past. We had to work to uncover pellagra's stories of starvation from glowing memorials of the southern table's abundance. And we had to pull apart the nostalgic grouping of biscuits and cornbread together in order to see how they enforced class disparities separately. Throughout the century, the idea of the South became especially useful for people outside the region, as it had already done in the moonshine literature. Theorist Tara McPherson follows the lead of scholars like Grace Hale and Nina Silber who had encouraged, in Silber's words, the examination of the "ideal and desired South" as well as the realistic one. All three scholars remind us that the idea of "the South" became useful to the rest of the United States—a helpful repository for what the nation no longer wished to be, a crucible for new political or social hierarchies, or a generator of nostalgia in media to export around the nation and the globe. At various times, such ideas allowed the South in imagination to hold, for instance, the nation's racism, George Wallace–style New Right as well as Civil Rights–style New Left politics, and an almost endless supply of blockbuster movies, books, and music reimagining womanhood and manhood across the races.[12]

Food scholar Warren Belasco, from a different scholarly tradition, carefully tracks how American pro-agribusiness celebrations of abundance and pro-environmental panics about food shortages have relied on differing interpretations of the exact same data. Utopian and dystopian interpretations of American food policies in the twentieth century operated much like the "ideal and desired South"—helpful repositories for what the nation no longer wished to be, crucibles for new political or social hierarchies, or generators of nostalgia in media to export around the nation and the globe. At various times, food was the repository of dust-bowl tumbleweeds and food lines, 1970s right-leaning agricultural policies encouraging consolidation as well as left-leaning Environmental Protection Agency regulations, and films, music, and books about the (sometimes vanishing, sometimes flourishing) family farm. Given the stakes in each strand—ideas of the South and ideas of food—no wonder the combined product, southern food, is so evocative in twenty- and twenty-first-century America. Southern food coheres as a cuisine, a media phenomenon, and, to borrow Grace Hale's phrase, a central cultural category precisely because in the interpretations of ideal and desired southern food resided national fights over who and what we were.[13]

Finally, we should dismantle any unquestioning sense of historical convergence (whether progressive or regressive) in the southern food story. In other words, all the data never fit into a perfectly straight line, regardless of whether that line pointed up or down. Southern corporate giant Wal-Mart makes strange bedfellows with organic food companies in our present era and the most dedicated southern food enthusiasts celebrate corporate products like MoonPies and Big Red, to name just two examples.[14] There always were moments of resistance, people and places in alternative relation to the mainstream. History rarely consolidated into such lockstep progression—moments of resistance, alternate practices, and work-around solutions were always simultaneously present and developing. And yet we should not trust those moments of resistance because the same forces of consumer culture and national heterogeneity worked within the alternative sites as well.

ALTERNATIVE ENDINGS, EMBRACING MESSES

Scholars, including myself, can be so hyperaware of the risks of prediction or the blinders of our own particular moment that we retreat to a critical distance, hesitate to take a stand, and find it easier to doubt and complicate than jump into the mess with our sources. Indeed, it might be safer to end the book with this list of complexities. Yet, the story of southern food and gender explored in *A Mess of Greens* deserves not to be tied up so easily. Just as the relation between food on the table and the people around it began in a vexed and sometimes tense way, the story remains fraught—perhaps necessarily so. We will keep those cautions in mind, but we nevertheless proceed.

Not doing so teeters on the edge of paralysis. It makes it almost impossible, for instance, to read the potential and possibility of self-definition that drove so many community groups, women's clubs, and church fund-raisers to collect their recipes and publish their cookbooks their ways. Those cookbooks remain silent if too much of the cynicism enters our perspective. We cannot speak, if we only use scholarly caution, about Granny Starkweather's recipe collection or the Junior League cookbooks. We notice them, but we cannot take them seriously or without irony. The friendship and self-education of white and black women in curb markets, selling vegetables, talking with each other, and forging connections across town and country would be dismissed as impossibly naïve. Blanche Elliott's memories of how liberating curb market conversations could be stay locked in the archives if we only doubt such connections. What Jane McKimmon called the Country Woman's College—which she argued was a racially integrated, cross-class effort—is hard to believe in the context of that academic chapter. Reminders of the near impossibility of genuine connection in the racially and class-charged South should not preclude seeing the instances that defy the odds.

Let us instead listen to the messages in the recipes, the signatures, and the organization of cookbooks from women's groups in places large and small. Let us reconsider the talk so often dismissed as foolish gossip beside the tables of the Saturday curb markets as potentially transformative political debate. Let us take seriously the connections between town and country in the recipes and market stands. The mess of greens hiding in plain sight—the connections between people and places that nourish and value both—might then be unearthed.

The chapter thus acknowledges but is not silenced by what made those brief moments of genuine connection so fragile—the same politics of race, class, gender, and region that have troubled each of the events in preceding chapters. This chapter is necessarily partial and tentative at times. It is vulnerable to charges of hopefulness. Yet it imagines along with the gardeners, sellers, and cooks a different outcome, one that is messy and untamed, but also nourishing.

COOKBOOKS

> Civil Rights Cake: One pound of sugar, 1 pound of flour, one-half pound of butter, whites of 12 eggs, one-half cup of sweet milk, 1 ½ t. of baking powder. Take one half of batter and bake in lakers [*sic*]. Then add to the other half one pound of seeded raisins, 1 t. of each cinnamon, cloves, nutmeg and spice. Bake in layers same as white and put all together with very stiff icing. This makes a delicious cake.
>
> MRS. W. H. MCQUISTON, *The Rest Room and Library Cook Book*, Monticello, Arkansas, 1924

Throughout the South, the early twentieth century saw an explosion of printed cookbooks. Mrs. McQuiston's "Civil Rights Cake" recipe appeared in a book produced for sale by a group of Arkansas women raising funds to build a local library. Founded in 1902, the Sorosis Club successfully opened the town library in 1928 (though, of course, Arkansas's segregation laws limited library access). From local chapters of the Junior League, to women's clubs, to church groups, publications of cookbooks such as *The Rest Room and Library Cook Book* followed a fairly standard format: advertisements from local businesses, a running header or footer urging proper behavior, such as "patronize our advertisers" or "go to church," some kind of standard measurements or weights page, and a brief introduction penned by the chair of the cookbook committee. Many of the recipes had a prominent citizen's name attached to them, though in most cookbooks some remained unattributed. Special foods, such as prized cake recipes, novel dishes like McQuiston's "Civil Rights Cake," or party punches, dominated, whereas everyday foods such as beans or greens rarely appeared. Some of the committees went to great pains to standardize the serving size of recipes, style of ingredient lists (in other words, they decided between narrative paragraphs or lists of ingredients with directions to follow), and assumed cooking skills of their audience. The best among these became regional classics and went through multiple editions.[15] In some ways cookbooks were the opposite of the messes with which this chapter is concerned—built as they were on formalizing the practice of cooking—nonetheless, in them the mess of the communal and the multivocal was very much present. Thus, cookbooks are the first case study to which we turn.

Cookbooks themselves were not new to the southern United States. Mary Randolph's *Virginia House-wife* from 1824, while not the first American cookbook, was wildly influential in the nineteenth century with its blend of English, Native American, and African American ingredients and techniques. The previously mentioned 1881 publication by Abby Fisher, *What Mrs. Fisher Knows about Old Southern Cooking*, joined Malinda Russell's 1866 *Domestic Cook-book* (Russell's last known address was Michigan, but she described her career cooking in Tennessee and Virginia) as crucial to southern food traditions in part because they emphasized the professional training and approach of accomplished black women.[16] McCulloch-Williams's *Dishes and Beverages of the Old South*, with its beaten biscuits, was typical of early twentieth-century white southern women's publications. All four authors, Randolph, Fisher, Russell, and McCulloch-Williams, despite their differences in class and race, published their own cookbooks in hopes of supporting themselves.

The tradition of community-authored cookbooks also traces its roots to the Civil War years and the period immediately following, as both northern and southern women's groups produced cookbooks to support others. They raised money for soldiers and veterans and to fill gaps in the broken postwar social safety nets. Cookbooks like *Housekeeping in the Bluegrass* (1875), *The Laurel Cookbook* (1900), and *Dixie Cook-Book and Practical Housekeeper* (1879) raised money for churches, women's guilds, and community groups. Scholars have suggested that up to the mid-twentieth century, community cookbooks in the South were very invested in policing class boundaries and demonstrating mainstream values.[17] Certainly, they reflected the class, race, and gender politics of the region at the time.

Individually authored cookbooks and group publications were not the only options for potential customers. The crowded early twentieth-century southern marketplace also had cookbooks produced by companies advertising their food products or kitchen appliances. Rumford Baking Powder, Godchaux Sugar, the National Association of Margarine Manufacturers, and the Armstrong Manufacturing Company all produced cookbooks. Newspaper columnists and celebrity chefs started producing their own cookbooks at the time, as did health and educational advocates, including the extension agents and early home economists.[18] Many of these publications also were invested in the social hierarchies of the South—or at least in not disturbing the values of the white residents they imagined as their prime consumers.

Lines between the different types of cookbooks blurred significantly, as companies supported individual authors, community groups embraced commercial products, and southerners shored up, rebuilt, or constructed anew identities that were regionally identified even with national affiliations. For instance, Mrs. M. Fauntleroy, writing in her McGehee, Arkansas, *Garden Club Cook Book* in 1936, blended regional colloquialisms and locally available ingredients for "Red Hot Apples." Fauntleroy's recipe directed the cook to "Peel, quarter and core tart apples. Drop in a rich heavy syrup which has been colored with little red hot candies." She commented, "I generally make mine a rich red and syrup so thick that before it is gone, it jells beautifully. Boil until apples are tender." The mass-produced candies did not necessarily come from the South, but applesauce like her distinctive "Red Hot Apples" is still available in some Arkansas Ozarks restaurants today.[19]

Among our two "messes" for this chapter, cookbooks have been most discussed by scholars.[20] Yet, scholarship on cookbooks often gets bogged down in what we cannot know with certainty about them as texts. For instance, as previously discussed, we cannot assume that "the South" in cookbooks such as *The Rest Room and Library Cook Book* mirrored conditions on the ground; cookbooks cannot tell us much about what Silber would call the "real South." In addition, we cannot know the color (or religion, or gender) of the hands that paged through and cooked from the finished cookbook. Just as the Sears catalogs circulated in both white and black communities, local cookbooks passed through kitchens with racially diverse women in them; they do not tell us into whose hands they fell. The list continues: we do not know whether the person holding the cookbook felt included or excluded by the book. Did the cookbooks successfully police race and class segregations in the twentieth-century South? Did they want to? We do not know whether the women who created the cookbooks were telling the truth; in particular, we do not know how often they cooked the recipes included. How often, in other words, did they cook a pot of greens and a simple pan of cornbread rather than a multi-course meal featuring imported ingredients and garnishes? Finally, we do not know how the people holding the cookbooks actually cooked—which recipes in the publications they used, whether they preferred to read for inspiration or aspiration or careful direction, or whether they simply purchased the book out of community spirit (or guilt) and then shoved it unceremoniously on the top shelf. Sherrie Inness qualifies her study of cookbooks like this: "I analyze texts that might or might not have influenced living women" because she worries she cannot prove the manuals and published accounts were taken seriously. Similarly, she says, "In many ways, it does not matter how often women in the early 1900s followed such recipes in their homes; the recipes suggested an idealized upper-middle-class vision of what women were expected to achieve in the kitchen."[21] Scholarship on cookbooks has often foundered here.

Some of that long list of questions can be partially answered: the provenance of a copy can tell something about to whom it circulated; the history of the organization behind a publication can tell us more about their intentions with their books; stains or annotations on particular recipes can suggest which were most used; memories and careful passing on of a volume can suggest its worth to an individual family. More theoretically, scholars argue that the broad developments in community cookbooks tell us something about the changing century. Standardizing recipes, for instance, was not just a stylistic choice when more and more publications adopted the practice: the practice signaled changes in women's roles (as they became comfortable with scientific precision in cooking) and reflected the mobility of family members (as the cookbooks no longer assumed a previous oral transmission of basic mechanics of cooking). As Ann Romines argues about baking in Eudora Welty's novels, "Such controversies about recipes and writing are far from trivial; they dramatize crucial questions about the changes in traditional women's lives at the end of the nineteenth century and about the relation of writing and women's domestic culture."[22] At the least, we can assume from their popularity that the cookbooks communicated something important to authors and consumers—even if we do not know precisely what that something was.

In fact, it is more than possible that the creators of cookbooks intentionally were only trying to communicate within their circle or community. For instance, in 1950, the women of the Brevard-Davidson River Presbyterian Church published a cookbook very similar to the earlier ones in which McQuiston and Fauntleroy participated. Interspersed advertisements from local companies—the town's one big paper mill, the taxi company, competing grocery stores, plumbers, dry cleaners, car dealerships, banks, jewelers, newsstands, drug stores—supported the Brevard women's printing costs. A header on every page exhorted "Go to church every Sunday." A grainy photo on the front cover of the *Presbyterian Women's Cook Book* showed not the church itself, but instead (it is hard to tell) either the church's rectory or the Silversteen mansion in town, famous for its elegance still today. Mrs. Edwin L. Happ, cookbook chair, provided all the commentary the book had, saying, "It has not been our intention to produce a complete Cook book; instead we have tried to publish a collection of favorite recipes of well-known cooks in the church." She thanked the advertisers and urged people to patronize them.[23] A page of standard measurements followed, after which the recipes commenced.

Sections of the cookbook included beverages, breads, casseroles, meats and "sea foods," salads and salad dressings, sauces, preserves and pickles, sandwich fillings, and vegetables. Sweets were intermixed in the table of contents: "cakes—cookies and frostings" and candies were the third and fourth sections. Desserts had a section in the middle of the book; pies and pastries came later on, and sweet recipes snuck into many other sections ("sweet sandwich" and "foamy sauce," for instance). Some recipes were anonymous, but most concluded with the contributor's name. The messages of the cookbook were fragile, however. It had no other commentary, very little narrative, and my copy, at least, is missing its back cover.

At the same time, my copy comes with written annotation and commentary—from my grandmother, who was the original owner, and from my mother, who inherited the book. From them, we learn that the town's young home economics agent contributed the icing recipe that used commercial Karo syrup. We learn the harried schoolteacher, the one not given the gifted students, offered the simplest banana bread recipe. We understand why families with distinctively Jewish-sounding names were in the Presbyterian cookbook (because of the German background of the mill management who were welcomed into the higher classes of the town, of which this church was also a member). We learn that at least some of the men listing recipes were actually boys, probably helping their mothers round out the table of contents without dominating the contributors' lists.[24] We glimpse who might suggest fresh seafood because they could afford it and who might be posturing with such a recipe. We learn which town eccentrics advertised but did not contribute recipes. The book, in other words, had a lot to say to readers who knew (or were learning) the codes.

In *Along the Archival Grain*, a book about nineteenth-century colonial Netherlands Indies, theorist Ann Laura Stoler suggests that rather than shying away from the "unsure and hesitant sorts of documentations and sensibilities" that cluster between the lines, in the margins, and around the edges of official texts, we should instead embrace them.[25] Even though early Dutch colonies were far from mid-century Brevard, North Carolina, Stoler's framework encourages us to dive into the mess of the recipes, partial attributions, and marginalia of the Presbyterian women's publication. For our purposes, what are interesting are the disruptions, the possibilities of subversion and conversation between the lines of food writing like these cookbooks. I do not own the key (however fragmentary) to the Sorosis Club's Arkansas cookbook in which McQuiston's "Civil Rights Cake" resided. Published five years after the founding of the NAACP, but well before the modern era brought the phrase,

"Civil Rights" into common use, the recipe holds tight to its mysteries. Was it a bad joke with its segregated layers of white and black? Was it a recipe made by a white woman's black cook, holding an embedded political critique of that segregation? Why did it not use chocolate, blackstrap molasses, or some other, more effective darkener if the goal was to distinguish the light layer from the black? Why did McQuiston leave the choice of the icing's color to the individual cook? What did the rest of the ladies of the club think of this recipe?

It is hard not to notice race and ethnicity in the South's cookbooks. Brevard's used a racial slur in one of its cabbage recipes. A cookbook from Laurel, Mississippi (popular enough to be republished five times by the 1949 edition), included recipes for "bortsch," "Egyptian soup," "frijole soup," and liberal calls for Caribbean, Creole, and Southwestern ingredients such as dasheens, mirlitons, fried bananas, and Tabasco peppers. Its corn and tamale casserole, attributed to an original contributor from the 1900 edition, called for more than a dozen tamales, so someone in the Mississippi town must already have been making them (Delta tamale traditions combined African American foodways and Latino ones, so it is hard to say from whom the Laurel women were getting tamales—if they did not make them themselves). Scholars have generally concluded along with Jessamyn Neuhaus and Sherrie Inness that the racial diversity in community cookbooks, in Neuhaus's words, "revealed how virtually all cookbook authors assumed a white readership." She points to stereotyped "Mammy" and "Juanita" figures in the ones she examined, and concludes that the cookbooks could not afford to "imply that their readers might already have family or cultural connections to 'foreign' cuisine." Inness agrees, saying that foreign food, including Mexican and Italian, "provided the media with a way to indoctrinate women readers with the belief that the ideal American woman was white and middle class."[26] Although the *Laurel Cook Book* partially countered their arguments in terms of familiarity with dishes like tamales, Neuhaus and Inness's cautions are important. Policing racial and ethnic hierarchies certainly occupied time and effort of many white women in the twentieth-century South.

Such a perspective would view McQuiston's "Civil Rights Cake" as an inside joke for white southerners—separate but equal in the cake and in society. But perhaps as scholars we have made an error in the other direction—we cannot prove the moments of diversity or inclusion in the cookbooks were not genuine. Surely some white women concluded from the cookbooks (or were confirmed in their existing belief) that they were superior; but it does not follow that every reader did, or that every cookbook committee included diverse cuisines to belittle them, or even that communities were new to these recipes. Nor does it follow that only aspirational middle-class white readers held the cookbooks and interpreted them. I suggest we carefully embrace the uncertainty—cookbooks could enforce the status quo, but they could also offer pathways to cooperation and communication. They could hold the faintest traces of an unironic "Civil Rights Cake" bringing a diverse community into conversation.

We can safely say that most of the time those traces were so faint as to be unworkable. The twentieth-century South practically had to explode before anything resembling racial equality could be achieved. Racial and class divides, despite the changes, still surface today to privilege the old hierarchies of whiteness, wealth, and masculinity. I am not naïve about the daily politics in which we live in the South, in the United States. But some change happened, some moments of communication laid the groundwork, and some people forged connections despite the divides. The act of sharing a recipe, eating each other's favorite foods, laboring in similar ways to make a dish, preserving forgotten pasts, and imagining unexpected futures all could happen between the pages of the cookbooks flooding the scene and in the exchange of recipe cards too numerous to count. This mess could serve unexpected purposes, in other words. The fact that we cannot prove it, however, may be the point. The key is lost; the sources remain opaque; but that does not mean we should decide they have no value or did not perform transformative work. In the history and memories of the women's curb market movement, a little more transparency appears. Its communal practices and undercurrents can be unearthed. It is the second mess to which we turn.

CURB MARKETS

Women's curb markets grew out of the home demonstration work across the South. They began as once-a-week, informal streetside gatherings with countrywomen bringing extra produce, eggs, and flowers to sell curbside to town women shoppers. Even as the markets expanded, acquiring covered building spaces, permanent tables, the assistance of the women's husbands and children, and longer hours, the name remained. It signaled the roots of the practice, as well as reminded customers, competitors, and producers of the differences in the markets from permanent businesses.

When sitting down to celebrate the fiftieth anniversary of North Carolina's Henderson County Curb Market in the 1970s, the area's preeminent memory keeper, Frank FitzSimons Sr., narrated the civic history of the market. The author of three volumes of town history, *From the Banks of the Oklawaha*, FitzSimons (also a dairyman, football coach, and banker) recalled writing a letter to the newspaper that argued the county needed a market like the European ones he observed during World War I. The editor of the newspaper, Noah Hollowell, joined with FitzSimons. Working with "Mr. Arnold, the country farm agent and the home demonstration agent, whose name I have forgotten," the city men persuaded seven farm families to create the first market. Remember FitzSimons's phrasing here; we will return to it soon. As they formally organized, the local newspaper reported the curb market's "governing board will consist of at least three representatives from the farmers. They will ask for one from the Merchants Association, one from the Chamber of Commerce, one from the city commissioners and one from the Woman's Club to help make regulations for conducting the market in a way that it will prove attractive to the producers as well as the buyers and objectionable to no one."[27] First occurring in 1924 and 1925 on Main Street under donated buggy umbrellas, the market eliminated the need for farmers to travel the streets of the town peddling at individuals' doors. Instead, city buyers came to the sellers. Soon after, businesses donated materials for a more permanent location (farmers provided the labor). The curb market moved to a wooden building on King

Street and, later, to the even more prominent location of its current concrete building on Church Street.

A second way to tell the story of the curb market hid in plain sight in FitzSimons's account. The same advertisement that proclaimed the death of peddling in the county gave a hint of the market's other history, saying, "The market had its beginning 12 years ago when a number of farmers, mostly farm women, through the co-operation of the county farm agent and home agent, united their efforts to make a better retail outlet for produce."[28] It was the story of the home demonstration agent whose name FitzSimons has forgotten, the "mostly farm women" who united to make a retail outlet, and the representatives from the Woman's Club who served on the original board—and it was the story of the women who have been behind the scenes of the market managing its daily operations for the eighty-five years of its existence. Both stories held kernels of truth. Given the social and cultural mores of the 1920s, the curb market needed the newspaperman and the city council member. It needed the commitment and the labor of male farmers to park their buggies and cars and let the city buyers come to them rather than peddle to each door. Still, most of the buyers (who made purchases and ran the kitchens of boarding houses and homes in town) and most of the sellers (who did the daily work of staffing the curb market tables every time it convened) were women, and the curb market could not exist without them. The conversations they had, forgotten or overlooked like their names in official histories, are the messes drawing our attention here.

In the 1920s in the rest of North Carolina, a coalition of farmwomen and the new home demonstration agents founded curb markets everywhere. McKimmon focused on the social aspects of the movement. She echoed Blanche Hanks Elliott, whose memories of the friendship growing up between city and country served as an epigraph for this chapter. McKimmon described the interaction country women and city women had on market day, especially mentioning the "friendly chats while sales are being made [that] give both buyer and seller a clearer understanding of each other's worth." She named the Henderson County market as one of their successes, using data gathered by the home demonstration agents whose names FitzSimons forgot. McKimmon documented more than $570,000 in profit made by state markets in 1945; the Henderson County market was in the second largest tier of profitable markets, the only one from the mountains to achieve such size; in other parts of the state, large markets made significant profits for the women involved. Men helped found the markets and have served on the boards and participated in their histories, but women always did the behind-the-scenes, daily work of sustaining them.[29] The Henderson County market's only paid position has traditionally been the manager; women have always staffed this position, most staying in the post for decades.

McKimmon was clear in her account that from its beginning the curb market movement was in deliberate opposition to mere capitalist market efficiency. She told of "several economists" who offered free advice to the women involved. The experts wanted a "selection or election of ten or fewer persons to do the selling for all the communities of a county." McKimmon continued, "This, they say, would release the many people now marketing their own products for other duties and place the selling in the hands of the efficient few, who would be paid for the service." To McKimmon and the women involved, the conversations between women, the exchanges of ideas, and the nurturing of friendship would be materially damaged if the curb markets were reorganized to look like traditional businesses. She argued, "This plan might be wise if the market was a commercial enterprise only, but these economists miss the point. The farm woman's market is not planned for economic value alone; it furnishes a social opportunity as well; and both are important." McKimmon's conclusion was that "the few selected sellers which economists advocate might be able to turn over the money paid in, but they would scarcely be able to transfer to the farm women at home the joy to be had from that weekly mingling with interesting people at the market place."[30] At first, the mingling and the talk appeared to mainly stay on the topics of food.

One farmwoman told McKimmon, "Town women need what we have to sell, and the Lord knows we need the money they will give us for it. When we women get together on a proposition like that, the matter of ways and means is pretty thoroughly thrashed out, and the thing is apt to be done." Another got more specific about how the groups needed each other, saying, "I did not know city folks could be so nice as my customers are. They look out for me no matter who else is selling, and we have become very good friends." She gave a glimpse of their topics of conversations: "But I will have to tell you a little secret: some of them don't know much about food, and that gives me an opportunity to pay back part of the nice things they do for me." This particular woman employed her knowledge of childrearing and nutrition to help her new friend. She said, "Right now I am showing a young mother how to feed her baby and am bringing her tomato juice which I canned in small glass jars and which she gives her little boy every day. When I showed her how to cook spinach in very little water to save the minerals and the vitamins and how to mash it through a sieve before feeding him, she was afraid to give him vegetables, but she did it and is delighted with his improvement. That kind of thing pleases me very much." This was a real switch from town women in the strike novels blaming the pellagra of mill women just in from the country on the mill women's ignorance. These rural women were scientific experts in McKimmon's account. McKimmon concluded, "And so it comes about that the country woman is on a wholesome footing with the town woman at the market . . . the friendly chats while sales are being made give both buyer and seller a clearer understanding of each other's worth."[31] Some of that worth specifically clustered around time for pleasure and care. The women with knowledge of vegetables and babies indulged in the pleasure of conversation. It was not efficient or money making per se; the rewards were not on the surface of the record. Much like the cookbook codes, the curb markets rewarded in a less obvious, but no less profound, manner.

Other pleasures involved ways that town women, the very ones whose time was so standardized by clocks, railroads, and the mechanized world, could actively resist what proved in the pellagra story to be a soul-draining efficiency. Interestingly, the benefits did not just go in one direction. Rural women benefited from being around the town women, but the town women not only benefited from the knowledge of the farmwomen, they also enjoyed the opportunity to slow down and spend time with each other. The curb markets were "fostering friendly relations between town and country" and, according to one of the rural women, "it was an interesting thing to see the town women with their market baskets. They drove down and did their own marketing and seemed to enjoy meeting each other as much as we enjoyed meeting them. One of them told me the other day she wouldn't miss the market for anything." McKimmon stepped away from her official role in her memoir to insert a truly personal anecdote about what she bought at her local market. She made clear that in terms of curb markets, she belonged to the community. Jane McKimmon loved sweet potatoes; her guilty pleasure (she said it was no good for her figure but she did it anyway) was bringing a bag of cooked ones home quickly to fry up with butter at the end of her long days working with North Carolina's women.[32]

In addition, McKimmon made a larger point about the kinds of foods that could be shared. Our mess of greens gets very literal here:

> I am now one of those apartment dwellers who cannot be at home all day, and I believe a good market for home-cooked food can be developed with people like me. All of us in apartments are up against it when it comes to long, slow cooking, and sellers on the woman's market are taking advantage of the fact and bringing cooked or partially prepared foods to the market to meet the need. For instance, Mrs. Sauls of the Raleigh market has developed quite a trade in cooked collards, six to ten pounds every Saturday. The apartment dweller knows that those collards have left most of the odor of boiling greens where they were first cooked and that she can reheat them for serving without scenting her own living quarters. A Southerner, you must know, thinks a dinner is incomplete if it lacks greens of some kind, and for that matter so does the nutritionist; and now cooked kale, turnip salad, and spinach all find their way to the woman's market.[33]

Partly, McKimmon targeted how blurred the distinctions between urban, city, town, village, farm, country, and rural were in the second half of the twentieth century in the South. Women lived in new city and town apartments, but they were not separated in terms of diet from their counterparts on farms. Together, they were southerners linked by preference and taste to the greens at the market.

Yet another part of McKimmon's paean to greens suggested the importance of foods that were not visible in the cookbooks from the era. Williams-Forson documents how rarely certain everyday foods appear in the middle-class cookbooks produced by African American women in the early century—fried chicken, hambones, and, significantly, greens—because such women were trying carefully to craft a new public persona less confined by the stereotypes of sights, smells, and sounds clustering around the foods. McKimmon's worries about the smells of apartment greens spoke of parallel anxieties. Flannery O'Connor's short story "A Stroke of Good Fortune" featured a social-climbing white woman similarly agonizing over her rural brother's insistence on eating greens; the smell, she feared, would offend her neighbors and reveal her own background to them. But a wide range of eaters simultaneously loved their mess of greens. Companies tried to can and profit from the preferences for greens (one in Arkansas even tried canning pokeweed, also called poke sallet, or poke greens), but they never really eclipsed the persistent preference for fresh. Perhaps greens such as the ones at curb markets were popular precisely because the practices of going for a walk in the woods, or picking them from a low-labor garden, effectively resisted tyrannies of time clocks, social pressures, and gendered workdays.[34] In any case, greens and curb markets were entwined in McKimmon's and many southerners' everyday lives, regardless of whether we can easily document them.

There are hints, moreover, that the conversations at markets involved more than food and included diverse women however they identified. An "Ambassador Daniels, back home from his post in Mexico," appeared to get hints of this potential when he said, "it is a social institution with town and country mingling. They talk politics and church and books, but mostly babies and housekeeping, and if you want to know the neighborly chat of Nash and Edgecombe counties you can go to the curb market to get it." Susie Powell in Mississippi was more explicit about the unstated power in gatherings of women and girls. She pointed out the political discussions that always could emerge. Striking a deliberately political note, Powell wrote in 1936 to a Jackson, Mississippi, newspaper, "Masses also need knowledge and training to prevent exploitation... Women welcome news, for women are close readers."[35] Rather than merely dismiss the conversations as gossip, we may acknowledge what else could be said, in the safe spaces of the market. Women and girls, in discussing politics and church and books, could easily have formed opinions and strategies around the edges of the curb market tables.

The curb market world was one of new introductions, unrecorded conversations, safety in numbers, and shared knowledge. It was even a world of passed notes. McKimmon claimed, "It is desirable that a producer put a slip containing her name in every package" so unsatisfied customers could have recourse. However, "These slips also serve many times to introduce seller and buyer."[36] Simply put, who knows what else the notes contained? Who knows what women were talking about at the markets? McKimmon suggested the lines of communication were robust and well exercised. She documented the percentages of what was sold on a typical day, packages in which those notes were tucked. She found that 25 percent was poultry; 16 percent, eggs; 13 percent, vegetables; 12 percent, meat; 7 percent, butter; 3 percent, flowers; 2 percent, fruits and berries. That left 11 percent in her miscellaneous category, which "covers almost anything from puppies to wild flowers, from walnuts to watermelons, and from rising dough to garden soil and house plants."[37] Miscellaneous, in other words, was a mess.

McKimmon hinted that an effort was being made by the women communicating at curb markets to put some order into that mess. They worked to define their own standards—for goodness, for fairness, and for local values—and establish what food scholar Amy Trubek calls, in part, the "taste of place" or *terroir*. McKimmon's examples were hams and grapes, illustrations of the measures that women developed. McKimmon said, "A young marketing specialist said to me once, after seeing women buying in a big grocery store, 'It's a strange thing that women here in the South will pass by all the standardized hams from the big packing houses and go over to those rusty looking hams from the farms for their purchases.'" McKimmon continued, "'There's a good reason,' I replied, 'and I could prove it to you if I had a slice from one of those rusty old hams after it is baked to show you its delicious flavor. Certainly the commercial hams are uniform in size and packaging, but those women buyers have a different standard of excellence and demand a recipe for curing with ingredients which will produce the piquant flavor they are accustomed to, and that the ham shall have been left long enough in that cure to assure them of the fine flavor.'" McKimmon argued that local women wanted standards, but ones based on flavor and quality, not on size or uniformity in appearance. Similarly, scuppernong grapes inspired poetic language from McKimmon: "when September rolls around, the rusty, ripe scuppernong is a thing to dream about. There is no more delightful experience than to be under a far-stretching arbor picking these luscious grapes from the vines, and next best is getting ripe scuppernongs from the farm woman's market." She added, "These grapes do not ship well, and in consequence outsiders know little of their tempting juiciness." Women's political, book, and church opinions might have echoed the mainstream South or nation. But they just as plausibly could have reflected local, place-based, community tastes—the traces, imperfectly recorded, of southern women's sense of *terroir*.[38]

CONCLUSION

Whether we are reading the mess writing, cooking up our own mess of greens, whispering to each other about the mess before us, or sitting in the mess hall and writing together, tracks of resistance can be unearthed. We may not know exactly how they worked, what their goals were, and who walked along them. Yet we can glimpse southern identities—some inclusive, some exclusive, some nostalgic, and some situational—being rebuilt over and over in those places. We get hints of some communication beyond the cynical to explain the persistence of southern food traditions. Always functioning against the backdrop of unequal social hierarchies of race, class, gender, and region, the mess of greens, nonetheless, was a story of possibility and promise if we wish to listen to it. Food. People. Places. Shared stories.

CONCLUSION

Market Bulletins

WRITING THE MESS OF GREENS TOGETHER

> Dear Friend, Received your letter with the leaf. No red shank is a shrub herb and don't have leaves like your leaf... Be sure to write again. I am a friend to all. Write me about yourself, a letter helps a lonely person. Love, Mrs. Fergusson.
>
> ELIZABETH LAWRENCE, *Gardening for Love*

Cookbooks and curb markets continued across the twentieth century and into our own. From the 1930s to today they have been simultaneously places of containment and exclusion on the one hand, and possibility and potential on the other. To conclude our exploration of moments in the southern food and gender story, we turn to one final example of mess writing, one final hidden archive. With the perspective garnered from female moonshiners in literature, battles over biscuits and cornbread, economic stores of the garden-variety tomato, ghostly pellagrins in strike novels, and the hopeful possibility encoded in cookbooks and curb markets, we now have the skills to understand a peculiar book published posthumously in 1988 by a garden writer named Elizabeth Lawrence.[1] The direct project that resulted in *Gardening for Love* did not even begin until the late 1940s, when Eudora Welty subscribed her friend Lawrence to the *Mississippi Market Bulletin*. Yet, the decades-long, collaborative writing project of *Gardening for Love* was the spiritual and historical progeny of all the messes of greens we have explored. It is also a concluding chapter in the southern food and gender story that has the potential to bring us, its descendants, into our own future, redefining our own mess writing beyond these pages.

Without our change of perspective we could not even hear the soul-saving friendship between a gardener in urban, thriving Charlotte, North Carolina, who wrote for the city newspaper and Mrs. Fergusson, a plant lover seeking an herb from her own childhood that might have helped her sick friend. Despite Eudora Welty's direct influence, southern literary scholars mostly missed the dialogue despite or beyond class, race, or place that *Gardening for Love* contained.[2] The friendship of those Elizabeth Lawrence, the Charlotte gardener, described as "gardening for love" disappeared for years. Gardeners and seed savers advertised their flowers and friendship in farmers' bulletins that were designed to be about agricultural business but which became places for women to meet over shared passions. They spoke in the bulletins, in letters with Lawrence, and through her book to us. The market bulletins became a region-wide repository of what McKimmon called the miscellaneous at curb markets. The "we" of the North Carolina or Arkansas cookbooks, as well as of McKimmon's curb market memoir, *When We're Green We Grow*, fits well with Lawrence's argument that "no one gardens alone"—and no one exchanges seeds and preserves plants without reaching out to others in collective, shared, messes of talk.

MARKET BULLETINS

The market bulletins were not designed to be vehicles for women's intimate connections and communication. Rather, they were, as the Web site for the Louisiana Market Bulletin says, "for the purpose of disseminating market information." Louisiana, Georgia, and South Carolina had some of the earliest bulletins, with the idea discussed as early as the first decade of the twentieth century, and full publication commencing around 1916. West Virginia and Florida followed quickly in the late teens, with North Carolina, Mississippi, Tennessee, Virginia, and Alabama joining in by the 1920s and early 1930s.

When garden writer Lawrence set out to subscribe to all of the bulletins, she could only find one vigorous state publication outside of the South, in Connecticut. Like girls' tomato clubs and extension-based women's curb markets, market bulletins were a primarily southern phenomenon. In general, residents within the states advertised for free; outside folks subscribed or listed want ads only; most states limited advertisements to around twenty-five words.

Regardless of what the states thought they were supporting, residents soon noticed some flexibility in the mission of the bulletins. For instance, Louisiana's assisted "in marketing Louisiana products and services not normally available through commercial channels." The bulletins soon overflowed with nontraditional products and services, the miscellaneous elements of farm life. Everything from a "widow with no family ties" looking for "a home with an elderly couple needing someone to take care of them," to a "family of cotton pickers" seeking "work and a house near school and church," to a "bachelor with no bad habits" who wanted "a congenial job where the hunting and fishing were good" was advertised in the bulletins. Reading Mississippi's bulletin, Lawrence was left wondering "whether puppies got homes and lost dogs were found. And I wonder who bought the little farm with the pecan trees and good clear well water." In fact, Lawrence claimed, "I have an idea that if someone sat down and read all of the market bulletins since 1928, he would have a rich sense of the social history of the rural Deep South."[3] More than simple want ads, the bulletins expanded beyond material objects to be the voices, hopes, and dreams of their readers' lives.

Even though Lawrence used the generic male "he" in the previous quote, she herself was especially interested in the "hard-working farm women" in the bulletins. Whatever the states intended, women soon found their way into the bulletins and populated them with their specific concerns and ways of communicating. They advertised their garden seeds, yard plants, window plants, and box plants. They became Lawrence's faithful correspondents and friends over the exchange of vegetables, flowers, herbs, and wild plants. (Some women complained to Lawrence about the space given to advertise dogs, which never seemed edited for length, versus their own listings of long country names for plants, which got mysteriously shortened.) The communication that began in the miscellaneous categories of the bulletins transferred to letters exchanged between Lawrence and the women along with the seeds. Lawrence, with her correspondents' permissions, labored to turn their letters into a book. *Gardening for Love* expanded beyond the advertisements into the friendships—and much as the cookbooks and curb markets came to life in the collective voice, the bulletins proved a shared mess of greens as well.

Lawrence was born in 1904 in Marietta, Georgia, but she spent most of her childhood in the Piedmont region of North Carolina. After receiving a degree in English literature from Barnard College, she returned to Raleigh. A class in landscape architecture at North Carolina State led to her career as a garden writer and designer. Resisting labels, Lawrence said about her work, "I design gardens but cannot bear to be called a Landscape Architect; lecture and write about gardening, but cannot bear to be called an expert. Cannot bear to be called an amateur, but like to be taken seriously as a gardener and a writer." Most of that career took place in Charlotte, North Carolina, where she moved with her mother to be near her sister. From 1959 to 1975, she was the weekly Sunday gardening columnist for the *Charlotte Observer*. Along with the column, Lawrence wrote books that pioneered the field of southern garden writing; she devotedly corresponded with other gardeners around the country; and she cultivated a home garden significant enough to be listed on the National Historic Register of Places.[4]

Interest in Lawrence has increased since her death in 1985, with more of her books in print today than when she was alive. In part, this is because of how intimate and inviting her garden writing is. Lawrence was always in conversation with her plants, with other gardeners, and with her armchair readers; she wrote as if we were all already friends. In fact, her first column for the *Observer* was illustrated with a photo of her at her own garden gate, inviting readers to come through and join her.[5] Much like Jane McKimmon's autobiographical "we," Lawrence created intimacy in dialogue and collectivity, rather than in solo personal revelations.

Lawrence did not finish her book on the market bulletins before she passed away. Fellow garden writer Allen Lacy inherited "a huge pasteboard box" and the charge to see if he could make a final book out of it. In that box were issues of bulletins, packages of seeds, newspaper clippings, typescript and handwritten manuscript pages from Lawrence, and bundles of letters sent to Lawrence from around the South. Lacy described the letters as "tracing out not only the love for plants but also the stuff of life—the deaths of spouses or of children, the onset of serious illness, the loneliness of elderly women for whom writing letters to Miss Lawrence was obviously a lifeline." Lacy noted that while Lawrence used the first person, she said little about her life with it. Unlike Lacy, however, I argue that Lawrence *was* telling her autobiography; but we can only see it by shifting our definitions to view her story as inseparable from those of her plants, her correspondents, and her community. While it is easier for us to hold *Gardening for Love* in its current form as a book, it was perhaps in a truer form in that big, jumbled box of materials. Lacy hinted at such, saying "some of the enormous pleasure I have found in editing this book cannot be passed on to readers, except indirectly." He called it a treasure, and magic; Lawrence's carefully chosen word "love" seems just as apt. As Lawrence wrote in the preface to *The Little Bulbs* in 1957, "Gardening, reading about gardening, and writing about gardening are all one; no one can garden alone."[6] In *Gardening for Love,* Lawrence not only gave voice to her story but also to those of southern farm women speaking through the bulletins.

The names of the people in the market bulletins and the book were otherwise "recorded only in family Bibles, in the records of county courthouses, on tombstones in country cemeteries—and in the yellowed pages of the market bulletins where they sold their mules and their cordwood, their bales of sweet-smelling alfalfa, their old-fashioned daffodils and their yard plants with their poetic country names." They lived in places that even by 1928 were no longer on maps "in this, the era of ZIP codes," according to a Mississippi writer Lawrence quoted. That person continued, "Sadly, the names of yesterday's crossroad communities read like an obituary of promise."[7] Lawrence's source was nostalgic for the promise of new growth, of places taking hold.

In the South of the mid-twentieth century, in which races were separate, genders lived divided lives, and class demarcated who could talk to whom in small towns and large, the promise and possibility of the correspondences spawned by bulletins extended even further. Lawrence admitted that she did not know for certain whether the person nostalgic for lost towns, Terry Megehee, were a man or a woman. It did not matter, since what she and Megehee shared was a dedication to the bulletins. Over the course of the four decades of her experience with the bulletins, Lawrence met only a handful of her correspondents in person. Through their mutual love of plants, gardens, and place, they formed friendships outside of the traditional social hierarchies. We cannot know for certain if, for instance, some of the letter writers were African American (Lawrence herself was white), or from mill villages (Lawrence was a middle-class town woman), or otherwise crossing conventions. The possibility existed that they were, and that, therefore, communication between groups said to be taboo could have been happening out of sight of traditional recordkeeping. Just as we cannot know for certain what was meant by and whose hands held the recipes in cookbooks, or what was said by whom beside the tables of the curb market about politics and books, we cannot know for certain who was forming friendships across the market bulletins.

We do know that *Gardening for Love* documented working lines of communication between city and country—and pointed out how blurry those differences could be in individual lives. In a remembrance of his parents, Dudley Clendinen, a newspaper journalist in Atlanta, talked about keeping their subscription to the Georgia bulletin in their memory. Clendinen described the bulletin as "the one paper anyone could afford" and "a connective tissue between farmers isolated from one another, and later between city dwellers and their country roots."[8] Persisting through decades during which masses of people moved from the rural South to urban areas in both the South and the nation, the market bulletins both preserved and built anew southern regional identities around the edges of homogenizing national food and cultural scenes.

In the world of the market bulletins, women claimed their own voice and expertise as they reworked connections. For instance, Lawrence pointed out that plants in the bulletins were not classified as botanists would classify them (even though her letters proved that some of the women advertising knew the Latin names). Instead, the women classified plants according to usage: yard plants for outside, window plants for inside, and box plants for growing in containers on the porches of the South. The women criticized the scientific methods not only by rejecting them in favor of their own agreed-upon system, but also explicitly, saying, as Mrs. U. B. Evans did, that "exchange with other gardeners is the only way to clarify the information we get from books." Similarly, the women chose methods of measurement useful to them—and standardized across their experiences, even if their methods were unacceptable to scientific authority. They sold seeds by the snuffbox, matchbox, soda box, or teacup—and within the community of bulletins, everyone agreed to the sizes.[9]

In addition, lines between garden vegetables and fruits, herbs and medicinal plants, and decorative or aesthetically pleasing plants blurred throughout the bulletins as both Lawrence and the farmwomen expanded definitions. They included items useful for the soul and for pleasure. The women clearly had few other ways to value this kind of nourishment. Lawrence described them as "the hard-working farm women who are never too tired, when their farm work is done, to cultivate their flower gardens. They always find time to gather seeds to dig and pack plants, and to send them off with friendly letters . . . Reading the flower lists is like reading poetry, for the flowers are called by their sweet country names, many of them belonging to Shakespeare and the Bible."[10] Lawrence's own interest in flowers pulls us away from a focus on food only, but the foodways of her world encompassed the practices, processes, and connected rituals of gardens, tables, and atmosphere—in which the garden flowers played a role.

In addition, the poetry of which she spoke existed against a background of increased availability of processed food, neat but sterile packages from grocery stores, and increasing distances between producers and consumers of food. The shifting to group vegetables and flowers together and the holding up both with the poetry of old names could be the women's resistance to the changes in the food around them. McKimmon argued as much, saying "when

I see the beauty-starved apartment dweller, who has no garden to look upon, going out of the market with great bunches of jonquils or roses in the spring and summer, chrysanthemums and cosmos in the fall, and holly and long leaf pine in the winter, I think not only is the market blessing those who sell but those who buy."[11] In market bulletins as well as curb markets, we glimpse even if we cannot fully explore, meaningful connections between places, plants, and the joint nourishment of food and soul.

Saving plants in the bulletins resisted pressures to homogenize the southern food supply and make it look more like that which was filling the nation's grocery bags. Although we cannot document the women's growing practices perfectly (did they use fertilizers?; did they compost or use organic mulch?), today we might view the women's offerings as heirloom vegetables and native plants; their knowledge closely resembled that valued in contemporary local foods movements—but it developed in unexpected and out of the way places. It also developed outside traditional money economies. Whereas some women advertised in the bulletins to make profits, much as some women at the curb markets did, many others conducted their trades by swapping and bartering. They would take feed sacks for flowers, plants they had not seen for their familiar ones, or even a good letter for cups of seeds. They wrote in their advertisements, "Will swap even. I don't have money," and they frequently returned what they viewed as overpayment or unearned generosity.[12]

The timeline for the exchanges and communication through the bulletins could be very leisurely—stretching from the back and forth of rural letter delivery to extremes of decades or lifetimes. For instance, Mrs. Fergusson, the lonely Alabama woman in the epigraph to this conclusion who was seeking "redshank," suffered from pellagra as a young woman in the 1930s. A Cherokee man at the time gave her the herb to make into a tea that cured her. Now, decades later, Fergusson had a friend with digestive troubles, and she wanted to return the favor.[13] The communication between the man who helped her through his knowledge of plants and the friend she, in turn, wished to help spanned decades. For the market bulletins, that timeline was natural and expected.

Sometimes the exchange in bulletins, slow as it was, was the last significant public communication in the women's lives. Such final, quiet moments occurred again and again, as Lawrence, who died before completing the book, had letters returned or received final updates from surviving family members of the market bulletin women who passed away. Novelist Eudora Welty not only played a pivotal role in *Gardening for Love* by introducing Lawrence to the market bulletins, but she also featured the bulletins in at least two of her works, *Golden Apples* and *Losing Battles*. The significance of market bulletins to the long passage of southern women's lives did not escape her. For instance, in "The Wanderers," a story in *Golden Apples*, the life and death of Miss Katie Rainey were inseparable from her relationship with the bulletins. Rainey used the proceeds from the bulletins for her daughter's wedding dress; but she also used her knowledge of her listings to mark her last breaths. Her daughter grabbed something with which to fan her mother as she died; it was the market bulletin. Welty wrote:

> Dying, Miss Katie went rapidly over the list in it, her list. As though her impatient foot would stomp at each item, she counted it, corrected it, and yet she was about to forget the seasons, and the places things grew. Purple althea cuttings, true box, four colors of cannas for 15¢, moonvine seed by teaspoonful, green and purple jew. Roses: big white rose, little thorn rose, beauty-red sister rose, pink monthly, old-fashioned red summer rose, very fragrant, baby rose. Five colors of verbena, candlestick lilies, milk and wine lilies, blackberry lilies, lemon lilies, angel lilies, apostle lilies, Angel trumpet seed. The red amaryllis. Faster and faster, Mrs. Rainey thought: Red salvia, four-o'clock, pink Jacob's ladder, sweet geranium cuttings, sword fern and fortune grass, century plants, vase palm, watermelon pink and white crape myrtle, Christmas cactus, golden bell. White Star Jessamine. Snowball. Hyacinthus. Pink fairy lilies. White. The fairy white... She put her hand up and never knew what happened to it, her protest.

Welty's full passage, with its insistent listing, arrestingly captured the death of a particular kind of southern woman who intimately connected foodways to her sense of self. It also documented all of the knowledge that threatened to vanish in her death.[14] We may not be able to connect the items in the list in the ways Miss Rainey would, or in the ways the actual market bulletin women did, but we can recognize the knowledge, communication, and sharing they represented.

Lacy told us that the city woman, Lawrence, practiced this same list making. He called it "Homeric," because she categorized and memorialized for posterity all of the details lest they be lost. Within the box that became *Gardening for Love*, Lawrence documented mountain names for plants, fine distinctions between hunting dogs, how many bulletins survived, and which correspondents waited somewhere for their next letter from someone who still cared to talk about the muscadines and the seasons.[15]

In many ways, the bulletins recorded early locavores: people who not only ate locally but also explicitly celebrated their connection to their place. Vegetables and fruits advertised in the bulletins' pages "are mostly local and old timey," in Lawrence's words. She gave the farmers in the bulletins credit for keeping plants from being lost and providing "a reservoir of stock material that could never be collected in any one place, even an institution."[16] Well before it came to be called seed saving, the community of the bulletins formed a library, dispersed in location, communal in ownership, but serious in effect, of plants outside of mass-market cultivation. This mess writing necessarily celebrated what we saw as unproved potential in the cookbooks and as unrecorded gossip in the curb markets—collaborative memory keeping, collective conversation, and largely invisible but strongly supported mutual communication.

CONCLUSION

In the 1970s, French feminists explored an *écriture féminine*—they asked what communication by and between women would sound or look like if we could be free from, outside of, constituted before, or untouched by patriarchal structures of culture, language, and self. That effort, always a mostly theoretical exercise, proved difficult to enact under the weight of other structures dividing women from each other (race, class, sexual identity, and place, for instance) and the ways masculinity and femininity blur into each other so that the categories of difference do not hold.[17] Yet perhaps we can borrow a bit of the term.

All the stories of southern gender and food we have explored in these pages hint at *écritures féminines* of southern food—practiced by men and women, but clustering around the practices and intimate connections between women and food. They remind us to ask what is at stake when we ban some foods or drinks and embrace others. To query what we are talking about when we fight over our biscuits and cornbread. To wonder who is part of the conversation when we offer a jar of home-canned tomatoes. To see how we are all complicit and damaged by the absence and lack of food. To listen to what is being said by gardens, fresh foods, and the people who love them.

There are strong reasons for us to be rigorous, concrete, and even suspicious as we examine the stories of southern food and gender. By so doing we can unearth what divided us, how we defined ourselves, who was excluded and why, what we wished to change, and what we wished to forget. Just as the 1970s feminists suggested, much of what we are saying when we talk about food is communicated without words. It is in the exchange of an extra helping or the presentation of a dish. I have tried to get at those moments here with our frequent turns to literature, recipes, ingredients, markets, images, and life stories. And I have now turned to acknowledge the things we cannot know with certainty but can see in their remaining traces—the hidden, collective repositories of communities like that of the market bulletins. Such pockets of food and gender are where the rest of our conversation takes place—but we will have to go beyond the confined pages of a book. Fortunately, with Lawrence's "love" and Lacy's "magic," we will still be talking about and talking through our food at the end of the day. The southern *écritures féminines* continue. It is a messy conversation, a collective conversation, a sustaining and yet never-ending conversation. The mess of greens is the mess of societies, of people, and of places, and it is gloriously, deliciously, collectively continuing.

NOTES

INTRODUCTION

1. See, for instance, Hale, *Making Whiteness*, 85–104; Ayers, *Promise*, 339–49; Jones, *Labor of Love*, 110–15; Williams-Forson, *Building Houses*, 80–90; Cowdrey, *This Land*, 103; Daniel, *Standing at the Crossroads*, 73–77; Manring, *Slave in a Box*, 110–48.

2. For one take on the Cherokee corn mother story, see Awiakta, *Selu*, 9–14.

3. Sauceman, "Social Class and Food," 104. Indeed, I myself am an inveterate forager, carrying my mulberry bucket all through spring when I lived in Atlanta and walked to my graduate classes, chewing on sassafras root on hikes in the woods as I worked in West Virginia, and always on the lookout for black raspberries or forgotten apple orchards on trips home to the North Carolina mountains.

4. Flagg, *Fried Green Tomatoes*, 398. For the story of how the novel popularized the recipe, see Best and Abbott, "Tomatoes," 277. McPherson describes the South's practice of disconnecting co-present whiteness and blackness as "lenticular"; she strives to "fashion new paradigms of vision and visibility" by refusing those separations. McPherson, *Reconstructing Dixie*, 7–8.

5. Reed, "Barbecue Sociology," 78. Edge, "Foreword" in Engelhardt, *Republic of Barbecue*, xv. Henry D. Shapiro, *Appalachia*, 264–65; Tullos, *Habits of Industry*, 3–4. Other social historians include, among many, Margaret Hagood, Ed Ayers, and Jacquelyn Dowd Hall; the Global South studies scholars include James Peacock, Kathryn McKee, and Jennifer Greeson, among others. American studies scholars such as Psyche Williams-Forson or Andrew Warnes join McPherson and Yaeger to round out the debates over a cohering and fragmenting South.

6. Engelhardt, *Tangled Roots*, 86–92.

7. Duke's Mayonnaise, "Duke's History"; Duke's Sandwich Company, "About Us."

8. White Lily, Martha White, and Coca-Cola were joined by many other distinctive southern food products: Dr Pepper, MoonPies, Tabasco, Mountain Dew, etc. See various entries, Edge, *Foodways*. Modern advertising, marketing, celebrity endorsement, distribution, and copyright were pioneered by some of these businesses; the full corporate story of food in the South has yet to be written. Levenstein, *Revolution*, 27. Gabaccia, *We Are What*, 37–38. Levenstein begins his study of "the transformation

of the American diet" with a meal given in 1880 in New York City at Delmonico's restaurant. Levenstein argues that meal happened because large food companies, the transportation infrastructure that supported them, and the consumer marketplace they supplied were already in place to dominate American foodways. By the 1930s, the excesses of the Delmonico's meal morphed into middle-class emphases on nutritional science, proper calories, and labor-saving food technologies. Levenstein focuses primarily on the Northeast and on class issues; he rarely turns his attention southward. Donna Gabaccia adds a complementary focus on race and ethnicity to the national food story. Gabaccia, still mostly avoiding the South, argues that national food companies were indebted to immigrant entrepreneurs who expanded both the palate of consumers and also the pool of available customers. To Gabaccia, the American food story is one of creolization through time. To both, companies with national reaches homogenized everyday food in the United States.

9. Sidney Mintz's claims there are no American cuisines notwithstanding (Mintz, *Tasting*, 97–98). For a counter to his argument, see Warnes, *Savage Barbecue*, 89–92. Egerton, *Southern Food*, 2.

10. Extensive genealogical research in the family has turned up no such stories, but neither were such stories meant to be found.

11. Hale, *Making Whiteness*, 94–98. Opie, *Hog and Hominy*, 1–15; Williams-Forson, *Building Houses*, 136. For discussions of food in colonial commodity chains, see, for instance, Mintz's *Sweetness and Power*, Harris's *Beyond Gumbo*, and Warnes's *Savage Barbecue*, among many others.

12. A fast-developing field, southern food studies more recently has reflected the emphasis of scholars associated, as I am, with the Southern Foodways Alliance—an inclusive and broadly defined vision of preserving the diverse cultures, practitioners, and ingredients of southern food, wherever and among whomever it occurred. See, for instance, www.southernfoodways.com.

13. Ferris, "Gender and Food," 58.

14. Sinclair, *The Jungle*, 1; DuPuis, *Nature's Perfect Food*, 67–89. On women and food, see especially Avakian and Haber, *From Betty Crocker*, 1–28; Haber, *From Hardtack*, 1–6.

15. Bower, "Bound Together," 6. Newlyn, "Challenging Contemporary Narrative Theory," 35.

16. Schneir, *Feminism in Our Time*, 125–29.

CHAPTER ONE. MOONSHINE

1. Since this project's focus is on foodways—by which I mean the range of ingredients, preparations, rituals, and cultural politics that make up food practices—the

fact that moonshine is a drink, not a food, while perhaps odd, is less counterintuitive. Just as the iced tea on the table for the meal discussed in the introduction was part of the practices, process, and ingredients of that celebration, moonshine as a drink is well inside the tent for a foodways study. On the regulation of butter and other items in addition to moonshine, see Price and Spillane, "Commissioner," 498. The story of moonshine's path to illegality was one of taxation in the young nation. Although taxes on liquor had been tried earlier in the country's history, most famously those leading to the Whiskey Rebellion of 1794 in western Pennsylvania, direct ancestors of modern liquor taxes can be traced to the Civil War. First put in place by both sides to defray war costs, then retained to pay off war debts, the taxes became so much a part of the national system that they remained even after Reconstruction. Then and now, selling is the most illegal part of moonshine; making small amounts for home consumption out of legal ingredients and equipment is generally overlooked. See Wilbur R. Miller, *Revenuers*, 5–6, and Ellis, "Moonshine." For memoirs on moonshine, see Abernethy, *Moonshine*; Maurer, *Kentucky Moonshine*; Wilkinson, *Moonshine*; and Gabbard, *Thunder Road*. For folklife perspectives, see Durand, "'Mountain Moonshining'"; Rehder, *Appalachian Folkways*; and Michael Ann Williams, *Great Smoky*. For an interesting examination of the North Carolina Klan and moonshine in the early 1870s, see Stewart, "'When Darkness Reigns.'"

2. Liquor appeared in stories about the South from colonial histories to modern discussions of trendy Appalachian cuisine. Such discussions of liquor began with Jefferson and Washington, continued through the Whiskey Rebellion, and emerge today with celebrations like that of the 2003 Southern Foodways Alliance Conference, which featured a moonshine toast hosted by Appalachia's top chefs (Southern Foodways Alliance 2003). Interest in the tragic case of Tennessee's Popcorn Sutton (Stephen Miller, "Marvin") and white dog whiskeys (Simonson, "Moonshine") demonstrates continued fascination with moonshine. See *Reader's Guide;* Poole, *Poole's Index;* and Collins, *Literary Tradition*, for examples of the range of publications.

3. Rehder, *Appalachian Folkways*, 199–200; Evans, *Appalachians*, 86.

4. Wilbur R. Miller, *Revenuers*, 5–6.

5. Ibid., 28; Michael Ann Williams, *Great Smoky*, 104.

6. Anderson's novel will be discussed in more detail in the final section of this chapter; Dame was the sister of Olive Campbell and will be discussed in chapter 2; Heyward was most famous for writing *Porgy and Bess*, but he split his time between Charleston, South Carolina, where *Porgy* was set, and Hendersonville, North Carolina, in the mountains that were the setting for *Angel* (Calhoun and Guilds, *Tricentennial*, 372). Daisy Dame, sister of the more serious Olive Dame Campbell, wrote home, "Dear Family: I am *busting* with excitement! That moonshine still I fancied I found *really is* in the place where I thought it might be ... tomorrow we are going to ride up to view

it." The next day, she continued, "I've 'done did it', and seven or eight snap-shots are reposing on my films." Dame described her emotions and expectations upon seeing the still: "I must say I had a delicious thrill of excitement when I first came in sight of the place, and I half hoped that I should see a Winchester sticking out from behind a log and a summons to stop—but instead, we rode up unmolested." Later in the letter, Dame made it clear that her ideas of moonshine and the moonshiner with the Winchester came directly from novels and stories: "It is a really romantic spot, trees and green moss, a sloping hill covered with timber, and the afternoon sunlight streaming in. As a stage setting it was perfect—just what I had always imagined! When I get some 'Moonshine' I shall be perfectly happy—Isn't this luck? . . . I can't possibly see any other such glorious excitement that we can have." Dame, "Dear Family," 18 and 19 January 1910, Dame Papers. Heyward, *Angel*, 48; Anderson, *Kit Brandon*, 218.

7. Mattingly, *Well-Tempered*, 13–38. Joyce, "Carrie Chapman Catt," 936, 942. Ownby, *Subduing Satan*, 50–53.

8. For a discussion of the range of what I term the "moonshine literature" and an explanation of the method I employed to gather it, please see Engelhardt, "Writing," 74. On the stereotypes of the moonshiner, see, for instance, Harkins, *Hillbilly*, 34–39, and Williamson, *Hillbillyland*, 1–4.

9. John Fox Jr., *Trail*; Murfree, *Tennessee Mountains*; Smith-Rosenberg, *Disorderly Conduct*, 245. For alternative discussions of New Women and clubwomen, see Richardson and Willis, *New Woman*, 1–38; Tarbox, *Clubwomen's Daughter's*, 13–28.

10. Smith-Rosenberg, *Disorderly Conduct*, 257. On southern New Women, see Gilmore, *Gender and Jim Crow*, 37–39 and 95–96; Johnson, *Southern Ladies*, 1–23; and Scott, *Making the Invisible*, 212–21.

11. Lucy McElroy wrote three novels in her short life, none of which are in print today. *Juletty* begins in the mountains of Kentucky, but most of the action of the story, including that around Juletty's still, occurs near Bowling Green, Kentucky (McElroy, *Juletty*, 130). Gill seems to have written only one book. According to the novel, a native of Kentucky, Gill set his book in fictional "Ginseng County." Catherine Frances Cavanagh wrote her piece, "Stories of Our Government Bureaus" in 1911 for *Bookman*, which also reviewed Gill's efforts. Little is known of Cavanagh's biography.

12. Walter Womble's *Love in the Mists* uses the revenuer main character (Womble, *Love*, 1–5). Also see, Woolson, *Blue Ridge*, 276, and Buck, *When "Bear Cat,"* 1. Juletty's father's deathbed scene is McElroy, *Juletty*, 267.

13. McElroy, *Juletty*, 274, 280. Although working here as a comic effect, at other times tragedy ensued when people assumed women could not brew moonshine, such as happens in "At Teague Poteet's: A Sketch of the Hog Mountain Range" when a moonshining widow's son is shot (Joel Chandler Harris, "At Teague," 123).

14. The full quote reads: "I had caught her in my arms, and stopped her mouth with kisses. *I*, the virtuous officer, who had almost hesitated to wed the *daughter* of a lawbreaker. *I* clasped the real culprit close, and laughed at the thought of her pluck and the wisdom of her plans for evading justice, and reveled in the bravery of her final confession. *I* called her a heroine, and my brave little darling, and said how proud I was of her, and how grieved to punish her. But grieved though I was, there was no escaping it, and I sentenced her to captivity for life—to the man who had raided her 'Licit Still" (McElroy, *Juletty*, 280). While the novel's ending could be read as a rejection of Juletty's choices and the rhetoric of New Womanhood, the final page cannot quite erase the 279 pages of freedom that came before. The sexual double entendre of the "'Licit Still" reveals, however unintentionally, another unsettling element of New Womanhood: the potential for sexual choice exercised by strong women, an element Grace MacGowan Cooke's "The Spy" explores. Tall Lodora Luster, with her "deep golden contralto" voice and "pride of strength," gazes "squarely, with frank blue eyes" into others' faces. She even has very short hair (Cooke, "The Spy," 475–76). Cooke's description strongly resembled that of prominent sexologist Richard von Krafft-Ebing, who described a woman with "masculine features, deep voice, manly gait, without beard, small breasts, [who] cropped her hair short and gave the impression of a man in women's clothes" (Smith-Rosenberg, *Disorderly Conduct*, 272). Moonshiners are the ones fooled by this New Woman because to explain her unsettling appearance they conclude she must be a cross-dressing revenuer. Not only is Lodora strong, but she also makes her own sexual choices—Lodora does not want to be kissed, and she punches men who try (Cooke, "The Spy," 477). Like McElroy, Cooke relied on a final-paragraph heterosexual marriage. Lacy, the only character who recognizes Lodora's New Womanhood as womanly and loveable, marries her. Yet, when confronted with his relatives' theory that she spied for the government, Lacy Mountjoy "opened his mouth—but words would not come. The subject was too immense; the gulf between what he knew and what they suspected was too vast to be immediately bridged by speech" as he asks himself, "Could a human creature look so different to different eyes?" (Cooke, "The Spy," 477). Lacy confronts what Lodora's strength, disinterest in conforming to gender-differentiated fashion, and willingness to look men in the eyes means for his own gendered identity. He and the reader consider the implications on heterosexual romance of partners being physically and sexually equal. And, yes, the double entendres continue with Mr. Mountjoy claiming Lodora Luster.

15. Gill, *Beyond the Blue Grass*, 86.

16. Cavanagh, "Stories," 53. Rose's pardon reads, "Whereas Adaline Rose was convicted in the United States Court for the Eastern District of Kentucky of unlawfully making and selling whiskey . . . and on May fifteenth 1907, was sentenced to pay

a fine of one thousand dollars and to be imprisoned for six months in the County jail at London, Kentucky; and... whereas, it has been made to appear to me that the said Adaline Rose is a fit object of executive clemency... [I] hereby commute the sentence of the said Adaline Rose to a term of imprisonment to expire September seventeenth, 1907" (Roosevelt, *Presidential Records*).

17. Eaker, Conversation with the author, 6 June 2005.

18. Barton, "Moonshiner's Judge," 58–59.

19. Cavanagh, "Stories," 52–53.

20. G. Stanley Hall, *Adolescence*. Nash, *American Sweethearts*, 17. Prior to Hall's era, children moved fairly quickly through their youth into adulthood; one's youth was judged more by apprenticeships than by the calendar years of teens. See, for instance, Rotundo, *American Manhood*, 56–74, and Hunter, *How Young Ladies*, 11–37. In this sense, teens were invented creatures. Gielow worked with the Southern Industrial Educational Association (SIEA) raising awareness and money for educational efforts among poor white southerners; to support her work, she published and performed stories on the mountains and southern plantation life; *Old Andy* was such a piece. For a discussion of the SIEA, see Kathleen Curtis Wilson, *Uplifting*, 2–3.

21. Stoneley, *Consumerism*, 2–4. Nash, *American Sweethearts*, 2.

22. Gielow, *Old Andy*. Other stories with teen characters include Harris, "At Teague"; Cavanagh, "Stories"; Buck, *When "Bear Cat"*; and Heyward, *Angel*. Some of these stories focus less on how girls could be helpful and more on how disruptive the teen is to patriarchy.

23. Gielow, *Old Andy*, 8–10. Harris, "At Teague," 56–57. For biographical details on Harris and an analysis of the cultural work his writing performs, see Hale, *Making Whiteness*, 54–59.

24. Gielow, *Old Andy*, 4–6, 14.

25. Ibid., 5–6, 31–40, 19. One should not have to note that by 1909 many Appalachian families baked cakes, used store-bought fabric, and listened to and played pianos. They certainly knew of (and many practiced) Christianity. Gielow's text inconsistently allows as much, for instance, mentioning mountain preachers (Gielow, *Old Andy*, 26). Here, her effort to justify the work of the SIEA trumped realism.

26. In a nod to moonshine as a de facto safety net, Sal's grandmother muses that she and Sal might have to turn to moonshine themselves if Andy is sent away permanently (Gielow, *Old Andy*, 24). Further, the details of Sal's conception are biting commentary on what can happen when teen girls are not tamed—her lawyer father, "when he was yet but a lad of eighteen accompanying a party of hunters and revenue officers," spent a "wild happy week" with a fifteen-year-old "simple mountain girl" (Sal's mother, who was exactly Sal's age when she met the lawyer) and "youth and passion and the wildness of nature, and its irresistible wooings must be responsible"

(Gielow, *Old Andy*, 36). Sal's mother died in childbirth refusing to reveal the father's name; as befitted a good melodrama, he sees the dead mother in Sal, the daughter, and is motivated to help her.

27. Harris, "At Teague," 168. Gielow, *Old Andy*, 40–45.

28. Gielow, *Old Andy*, following 46. Social Darwinism argued that European whites were the most evolved humans, but that limiting their reproduction could allow other (such as African or Asian) races to take over, resulting in the so-called race suicide (Bederman, *Manliness*, 170).

29. Gielow, *Old Andy*, 11.

30. Ibid., following 46.

31. The plotline Stoneley identifies followed "the 'backwoods' girl-heroine who achieves a love-match with a successful but disillusioned middle-aged businessman. In managing this, the girl also manages, in concentrated symbolic form, to enact the progress of fifty years" as she acquired goods, education, and sophistication (Stoneley, *Consumerism*, 1). Stoneley does not use Appalachian examples, but the plot was common in mountain novels, including those of Gielow, John Fox Jr.'s *Trail*, and Gill's *Beyond the Blue Grass*.

32. Mancini, "Messin' With," 209. For a discussion of consumer culture, see Cohen, *Making a New Deal*, 99.

33. Mancini, "Messin' With," 211, 215. Anderson was most famous for his Winesburg, Ohio, stories. Though born in Ohio, Anderson spent his later years in Appalachian Virginia, where he composed *Kit Brandon*.

34. Often in the novel we are left asking, is Kit talking?; is Kit quoting fellow moonshiners?; are these speeches by the narrator?; are they what the narrator imagines Kit said then? To help clarify, all ellipses used in quotes are Anderson's own, except when in square brackets. On the claim that Kit Brandon is understudied, see Dunne, *Grotesques*, 112.

35. Rejecting the separation of Appalachia from the rest of the nation, Anderson's narrator says, "mountain men and women walk through the pages of our literature. 'They are a brave people.' 'They are undernourished, dangerous, courteous, killers, chicken thieves,' this and that" (Anderson, *Kit Brandon*, 28). He lists the "tales of mountain feuds . . . the Hatfield-McCoys of West Virginia, stories out of Breathitt County, Kentucky . . . sentimental yarns . . . 'Trail of the Lonesome Pine'" and suggests these "yarns" are responsible for the many stereotypes about Appalachians. Countering the misperception that "mountain men were thought of, by tourists passing swiftly through the hills, as all of a type. They were dangerous, secretive, sly. They spent their time hunting 'federals' or shooting at each other," he adds, "It was of course all nonsense. They were of every type, incipient poets, honest hard-working men, killers, horse traders, liars, men faithful to friends unto death, stupid ones, smart ones, God-

seeking ones" (Anderson, *Kit Brandon*, 114–15). For a modern scholar qualifying the idea of Appalachia as isolated, see Dunaway, *First American Frontier*.

36. Anderson, *Kit Brandon*, 24, 29, 42, 191.
37. Ibid., 24.
38. Ibid., 28, 41–42, 102.
39. Ibid., 13–14, 108, 273.
40. Ibid., 39, 218, 273–74.
41. Ibid., 251, 269.
42. Ibid., 25, 173.
43. Racial and ethnic diversity in moonshine can be glimpsed in the historical record, but it was often just as slippery as Anderson proposed. Wilma Dykeman, in *The French Broad*, a nonfiction work about a river in North Carolina's mountains, described an African American version of Kit (or Kit's bosses): Maggie Jones was "black and smart too. She'd been selling liquor down there in Darktown for years and nobody could catch her. She had sharp eyes and a big iron bar half as big as my arm across the front door" (Dykeman, *The French Broad*, 303–4). From historian Wilbur R. Miller: "A black woman in Elbert County, Georgia, operated a still with a white partner. The white woman confessed that she had been moonshining for several years, but the revenuers let her go because she had a small baby with her. The black woman, though 'had to tramp the usual road paved for the violator of the revenue laws'" (Miller, *Revenuers*, 36). The layers of white privilege and domesticity at work in that story were unexplored by Miller. Often the diversity was left to vague descriptions of darker skins, "gypsy" or "Melungeon" blood, or "outsider" status. Anderson, *Kit Brandon*, 125, 263, 267.
44. Anderson, *Kit Brandon*, 354, 373. Anderson seemed discomfited by giving his heroine absolute freedom. At times he veered into gender essentialism, constraining Kit with biological urges for pregnancy or nurturing, as when he claims, "there is something else wanted, something very deep, often very subtle, hidden away, in all women who are women. It is the desire, the hunger, to bear the child within the woman's own body [. . .] 'Here is our woman thing. No man can ever go through this, feel this'" (Anderson, *Kit Brandon*, 202). Anderson also could not leave Kit so far outside mainstream society, so he gave her a late monologue in which she repudiates much of what she had enjoyed for the whole novel. But Anderson waffles and merely comments, "Kit had *for the moment* lost all desire for the adventurous life. She wanted only to disappear into the mass of people, no longer to be notorious, an adventuress" (Anderson, *Kit Brandon*, 350, emphasis added). Nonetheless, as with Juletty, a late recapitulation was not quite enough to counter the 349 previous pages of freedom.

45. Anderson, *Kit Brandon*, 23, 64, 169–70, 261. Mullett, "Women," 500. For other scholars examining women and automobiles, see Wintle, "Horses, Bikes," 66–78; Scharff, *Taking the Wheel*; Romalov, "Mobile and Modern," 75–88; Walsh, "Gender and the Automobile."

46. Anderson himself predicted the debate: "The reader should bear in mind that Kit Brandon was and is a real person, a living American woman. How much of her real story can be told? You, sitting and reading this book, have also a story, a history. How much of that could be told? How much do we writers dare let ourselves go in the making of portraits?" (Anderson, *Kit Brandon*, 181).

47. Welford Dunaway Taylor, *Sherwood Anderson*, 91. Anderson quoted in Salzman, et al., *Sherwood Anderson*, 267. Ray Lewis White, "Original," 197. As early as 1936, reviewer Hamilton Basso was already asking whether Anderson narrated the novel and if Kit were real (Basso, "Kit Brandon," 58).

48. Anderson, *Kit Brandon*, 340.

49. Ibid., 9, 155.

CHAPTER TWO. BISCUITS AND CORNBREAD

1. On "soul" versus "southern" food, see Opie, *Hog and Hominy*, 130–33; Williams-Forson, *Building Houses*, 109–10; Egerton, *Southern Food*, 9–50; Bolsterli, et al., "Soul Food," 104–7.

2. Cooper, *A Voice*, 142–43. On women and Progressivism, see (among many) Scott, *Natural Allies*, 141–58. On regionalism, see Fetterley and Pryse, *Writing Out*, 1–33.

3. Whisnant, *All That Is*, 34. Stoddart, *Challenge*, 26–27. Scott, *Making the Invisible*, 217; also see Scott, *Natural Allies*, for more on southern Progressive women's club work. For information on the lives of Pettit and Stone, see Whisnant, *All That Is*, 24–30, and Peck, "Katherine Pettit," 56–58. For general information on women activists in Appalachia, see Forderhase, "Eve Returns," 237–61; Blackwell, "Eleanor Marsh Frost," 225–46; Barney, *Authorized*, 71–99.

4. Recently the debate has heated up again over the degree to which Pettit and Stone were responding to or imposing upon the mountain residents they taught. The early journals kept by the women, since they were always meant to be used for fundraising, certainly should not be taken as solely the private beliefs of the two women—they are in some degree giving their audience what they expected in terms of picturesque and quaint mountaineers. For an outline of the debate, see Stoddart, *Challenge*, 225–31. For our purposes, it is enough that Pettit and Stone were willing to characterize mountain residents and their food habits as backward, immoral, and

unhygienic. The original journals have been republished as Stone and Pettit, *Quare Women's Journals*.

5. Beecher and Stowe, *American Woman's Home*, 19–20. Laura Shapiro, *Perfection Salad*, 47–70. Strasser, *Never Done*, 176–79. Fields, *How to Help*, 111–12. Levenstein, *Revolution*, 98–108.

6. Knight, *Citizen*, 179–98. On the links between Hindman and Hull House, see especially Stoddart's reseach on members of the Breckinridge family in both places (Stoddart, *Challenge*, 10–19). Note, the tomato club women who are the center of chapter 3 will prove to be progeny of both approaches, the cooking schools and the settlement houses.

7. Stone and Pettit, *Quare Women's Journals*, 59; Stoddart, *Challenge*, 28.

8. Dame, "Dear Family," 18 and 19 January 1910, Dame Papers. For a discussion of Olive Dame Campbell labeling the same photograph a "Georgia moonshine family" in one place and "Georgia mountain people" in another, see Engelhardt, *Tangled Roots*, 84. On Campbell visiting Hindman, see Stoddart, *Challenge*, 87. Stone and Pettit, *Quare Women's Journals*, 184–99.

9. McWilliams, "Distant Tables," 365–93. Frost, "Our Contemporary Ancestors," 311–19. The irony was rich since corn was an indigenous food, meaning anything native Inuits ate was no less American (Awiakta, *Selu*). On competing "missions," see Kaplan and Pease, *Cultures*, 22–40.

10. Kaplan, *Anarchy of Empire*, 23–50.

11. Stone and Pettit, *Quare Women's Journals*, 177.

12. Ibid., 213, 230–32. "Crusade" quote in Whisnant, *All That Is*, 25.

13. Neal, *Southern Cooking*, 34–35; McCulloch-Williams, *Dishes and Beverages*, 30.

14. Pool, *In Buncombe County*, 95.

15. Bass, *Plain Southern*, 37–38.

16. Cooke, "Andy Proudfoot," 6; Morley, *Carolina Mountains*, 161; Crim, "Strike at Mr. Mobley's," 378; Troubetzkoy, *Tanis*, 92; Stone and Pettit, *Quare Women's Journals*, 190.

17. Stone and Pettit, *Quare Women's Journals*, 63, 202.

18. Lang, *Syntax of Class*, 18, 23; Stoddart, *Challenge*, 152.

19. John C. Campbell, *Southern Highlander*, 201. Troubetzkoy, *Tanis*, 40.

20. Joe Gray Taylor, *Eating*, 21, 110; Bass, *Plain Cooking*, 40; Huie, *Mud on the Stars*, 42–43. Slang usage shows "cornpone" to mean hick, redneck, or behavior that is low class. Urban Dictionary, "Corn Pone," http://www.urbandictionary.com/define.php?term=corn%20pone. Accessed 15 July 2010.

21. Joe Gray Taylor, *Eating*, 21. Turner, "Demography of Black Appalachia," 237–61; Beardsley, *History of Neglect*, 11–41; Gregory, *Southern Diaspora*, 23–28. Joe Gray

Taylor, *Eating*, 21; Bass, *Plain Cooking*, 34. Stone and Pettit, *Quare Women's Journals*, 86.

22. Goodrich, *Mountain Homespun*, 40. Also see McKimmon, *When We're Green*, 1–2.

23. John C. Campbell, *Southern Highlander*, 201–3; Miles, *Spirit of the Mountains*, 22.

24. Furman, *Quare Women*, 7–8.

25. Stone and Pettit, *Quare Women's Journals*, 63.

26. Hale, *Making Whiteness*, 176–79.

27. Stone and Pettit, *Quare Women's Journals*, 233.

28. Dabney, *Smokehouse Ham*, 118. Fisher, *What Mrs. Fisher Knows*, 9.

29. McCulloch-Williams, *Dishes and Beverages*, 28–30. Hurston, *Their Eyes*, 22. Hale, *Making Whiteness*, 98–104. On Hurston, also see Marquis, "When de Notion," 79; Warnes, *Hunger Overcome?*, 36–79.

30. Stone and Pettit, *Quare Women's Journals*, 180. Scholars have, however, in recent years helpfully challenged the idea that slavery did not exist at all in the mountains. See, for instance, Inscoe, *Race, War, and Remembrance*. For a longer discussion of Stone and Pettit's washerwomen, see Engelhardt, *Tangled Roots*, 94–96.

31. For many middle-class African Americans, staying home symbolized freedom, not oppression (Jones, *Labor of Love*, 142–46). On Stone and Pettit enjoying the outdoors, see Engelhardt, *Tangled Roots*, 65–71.

32. Miles, *Spirit of the Mountains*, 54.

33. Crumpacker, *Sex Life of Food*, 3–5. Troubetzkoy, *Tanis*, 97; Cooke, "Andy Proudfoot," 8–10, 16, 17. Laura Shapiro, *Perfection Salad*, 6.

34. Troubetzkoy, *Tanis*, 92. One example of the blues song comes from Clifford Blake Sr. (Hatley, "Calling").

35. Stone and Pettit, *Quare Women's Journals*, 84.

36. Cooke, *Power*, 27; Gordon and McArthur, "American Women," 38, 35. McCulloch-Williams, *Dishes and Beverages*, 30.

37. Baker, *Cis Martin*, 89; Cooke, *Power*, 13, 368. Cooke's heroine may well be eluding classification, to use Lang's terminology.

38. See Charles Reagan Wilson, "Biscuits," 123; Martha White Flour, "History and Heritage."

39. Olive Dame Campbell, Diary, 1 February 1909. Hochschild, *Second Shift*, 1–10; Strasser, *Never Done*, 242–62. Stone and Pettit, *Quare Women's Journals*, 139. Furman, *Mothering on Perilous*, 61.

40. Charles Reagan Wilson, "Biscuits," 123.

41. Pool, *In Buncombe County*, 12; Morley, *Carolina Mountains*, 163; Beecher and Stowe, *American Woman's Home*, 176, 170.

42. Miles, *Spirit of the Mountains*, 24.

43. Ibid., 191, 196. On Miles's biography, see Whisnant, introduction, ibid., xix; Miles, Diary, 8 May 1915.

44. Fisher, *What Mrs. Fisher Knows*, preface. Opie, *Hog and Hominy*, 103–6. Charles Reagan Wilson, "Biscuits," 123. Fendelman and Rosson, "Old Biscuit Table."

45. Joe Gray Taylor, *Eating*, 111.

46. Her recipe: "Everyone knows Mrs. Jane S. McKimmon, a real North Carolinian and well known for her work with girls' and women's clubs. She makes wonderful beaten biscuits . . . 1 level qt. flour. 5 level tbsp. vegetable shortening (¼ cup). 1 level tsp. salt. Mix flour, shortening, and salt. Add enough very cold water to make a stiff dough. Roll in machine or beat until the dough blisters. Roll dough ½-inch thick. Cut into small biscuits. Bake in moderately hot oven." Notice that by the 1920s, it was unremarkable to use a machine to beat the dough ("Everyone Knows," *Farmer's Wife*). Warren, "Lifted."

47. Warren, "Lifted."

48. Ibid. Rather than beaten biscuits, McKimmon was demonstrating risen rolls or possibly loaves, since elsewhere she mentioned the yeast she took along. In 1945, McKimmon clarified, "I found that teaching people how to cook, sew, or improve the home was not dependent upon what was recognized as standard equipment; much could be done through the exercise of good, hard common sense and the ability to recognize usable substitutes in the things at hand." She also told the story of inviting women and girls to stay in touch and subsequently receiving rolls by the mail for criticism and suggestions—which she cheerfully provided (McKimmon, *When We're Green*, 6, 9).

CHAPTER THREE. CANNING TOMATOES

1. Tomato Club Songs, "See How We Can." This song from Mississippi's club girls, included because it was sung to a ditty still recognizable today, is a little deceptive—one of the few places that training for wife-hood was mentioned in tomato clubs. Most of the other songs were sung to tunes of popular songs from their day and emphasize state or club pride and competition. The speech Cromer heard was by O. B. Martin, one of Knapp's right-hand men, and a fellow South Carolinian. Knapp, a midwesterner, had recently relocated to Texas to begin a demonstration farm; although he died early, Knapp created the blueprint for the United States Department of Agriculture outreach programs and the national agricultural extension service. Knapp's breakthrough was to take university research on farming and translate it into on-the-ground demonstrations. Further, he trained farmers to teach other farmers. Rare at the time, Knapp

took Rockefeller's General Education Board funding and used it for programs across the South with minimum resentment (even though many agreed with the adage from labor activist Mother Jones: "God almighty made women, but that Rockefeller gang of thieves made the ladies"). He used private funding to push progressive ideas when government bureaucracy was not yet ready: Rockefeller funding paid the first female and African American employees. Knapp collaborated with Tuskegee Institute and Hampton Institute, with African American Jeanes teachers (more on them later in this chapter), and with clubwomen at a time when Jim Crow and gender and race paternalism reigned in the South. As his biographer says, "there is no blinking the fact that Knapp was in deep earnest about extending his work to all the back roads of the South" (Bailey, *Seaman A. Knapp*, 226). Knapp's work was not free of race and gender politics of his time, as witnessed by the thicket of competing claims about the early tomato club work: some suggest Cromer had the idea to focus on tomatoes by herself; (Cromer, "South Carolina's Tomato Lady," April 14, Newspaper Clipping, Scrapbook, Cromer Papers; McKimmon, *When We're Green*, 3–4); others claim Knapp had the plan worked out and Cromer just enacted it (Reck, *4-H Story*, 77–78); and still others say people in several locations had similar ideas around the same time (Creswell, "Home Demonstration Work," 242). For our purposes, the exact beginnings are less important; I have chosen when necessary to trust McKimmon, Powell, and Cromer's largely concurring accounts as a corrective to the subtle paternalistic sexism in earlier scholarship and in government organization at the time.

2. Cromer, "Miss Cromer's Address" and "Educational Column," Newspaper Clippings, Scrapbook, Cromer Papers. Powell, "How 4-H Club Work Started," Powell Vertical File. Knapp responded quickly and positively to Cromer's efforts, having "Miss Cromer made a special agent of the Department [of Agriculture], although no woman had ever before been appointed for field work" (Bailey, *Seaman A. Knapp*, 235). In the following two years, McKimmon, Powell, Agnew, and Moore, all of whom, like Cromer, were local to and active in their states, joined in the tomato club work.

3. For information on Ella G. Agnew, see McCleary, "Seizing the Opportunity," 97–102; Heinemann, "Ella G. Agnew." On Virginia Moore, see Hoffschwelle, "Better Homes," 51–53. One of Moore's tomato club girls, Myrtle Hardin, is featured in Crow, *American Country Girl*, 189–91.

4. For general background on agricultural South Carolina, see Ayers, *Promise of the New South*, 111–15; Walker, *All We Knew*, 8–32. More specifically, see Eelman, "Entrepreneurs," 77–106. Also, Simon, *A Fabric of Defeat*, 1–10. For perspective on Ben Tillman, see Kantrowitz, "Youngest Living Carpetbagger," 18–37. Cromer, "Letter to Girls," Newspaper Clipping, Scrapbook, Cromer Papers. Even this was understating: Knapp, in the following year, appointed Cromer, Agnew in Virginia, and Powell in

Mississippi; McKimmon and Moore followed quickly (Reck, *4-H Story*, 83). Queries came from across the United States and even South America. McKimmon's 1914 report said Austin Nichols, a food wholesaler in New York City, was interested (McKimmon, "Annual Report, 1913–1914," P.C. 234.1, McKimmon Papers). An article in the *Extension News* of North Carolina from 2 May 1916 titled "North Carolina Club Girls Going after Foreign Trade" discussed "a firm in Argentine Republic, South America" (McKimmon, Scrapbook of Newspaper Clippings, P.C. 234.22, McKimmon Papers).

5. See Ayers, *Promise of the New South*, 104–31; Walker, *All We Knew*, 98–142. More specifically, see Beeby, *Revolt of the Tar Heels*, 85–102. Cowdrey, *This Land*, 103, makes the argument about logging and extractive industries. See also Caldwell, *Tobacco Road*, 1.

6. See Ayers, *Promise of the New South*, 187–213. More specifically on Mississippi, see Cresswell, *Rednecks, Redeemers, and Race*, 12–36. On sharecropping and tenant farming for African Americans in the era, see Rosengarten, *All God's Dangers*, 1. Massy and Tanner, *Year Book for Boys' and Girls'*, 4-H Club Vertical File.

7. Cromer, "Miss Katie Gunzer [sic], Champion," Newspaper Clipping, Scrapbook, Cromer Papers. McKimmon, "Report of Girls' Canning Clubs, North Carolina, November 1911–December 1912," P.C. 234.1, McKimmon Papers. Bureau of Labor Statistics, "Inflation Calculator." Powell, "Report of Girls' Canning Clubs of Mississippi up to December 10, 1912," Annual Reports. McKimmon, "Annual Report 1913–1914," P.C. 234.1, McKimmon Papers. McKimmon, "Annual Report, December 1914–1915," P.C. 234.1, McKimmon Papers. McKimmon, "Annual Report July 1, 1917 to July 1, 1918," P.C. 234.1, McKimmon Papers. Powell, "Report of Girls' Canning Club Work, State of Mississippi for 1917," Annual Reports. McKimmon, "Annual Report, 1918–1919," P.C. 234.1, McKimmon Papers. "Negroes Make Progress," Mississippi Cooperative Extension Folder, 1910–1939, Vertical File. Creswell, "Home Demonstration Work," 245. Green 'N' Growing Project, "A Timeline of 4-H." McKimmon, Newspaper Clipping, *Oklahoma Farmer*, 25 August 1915, Conceit Book, 1915–1930, P.C. 234.23, McKimmon Papers. Tomato clubs evolved into home demonstration and home extension agencies; terminology can be confusing. The focus here is on the tomato clubs, but participants added new programs rather quickly. I follow their practice of using terms essentially interchangeably as they tried on new titles for the work they were doing.

8. McKimmon, Tomato Club Booklets, 1912–1915, P.C. 234.8, McKimmon Papers. The first report by Ethel Baggett, a member of the Mingo Club in Sampson County, said, "how I squalled[.] I had to take my hose off and let them dry so I was barefooted and the girls all said they wished some young man would come along and sure enough they did but he did not see my feet." Her second, shorter report made no mention of

the episode. North Carolina seems unique in having preserved the girls' reports, but girls in every state seem to have made them. See, for instance, Cromer, "The Tomato Girls," 10 October 1911 (handwritten date), Newspaper Clipping, Scrapbook, Cromer Papers. Cogdell, "Report of Mississippi." Note that many of the North Carolina girls' booklets have been digitized and are available on the beautiful Green 'N' Growing website, hosted by North Carolina State University: http://www.lib.ncsu.edu/specialcollections/greenngrowing/index.html.

9. Cromer, "Girls Tomato Club," Newspaper Clipping, Scrapbook, Cromer Papers.

10. McKimmon, "Annual Report 1911–1912," P.C. 234.1, McKimmon Papers. South Carolina began with girls nine to eighteen (Cromer, "Letter to Girls," Newspaper Clipping, Scrapbook, Cromer Papers); McKimmon noted that although in North Carolina they wanted girls no younger than twelve, they regularly made exceptions and, in fact, some ten-year-olds became star tomato club members: "Indeed, one little girl in Guilford County last year, only ten years old, made the best county record." McKimmon added that the girl made a $50 profit for herself (McKimmon, "Annual Report 1911–1912," P.C. 234.1, McKimmon Papers). Similarly, the one-tenth acre requirement varied in the beginning. The following section explains how the size was eventually rationalized. The question of plowing turned on assumptions about gender roles and age, as a story from Powell illustrated. In testimony before the U.S. Senate, "Mr. Lever asked the littlest girl who plowed her plat. She hesitated evidently thinking that he expected her to do this work and said apologetically, 'Daddy did the heavy work for me.' Mr. Lever quickly replied, 'I'd be ashamed of him if he didn't'" (Powell, "How 4-H Club Work Started," Powell Vertical File). Girls could be embarrassed to ask fathers or brothers for help plowing, yet the clubs also created a situation in which men in families were working for the girls. Or, as McKimmon slipped into an anecdote about playing baseball with her brother as a child, "I gained a wholesome respect for male prowess, though I was able to note with satisfaction that male superiority was mainly muscular—it couldn't always outwit, or even outrun its girl opponents, and this was not a bad thing to keep in mind" (McKimmon, *When We're Green*, 17). Surely in some instances, the girls themselves did the work.

11. Estelle Mauney's report was titled, "The Girls Canning Club and How I Raised My Tomatoes." It can be found in McKimmon, Tomato Club Booklets, 1912–1915, P.C. 234.8, McKimmon Papers. Anyone involved in 4-H work today recognizes the girls' clover symbol.

12. McKimmon, "Annual Report 1911–1912," P.C. 234.1, McKimmon Papers. For narrative description of the early agents, see McKimmon, *When We're Green*, 15. McKimmon and Powell patterned much of their early work on the successes of the

women's club movement in the United States (Scott, *Natural Allies*, 159–74). Powell was a charter member of the Mississippi Federation of Women's Clubs, affiliated with the national General Federation of Women's Clubs; McKimmon's early records are full of correspondence with both North Carolina and national federated clubs (Powell, "How 4-H Club Work Started," Powell Vertical File; Whitlow, *Susie Virginia Powell*, 5; McWhirter, *Work of Miss Susie V. Powell*, 25; McKimmon, Clippings, Conceit Book, 1915–1930, P.C. 234.23, McKimmon Papers). McKimmon's description fits the five original women almost perfectly: Powell, Cromer, Agnew, and Moore were all single when they began the work (only McKimmon was married), each was from the state in which she worked (Agnew had worked overseas but had recently returned to Virginia), and most were in their thirties when they began (Reck, *4-H Story*, 77–91; Moore, "To Make the Best Better," 106–8; McKimmon, *When We're Green*, 16–18).

13. Powell, "Report, 1914–1915," Mississippi Cooperative Extension Folder, 1910–1939, Vertical File. Powell, "How 4-H Club Work Started," Powell Vertical File. On Powell's life after tomato clubs, see Whitlow, *Susie Virginia Powell*, 4–5. Also see Moore, "To Make the Best Better," 107–9. Mississippi documents listed the outside qualifications of women hired to do early extension work, which included groups such as the Mississippi Federation, the Business and Professional Woman's Club, the Progressive Club, and the Woman's Club (Tanner, "County Extension Workers," Tanner Papers). Some stories of cooperation open up as many questions as they settle, however, as with this detail of clubwomen feeling girls needed and wanted undergarments for their big trip out of the state.

14. Sallie Jones's report was titled, "Girls Canning Club" (McKimmon, Tomato Club Booklets 1912–1915, P.C. 234.9, McKimmon Papers).

15. On clubs dedicated to other crops, see Bailey, *Seaman A. Knapp*, 230–36. Tanner also discussed them in Tanner, *Places of the 4-H Club Boy*, James E. Tanner Vertical File. Most of these other clubs reemerged in later 4-H work; girls asked to be included in as many of the clubs as would open to them, surprising some of the organizers with their ability to outproduce the boys (Reck, *4-H Story*, 78). I have not, however, found any evidence of a tomato club boy. Cromer, "Miss Cromer's Address," Newspaper Clipping, Scrapbook, Cromer Papers. McKimmon, "Annual Report 1912–1913," P.C. 234.1, McKimmon Papers. Powell discussed the lack of canning practices in one of her earliest reports (Powell, "Annual Report, 1912," Annual Reports). On the history of the tomato, see, among others, Andrew F. Smith, *Tomato in America*, 149–60; McGill, "Red Gold Ozark," 23–25; Dicke, "Red Gold," 5–6; Pitts et al., "Princely Tomato," 5947–49. The appropriateness of tomatoes for girls is reminiscent of the discussion in chapter 2 about gender roles and corn versus wheat.

16. Powell, "How 4-H Club Work Started," Powell Vertical File. Tanner, "Food Preservation," Tanner Papers. Reck, *4-H Story*, 81. Once pressure cookers became more

affordable, home demonstration agents taught more frequently with them. Also see Arkansas' *History of Home Demonstration Work*, 60, 117.

17. Cromer, "Miss Cromer's Address," and Fragment, 9 April 1911, Newspaper Clippings, Scrapbook, Cromer Papers. She added, "that is the only ambition I have—to see the south grow great in farming" (Cromer, "South Carolina's Tomato Lady," April 14, Newspaper Clipping, Scrapbook, Cromer Papers). Another profile commented that the tomato clubs are "attracting the kind of attention to South Carolina that is most desirable and ... helpful in developement [sic] of their State" (Cromer, "Tomato Clubs," Newspaper Clipping, Scrapbook, Cromer Papers). North Carolina's organizers were not above making a state's pride argument; they just did it less frequently. McKimmon, for instance, recorded a plea to a merchant: "if you bought from us, your dollar would be circulating right here in Anson County and not in Maryland" (McKimmon, *When We're Green*, 29). Mississippi and Arkansas, both farther from the seats of the canning industry, did not emphasize competition with other states, and Arkansas later joined the Ozark Canners and Freezers Association, an industry group. See Lucas, *Ozark Canners*, 40.

18. Hawkins, "Baltimore Canning," 2–3. Brown and Philips, "Craft Labor," 743–56. Keuchel, "Master of the Art," 355–57. On Baltimore cannery workers, see Brown and Philips, "Craft Labor," 744–46.

19. Levenstein, *Revolution*, 30–43. Sinclair, *The Jungle*, 1. Rydell, *All the World's*, 38–71. Garvey, *Adman in the Parlor*, 135–65.

20. On Booker T. Washington and farmers, see Reck, *4-H Story*, 135.

21. Cromer, "My dear Miss Cromer," W. W. Finley, President, Southern Railway Company, 14 December 1910, and "Tomato Expo Planned for Southern Growers," Letter and Newspaper Clipping, Scrapbook, Cromer Papers. McKimmon, *When We're Green*, 27–32. Burwell's report was titled "Tomatoes" and can be found in McKimmon, Tomato Club Booklets, 1912–1915, P.C. 234.10, McKimmon Papers. Tanner, "Food Preservation," Tanner Papers.

22. Yoder's report was titled simply, "Hickory, NC" (McKimmon, Tomato Club Booklets, 1912–1915, P.C. 234.8, McKimmon Papers).

23. Tanner, "Food Preservation," Tanner Papers. McKimmon, *When We're Green*, 34. Powell, "How 4-H Club Work Started," Powell Vertical File.

24. Cromer, "The Origin and Growth of Tomato Club Work," by Walter Duncan, Newspaper Clipping, Scrapbook, Cromer Papers. For Knapp on acreage, see Reck, *4-H Story*, 78.

25. Reck, *4-H Story*, 86. "Uncle Sam," SM13. Margaret Brown, "How I Grew My Tomatoes," and Charlotte Yoder, "Hickory, NC," in McKimmon, Tomato Club Booklets, 1912–1915, P.C. 234.8, McKimmon Papers.

26. Powell, "How 4-H Club Work Started," Powell Vertical File. This is a useful

contrast to the regular assertion in literature about Appalachia—some of which was written by the women of the beaten biscuit crusade—that Appalachians were too backward, poor, and inferior even to recognize the aesthetic beauty of the mountains that surrounded them. See Engelhardt, *Tangled Roots*, 75–86.

27. Talbott, "Splendid Work," SM16. Betty Van Tapscott, "History of My Tomatoes" (McKimmon, Tomato Club Booklets, 1912–1915, P.C. 234.8, McKimmon Papers). Gilman, *Women and Economics*, 7. On rural women and the stakes in earning potential, see Walker, *All We Knew*, 71; Hoffschwelle, *Rebuilding*, 32–33 (though note that Hoffschwelle's interpretation of the canning work in Tennessee finds more prescriptive emphasis than I do in North Carolina); Apple, "Liberal Arts," 86, 94; Jellison, *Entitled to Power*, xx–xxi, 18; Jensen and Effland, "Introduction," iii–iv; and Jensen, *With These Hands*, 64–99.

28. Reck, *4-H Story*, 86. Charlotte Yoder, "Hickory, NC" (McKimmon, Tomato Club Booklets, 1912–1915, P.C. 234.10, McKimmon Papers). Cromer, "Miss Katie Gunzer [sic], Champion," Newspaper Clipping, Scrapbook, Cromer Papers. McKimmon, "Annual Report, 1915–1916," P.C. 234.1, McKimmon Papers.

29. McKimmon, *When We're Green*, 286.

30. Cromer, "The Tomato Girls," 10 October 1911 (handwritten date), Newspaper Clipping, Scrapbook, Cromer Papers. McKimmon, Tomato Club Booklets, 1912–1915, P.C. 234.10, McKimmon Papers. Staking was one of the "scientific" farming advances introduced by the tomato clubs, and girls were asked to measure its success. An article in Jackson, Mississippi's *Clarion-Ledger*, "Canning Tomatoes Was a Real Task in 1912," argued that "Before joining the Tomato Club, [most growers] had just let the tomato vines run along the ground" (Tanner, Newspaper Clippings, Tanner Papers).

31. Apple, "Liberal Arts," 85. Powell, "How 4-H Club Work Started," Powell Vertical File. McKimmon, "Annual Report, December 1914–1915," P.C. 234.1, McKimmon Papers; the county is Moore County. Virginia Jones, "Marshville, NC," and Sadie Limer, "Warren Co., NC" (McKimmon, Tomato Club Booklets, 1912–1915, P.C. 234.9, McKimmon Papers). "Negroes Make Progress," Mississippi Cooperative Extension Folder, 1910–1939, Vertical File. The final Powell quote in this paragraph returns to Powell, "How 4-H Club Work Started," Powell Vertical File.

32. Tanner, "County Extension Workers," Tanner Papers. Powell, "How 4-H Club Work Started," Powell Vertical File.

33. McKimmon, "Unique Entertainment," Newspaper Clipping, 4 June 1915, Conceit Book, 1915–1930, P.C. 234.23, McKimmon Papers. The description of the girls being canned is reminiscent of the celebrations at Henry Ford's Greenfield Village of the same era in which immigrants entered a big melting pot in their indigenous clothes and came out as "Americans."

34. While the isolation of which Reck speaks is exaggerated, scholars have documented the growing consumer desire. See, for instance, Patnode, "What These People Need," 285–88; Hall et al., *Like a Family*, 237–39; Huber, *Linthead Stomp*, xiii–xiv; Hale, *Making Whiteness*, 179–89. Reck, *4-H Story*, 6. Cromer, "Improvement in Schools" and "School Improvement Ass'n," Newspaper Clippings, Scrapbook, Cromer Papers. Alma Tromberger, "Bessemer City, NC" (McKimmon, Tomato Club Booklets, 1912–1915, P.C. 234.8, McKimmon Papers). Other commentators argued the work would keep a nineteenth-century idealized domestic order in place, one where women and girls stay safely in the private home sphere, earning money only as supplemental income to the family support provided by fathers or husbands. An article in the *New York Times* expressed this viewpoint, saying, "The financial freedom it is bringing is making the girls contented to stay at home rather than to seek work in the city or town" (Talbott, "Splendid Work," SM16).

35. Cromer, "Miss Cromer's Address," Newspaper Clipping, Scrapbook, Cromer Papers. The Department of Agriculture letter is quoted in "Uncle Sam," SM13. Tanner, *Places of 4-H*, Tanner Vertical File. Implications of gender, labor, and food are explored in chapter 4.

36. McKimmon, *When We're Green*, 142. T. Roy Reid, "Factors Limiting Contacts," Dorris Vick Collection. *Year Book for Girls'*, Mississippi Cooperative Extension Folder, 1910–1939, Vertical File.

37. Reck, *4-H Story*, 80, 134. Campbell drove the Jesup Agricultural Wagon, named after its donor. The story of interracial interactions around food continues in the following chapters. Reck also discusses Lizzie Jenkins, the second Negro Home Demonstration agent hired in Virginia who explicitly credited her canning knowledge to her own Jeanes teacher (Reck, *4-H Story*, 137–38). African American Texans also benefited from expanded support during the war (Debra Reid, *Reaping*, 68–70). Although most of these sources consider race primarily in terms of black and white, some other ethnicities occasionally appear in the primary documents. See, for instance, Mae Blakeley Rosborough, who said, "Miss Margaret Callahan of Lake Village has done a beautiful piece of work with the Italians in her county, many of whom are there. She has given demonstrations in the care and feeding of children, bread making, canning and many other activities. These had to be interpreted by the Italian women and the Catholic priest" (Rosborough, "Extension Activities").

38. McKimmon, *When We're Green*, 137. Reck, *4-H Story*, 133–40. McKimmon, "Annual Report July 1, 1917 to July 1, 1918," and "Annual Report, 1920–1921," P.C. 234.1, McKimmon Papers. See also von der Heide and Pronovost, "Dazelle Foster Lowe."

39. Carmen V. Harris, "Grace under Pressure," 203; Johnson, *Southern Ladies*, 13. See also Carmen V. Harris, "Well I Just," 91–108.

40. Gilmore, *Gender and Jim Crow*, 196–99. McKimmon, *When We're Green*, 145.

Lowe in 1933 felt secure enough to turn her reports into dialogues with McKimmon, making them places to advocate for more resources: "The Negro agents have little opportunity for professional improvement. A. Their salaries are too low to allow a saving toward a leave for study. B. The summer schools do not offer courses required for their improvement" (McKimmon, Scrapbook of Newspaper Clippings, 1926–1939, P.C. 234.21, McKimmon Papers).

41. "Federation of Women's Clubs."

42. Darlene Clark Hine, "Rape and the Inner Lives," 915. Gilmore, *Gender and Jim Crow*, 199. Lucy Wade, "My Dear Mrs. McKimmon," 29 January 1923 (McKimmon, Conceit Book, P.C. 234.23, McKimmon Papers).

43. Moore, "To Make the Best," 113. Tanner, "Mississippi Extension Service among Negroes," A85–149, Box 4, Tanner Papers. For instance, in a letter supposedly requesting more support for the "Negro Work," Wilson wrote, "they must be impressed with the importance of Sanitation and better care of their bodies; since it is a well known fact that, as a race, they are deteriorating physically, due to the unsanitary condition in their home and their immoral way of living" (R. S. Wilson, "My dear Mr. [Bradford] Knapp"). Despite that, friendships between women did not happen only in North Carolina. White Arkansan Blanche Hanks Elliott wrote, "Here I was exposed to minority groups, since in Pope County there were rural black communities, with their own black home demonstration agent, with whom I worked very closely. I admired her as a leader of her people and became very fond of her as a personal friend" (Elliott, "Autobiography"). Without the voice of the African American agent Hanks discussed, however, it is hard to know whether to read any condescension into the "fondness" of which Hanks speaks.

44. T. Roy Reid, "Factors Limiting Contacts." Tanner (quoting Powell), "County Extension Workers." Reck, *4-H Story*, 45. Miss Hudson worked in Cleveland County, Arkansas; see *History of Home Demonstration*, 205.

45. On expansion of the demonstration work, see Creswell, "Home Demonstration Work," 244–49; West, "Yours for Home," 62–63; and Rieff, "Go Ahead," 134–52. On Powell and McKimmon, see Moore, "To Make the Best," 115–18; Gilmore, *Gender and Jim Crow*, 196–99.

46. McKimmon confirms (McKimmon, *When We're Green*, 4); Cromer, "American School of Home Economics Certificate of Membership" and "Green Acre Conferences, July 24–31, 1910," Scrapbook, Cromer Papers. Then and now, a Baháʼí retreat center, studying comparative religions and peace (Green Acre Baháʼí School, "History").

47. On the lifting motto, see Deborah Gray White, *Too Heavy a Load*, 54. Warren, "She 'Lifted.'"

48. The Mississippi Federation of Women's Clubs suggested Wilson shook a fist in the face of one of Powell's agents; she protested and ended up resigning, as did several of her staff. The dispute seemed to center on Wilson's expectation that work for male agents should always receive precedence and funding over work for women, and that the female employees in his office should always support his programs without any question or feedback. This is the same Wilson who exhibited such tepid support for the African American work. See Tanner, "Miss Powell's Letter" and "Concerning Miss Powell's Resignation." See also Whitlow, *Susie Virginia Powell*, 3–4.

49. Anderson, *Kit Brandon*, 365. Green, "Daughters of the New South." Annie Laura Peterson, "History of My Work Done at Canning Club," October 12, 1915 (Mc-Kimmon, Tomato Club Booklets, 1912–1915, P.C. 234.8, McKimmon Papers).

CHAPTER FOUR. WILL WORK FOR FOOD

1. Cleghorn (1876–1959), a peace activist, socialist, and well-connected New England poet, offered "Canned Childhood" for a Christmas publication of the National Child Labor Committee; her most famous poem also addressed child labor, but pointed out the irony of men on golf courses whose leisure time was financed by the mill children who never got to play outside. Cleghorn, "Canned Childhood," 14. Cromer, "South Carolina's Tomato Lady," April 14, Newspaper Clipping, Scrapbook, Cromer Papers. Jacquelyn Dowd Hall, "Disorderly Women," 354–82. On Cleghorn, see University of Vermont, "Sarah Norcliffe Cleghorn Papers."

2. Among many examples, see Lewis Hine, "Child Labor," 118–22. Philips, "To Blanche Hanks Elliott," 17 September 1917 and 10 October 1917, Elliott Papers. The letters in Elliott's collections were windows into Arkansas' teen girl culture from the period (one, from Henrietta Bennett, was written such that you had to hold it up to a mirror to read it). They all included comments on who was dating, who was fighting, and who was friendly again. Philips's October letter, for instance, ended: "So Van goes with Lillian and Orlin with Opal. I am glad to hear that."

3. Philips, "To Blanche Hanks Elliott," 17 September 1917 and 10 October 1917, Elliott Papers. Cleghorn, "Canned Childhood," 14.

4. For medical details of the disease, see *National Library*, "Pellagra."

5. Thompson, "Life in a Southern Mill Town," 9–10. After spending his childhood in the Piedmont of North Carolina, and after completing a degree at the University of North Carolina, Thompson (1873–1940) worked for four years as a high school principal in Concord. An essay he wrote on the transitions from farm to industry there won him the chance to do doctoral work at Columbia University. A book based on his dissertation, *From Cotton Field to Cotton Mill* (1906), established him as one of

the first "historians to make the New South a field of study" (Clyde Wilson, "Holland Thompson"). On pellagraphobia, see Etheridge, *The Butterfly Caste*, 30. For a discussion of the political fallout and importance of South Carolina, see Etheridge, *The Butterfly Caste*, 150, and Kraut, *Goldberger's War*, 123. Also see Marks, "Epidemiologists Explain Pellagra," 34–55. Caldwell, *Tobacco Road*, 1.

6. Etheridge, *The Butterfly Caste*, 7–8; Kraut, *Goldberger's War*, 164–67. Interestingly, female victims were more likely to drown themselves; male ones were more likely to hurt others (Etheridge, *The Butterfly Caste*, 38).

7. All of these theories were floated and subsequently discredited, but it took time to sort propaganda from lies. Writing during the heart of the debate in 1913, John C. Campbell worried, "In this mountain-mill discussion there is yet more of heat than of light, and it is with something of hesitancy that I seek to make my contribution." Campbell warned that too little sociological data had been gathered to sort out, for instance, how much sanitation mills really provided, how healthy people were when they were driven in desperation to mill life, and what role individual will played in prescriptive solutions (John C. Campbell, "Mountain Cabin," 75–79). Vorse, *Strike!*, 130. Page, *Gathering Storm*, 32.

8. Marks, "Epidemiologists Explain Pellagra," 38. Interestingly, Sydenstricker was the brother of West Virginia novelist Pearl S. Buck.

9. Much like later, more famous Tuskegee syphilis experiments, Goldberger's prison experiments have been criticized for racism and exploitation (Kraut, *Goldberger's War*, 121–24). Levenstein, *Revolution*, 147–60.

10. Edge, *Foodways*, 6; Opie, "Molasses-Colored Glasses," 84–85.

11. Post–World War II efforts to fortify flour and to establish food stamps and welfare programs made a huge difference in pellagra rates (Etheridge, *The Butterfly Caste*, 214).

12. Ackerman, *Heart of Revolution*, 67–75; Tullos, *Habits of Industry*, 286; Smith and Wilson, *North Carolina Women*, 218–24.

13. Founded by Mary Cornelia Barker, an Atlanta activist, the school described itself as "a nonsectarian, non-political experiment in Workers' Education sponsored by an independent committee of southern workers and educators." By its very existence and devotion to giving workers education and platforms from which to speak, however, it made a political statement. Sherwood Anderson's wife, activist Eleanor Copenhaver, served on the advisory committee of the school. On Barker, see Civil Rights Digital Library, "Barker." On the school, see "Southern Summer School," 1–2. On Atlanta's tradition of activists, see Hickey, *Hope and Danger*, 25–53. Beardsley, in addition to documenting the two hundred thousand victims of pellagra per year, argues, "Like a freight train gathering momentum . . . deaths reached an all-time peak"

(Beardsley, *History of Neglect*, 60). Stretch-outs combined Taylorism (a rationalization of tasks that frequently set impossible expectations for individual workers) with new technology that further automated the work; they resulted in massive lay-offs and increased burn-out of exhausted workers (Tullos, *Habits of Industry*, 198–204). Dredge explores the contradictions of corporate-sponsored benevolence, but notes that the themes emerged earlier than the time period of his study (Dredge, "Contradictions," 312). Novelists, including Van Vorst, Lumpkin, and Page, skewered the idealistic but duped or complicit club worker. In Page's novel, for instance, a librarian, horrified that a mill girl like Marge wants to read books like Upton Sinclair's *The Jungle*, instead gives her "sentimental love stories of rich girls and boys, or stories about college and the Wild West, an Elsie book, 'Three Little Women,' Thomas Nelson Pages, and 'Barriers Burned Away.'" When young Marge asks, "What did all of this have to do with a cotton mill girl?" and brings in Sinclair, "The librarian voiced her horror in a fifteen minute monologue, then pressed 'When Patty Went to Boarding School' into Marge's reluctant hands" (Page, *Gathering Storm*, 91, 103).

14. Smith and Wilson, *North Carolina Women*, 262–65.

15. Dargan, *Call Home the Heart*, 200. On the more common institutionalization of victims, see Monk, "A Plague of Cornbread," 4.

16. Cowdrey, *This Land*, 103–7.

17. Beardsley, *History of Neglect*, 43; Carlton, *Mill and Town*, 7.

18. Carlton, *Mill and Town*, 134.

19. Enstad, *Ladies of Labor*, 17–19; Peiss, *Cheap Amusements*, 5–7.

20. Van Vorst and Van Vorst, *The Woman Who Toils*, 173, 217. Responses to the Van Vorsts' style of investigation are discussed in Pittenger, "A World of Difference," 41, 46–50; Hapke, *Tales*, 45–49; Hapke, *Daughters*, 5–7. Eric Schocket describes writers such as the Van Vorsts as "proto-ethnographers" (Schocket, "Undercover Explorations," 116). One could read the Van Vorsts' writing and never know that working women and girls were activists in the 1890s and early 1900s. For a discussion of them, albeit in a more northern context, see Reitano, "Working Girls," 112–16.

21. Marie Van Vorst, *Amanda*, 339. Before her own death, Amanda's grandmother is driven to moonshine after the death of her husband and the failure of the social safety net.

22. Ibid., 33–36.

23. Page, *Gathering Storm*, 14, 32.

24. Lumpkin, *To Make My Bread*, 39, 140.

25. The classic argument about time by economic historian E. P. Thompson is reviewed and applied to the South in Marrs, "Railroads and Time," 435. Cultural studies scholar Michael O'Malley extends the argument to observe that time zones, easily

available watches, synchronized time, and factory clocks "established new patterns for self-discipline, social order, and the organization of knowledge," which in turn led to "on the one hand, outright resistance to clock time, or the desire to control it, and on the other a peculiar concern with internalizing clock authority and finding one's niche in the new framework of standardized time"—both of which could be seen in the strike novels (O'Malley, *Keeping Watch*, ix, 152).

26. Marie Van Vorst, *Amanda*, 44, 95.

27. Ibid., 129; Lumpkin, *To Make My Bread*, 199–202, 235, 329.

28. Chambers, "Stop-watches," 6; Lumpkin, *To Make My Bread*, 202–3; Dargan, *Call Home the Heart*, 219.

29. Marie Van Vorst, *Amanda*, 79, 111. Van Vorst did not romanticize the pre-mill life, admitting, "To eat corn bread, molasses, and ham, to hunt and smoke, to straggle down to the station and watch the scornful trains tear by, was the settlers' manner of passing their existences" (Ibid., 53). Nonetheless, once Amanda arrives in the mill village, the pointed critiques increase.

30. Ibid., 92, 96, 117, 211.

31. Ibid., 88–89, 125 (ellipses and emphasis in original).

32. Lumpkin, *To Make My Bread*, 147–150, 219; Page, *Gathering Storm*, 28.

33. Lumpkin, *To Make My Bread*, 246; Etheridge, *The Butterfly Caste*, 127.

34. Marie Van Vorst, *Amanda*, 129–33.

35. Wiggins's ballad has been published in several places, including the strike novels. See, for instance, Page, *Gathering Storm*, 336. Ackerman, *Heart of Revolution*, 79–80. Laura Hapke agrees with Ackerman's assessment of the uniqueness of the women strike novelists' perspectives (Hapke, *Daughters*, 154). Anderson's previously discussed *Kit Brandon* (1936) and Dargan's sequel *A Stone Came Rolling* (1935) more indirectly addressed the general labor unrest of the era.

36. Smith and Wilson, *North Carolina Women*, 262–65; Hapke, *Daughters*, 145–53. For more biography and an assessment of Wiggins as an artist, see Huber, "Mill Mother's Lament," 81–106. Contemporary newspapers such as the *New York Times* covered her assassination and murderers' trials; see "Gastonia Mob," 1, 26, and "Seven Men," 1, 12.

37. Sowinska, "Grace Lumpkin." See also Cratis D. Williams, "New Directions," 5–8, wherein Lumpkin's work is compared with that of the other strike novelists. Another take, which emphasizes critical reactions to her novel, can be found in Gray, "A Southern Writer," 187–89.

38. For more on Dargan's biography, see Ackerman, *Heart of Revolution*, 1–17; Shannon, "Biographical Afterword," 433–46. Dargan, *Call Home the Heart*, 295; Ackerman, *Heart of Revolution*, 109.

39. Page, *Southern Cotton*, 9–94. Hapke, *Daughters*, 163; University of North Carolina, "Myra Page Papers."

40. Wayne State University, "Mary Heaton Vorse Papers." Vorse, *Strike!*, 176. Wolfe, *Sherwood Anderson*, 253–69. Penzler, *Pulp Fiction*, 317.

41. Yaeger, *Dirt and Desire*, 222.

42. Lumpkin, *To Make My Bread*, 201.

43. Ibid., 203, 253.

44. Ibid., 246.

45. Ibid., 253.

46. Ibid., 254, 276.

47. Ibid., 298, 302 (ellipses in original).

48. Marie Van Vorst, *Amanda*, 111.

49. Lumpkin, *To Make My Bread*, 311.

50. Vorse, *Strike!*, 82, 143, 228.

51. Page, *Gathering Storm*, 95–98.

52. On patent medicine shows, see Hale, *Making Whiteness*, 169–71. Yaeger, *Dirt and Desire*, 219. Page, *Gathering Storm*, 29. Interestingly, Page made sure to note that women knew how to help their children, gathering, foraging, and sharing food when they could (Page, *Gathering Storm*, 92, 108); however, the mill pressures kept that from consistently happening, spurring a turn to medicines and damaged children.

53. Page, *Gathering Storm*, 117, 179, 245–53.

54. Ibid., 280, 313. The destruction of milk and food appeared in other novels as well; see, for instance, Lumpkin, *To Make My Bread*, 355–56.

55. Ackerman, *Heart of Revolution*, 80.

56. Dargan, *Call Home the Heart*, 7–10.

57. Ibid., 9–11, 67, 92, 345.

58. Ibid., 12.

59. Almost all of the women's strike novels criticized the lack of birth control for working women who wanted it. Dargan, *Call Home the Heart*, 199.

60. Hall et al., *Like a Family*, 150–51.

61. Marks, "Epidemiologists Explain Pellagra," 35. Hall et al., *Like a Family*, 150–51. Marks continues, "Sydenstricker's ingenuity in measuring families' ability to purchase food came at a price. Although his method improved substantially on existing research practices, it left him with no way of knowing how food was actually distributed within families" (Marks, "Epidemiologists Explain Pellagra," 46). Beardsley expands on the particular challenges facing African Americans during the era (Beardsley, *History of Neglect*, 11–41). For voices of both white and black women mill workers, see Byerly, *Hard Times*, 75–162.

62. Dargan, *Call Home the Heart*, 200–201.

63. Ibid., 199. Anderson, *Beyond Desire*, 72. For a more thorough examination of Coca-Cola and the South, see Michael M. Cohen, "Jim Crow's Drug War," 55–62.

64. Dargan, *Call Home the Heart*, 213–14 (emphasis in original). Yaeger, *Dirt and Desire*, 210. Yaeger also points out, as some of the mill novelists already had, that this new identity was supported by the New South's system of white privilege. African American mill residents were few, and their ability to acquire consumer goods was lessened by their lower wages. Grace Hale would add that their too easy purchases were likely to trigger the violence of Jim Crow lynch mobs, as the goods soon were thought to distinguish white from black. Hale, *Making Whiteness*, 168–79.

65. Dargan, *Call Home the Heart*, 429–30.

66. Yaeger, *Dirt and Desire*, 25–28.

CHAPTER FIVE. COOKBOOKS AND CURB MARKETS

1. Dargan, *Call Home the Heart*, 9. Elliott, "Women in Different Sections."

2. *Oxford English Dictionary*, Online ed., s.v. "mess."

3. I am, of course, oversimplifying the prolific work of three very different intellectuals. Barthes, *Mythologies*, 11; Douglas, *Food*, 1–39; Brillat-Savarin, *Physiology*, 1. Crumpacker, *Sex Life of Food*, 23–32.

4. *Oxford English Dictionary*, Online ed., s.v. "mess-writer."

5. For a survey of the scholarly debates over agricultural economics in the South, see Walker, "Agriculture," 18–25.

6. Gregory, *The Southern Diaspora*, 43–54.

7. McKimmon, *When We're Green*, 182. On the history of the Piggly Wiggly, see Piggly Wiggly, "About Us"; on the growth and race politics of similar businesses, see Stanonis, "Just Like Mammy," 209–11.

8. McCulloch-Williams, *Dishes and Beverages*, 11–12. On the changes leading to the Sunbelt, see the essays in Cobb and Namorato, *The New Deal and the South*. On Claiborne, Dull, restaurants, and *Southern Living*, see various entries in Edge, *Foodways*. Also see Stanonis, "Just Like Mammy," 223–26; Laura Shapiro, *Something from the Oven*, 129–44; Nickles, "Preserving Women," 695–98.

9. Laura Shapiro, *Something from the Oven*, 43–49; Pollan, *The Omnivore's Dilemma*, 32; Effland, "Migrant Labor," 178–81; Jakle and Sculle, *Fast Food*, 1–19.

10. Minnie C. Fox, *Blue Grass Cook Book*, xii–xiv; Williams-Forson, *Building Houses*, 166–71.

11. Edge, "Lunch Counters," 77–79; Cameron, "When Strangers," 413.

12. McPherson, *Reconstructing Dixie*, 1–8; Silber, *The Romance of Reunion*, 2; Hale, *Making Whiteness*, 281–96.

13. Belasco, *Meals to Come*, 20–60; Hale, *Making Whiteness*, xi–xii.

14. Warner, "Wal-Mart Eyes Organic Foods"; Rankin, "MoonPies," 199; Engelhardt, *Republic of Barbecue*, 26.

15. *Rest Room and Library Cook Book*, 103. On the classics of the South's community cookbooks, see Edge, *A Gracious Plenty*, 2–3.

16. Randolph, *The Virginia House-wife*, i–ii; Fisher, *What Mrs. Fisher Knows*, 9; O'Neill, "19th-Century Ghost"; McCulloch-Williams, *Dishes and Beverages*, 30.

17. Tartan, "Community Cookbooks," 41–45. Also see Longone, "Tried Receipts," 18–25; Floyd and Forster, "Recipe in Cultural Contexts," 1–8.

18. Neuhaus, *Manly Meals*, 1. For corporate cookbooks, see Nicole di Bona Petersen Collection, "More About."

19. *Garden Club Cook Book*, n.p. I first ate red-hot applesauce in a restaurant in Fayetteville, Arkansas, in 2005.

20. Joining the scholars already mentioned, see Leonardi, "Recipes for Reading," 340–47, who essentially fired the first salvo in the scholarly revaluation of women's recipes and cookbooks. Also see Newlyn, "Challenging Contemporary Narrative Theory," 35–44, for a discussion of manuscript cookbooks. Prenshaw, "Introduction," 6–12, lays out the scope of the articles in a double issue on southern food from *The Southern Quarterly* that represented major advances in southern food studies. Gantt, "Taking the Cake," 63–82, extended Prenshaw's framework to discuss Eudora Welty's writings, helpful to the conclusion of this book.

21. Hale, *Making Whiteness*, 177; Ferris, *Matzoh Ball Gumbo*, 189–215. Inness, *Dinner Roles*, 11, 54.

22. Romines, "Reading the Cakes," 603.

23. *Presbyterian Women's Cook Book*, 2. On the Silversteen house, see Todd, "Memories."

24. The boys, of course, might have wanted to be chefs some day. Boys willing to admit to a love of cooking and domesticity in the mid-century South could also have been speaking in codes meant to signal queerness.

25. Stoler, *Along the Archival Grain*, 1–2.

26. *Rest Room and Library Cook Book*, 103; *Laurel Cook Book*, 11–50. Neuhaus, *Manly Meals*, 37–38; Inness, *Dinner Roles*, 89. Inness continues, "These racial slurs show how cooking literature often instructed readers to treat other ethnic groups in a patronizing or belittling fashion. Cookbooks indoctrinated women about the desirability of cooking and staying in the kitchen; they simultaneously taught them that Anglo-American mores and foods were superior to all others" (Inness, *Dinner Roles*, 103). On tamales in Mississippi, see Streeter, "Hot Tamales."

27. FitzSimons, "Henderson County Curb Market," 25–26. "Saturday, May 30," (Hendersonville, NC) *Times News*, 20 May 1925.

CHAPTER FIVE AND CONCLUSION

Sections." McKimmon, *When We're Green*, 178,
ents were similarly excluded from the market's
os was a segregated state, with distinct institu-
he curb market's founding and patronage fell
early days. Despite its vibrant African American
on, who then passed through picking the local
in the county), the county's curb market did
y in its sellers.
n, 177.

uses, 94–99; O'Connor, *The Complete Stories*,
Collection. On using wild greens in mill vil-
th, see Blythe, "Unravelling the Threads," 137;

n, 155. "Miss Powell Writes Best Club Essay,"

n, 163.

e of Place, 6.

CLUSION
4–96.
he Southern Vernacular," 160–69.
alture and Farming, "Market Bulletin." This
isiana bulletin was in 1906, though Lacy says
the 1918 edition scanned on the Web site is
e, 32–36.
8. For these and more details on Lawrence,
No One Gardens Alone; market bulletins are
–78). Also see Wilson's volume of letters ex-
B. White's wife and a significant gardener in
Two Gardeners, 184–216). Lawrence wrote a
ce, *Garden of One's Own*, 3–4). In the preface
Lawrence added "An Apology for Myself as a

BIBLIOGRAPHY

Abernethy, Arthur Talmage. *Moonshine: Being Appalachia's Arabian Nights*. Asheville: Dixie Publishing, 1924.

Ackerman, Kathy Cantley. *The Heart of Revolution: The Radical Life and Novels of Olive Dargan*. Knoxville: University of Tennessee Press, 2004.

Anderson, Sherwood. *Beyond Desire*. New York: Liveright, 1932.

———. *Kit Brandon: A Portrait*. New York: Charles Scribner's Sons, 1936.

Apple, Rima D. "Liberal Arts or Vocational Training? Home Economics Education for Girls." In Stage and Vincenti, *Rethinking Home Economics*, 79–95.

Avakian, Arlene Voski, and Barbara Haber, eds. *From Betty Crocker to Feminist Food Studies: Critical Perspectives on Women and Food*. Amherst: University of Massachusetts Press, 2005.

Awiakta, Marilou. *Selu: Seeking the Corn-Mother's Wisdom*. Golden, Colo.: Fulcrum, 1993.

Ayers, Edward L. *The Promise of the New South: Life after Reconstruction*. Oxford: Oxford University Press, 1992.

Bailey, Joseph Cannon. *Seaman A. Knapp: Schoolmaster of American Agriculture*. New York: Columbia University Press, 1945.

Baker, Louise R. *Cis Martin, or, The Furriners in the Tennessee Mountains*. New York: Eaton and Mains, 1898.

Barney, Sandra Lee. *Authorized to Heal: Gender, Class, and the Transformation of Medicine in Appalachia, 1880–1930*. Chapel Hill: University of North Carolina Press, 2000.

Barthes, Roland. *Mythologies*. Translated by Annette Lavers. New York: Noonday Press, 1972.

Barton, Bruce. "The Moonshiner's Judge." *American Magazine* 79 (April 1915): 58–59.

Bass, A. L. Tommie. *Plain Southern Cooking: From the Reminiscences of A. L. Tommie Bass, Herbalist*. Compiled and edited by John K. Crellin. Durham: Duke University Press, 1988.

Basso, Hamilton. "Kit Brandon." In *Critical Essays on Sherwood Anderson*, edited by David D. Anderson, 58–59. Boston: G. K. Hall, 1981.

Beardsley, Edward H. *A History of Neglect: Health Care for Blacks and Mill Workers in the Twentieth-Century South*. Knoxville: University of Tennessee Press, 1987.

Bederman, Gail. *Manliness and Civilization: A Cultural History of Gender and Race in the United States, 1880–1917*. Chicago: University of Chicago Press, 1995.

Beeby, James M. *Revolt of the Tar Heels: The North Carolina Populist Movement, 1890–1901*. Jackson: University Press of Mississippi, 2008.

Beecher, Catharine E., and Harriet Beecher Stowe. *The American Woman's Home: or, Principles of Domestic Science; Being a Guide to the Formation and Maintenance of Economical, Healthful, Beautiful, and Christian Homes*. New York: Arno, [1869] 1971.

Belasco, Warren J. *Meals to Come: A History of the Future of Food*. Berkeley: University of California Press, 2006.

Best, Bill, and Frances Abbott. "Tomatoes." In Edge, *Foodways*, 274–77.

Blackwell, Deborah L. "Eleanor Marsh Frost and the Gender Dimensions of Appalachian Reform Efforts." *Register of the Kentucky Historical Society* 94, no. 3 (Summer 1996): 225–46.

Blythe, Robert W. "Unraveling the Threads of Community Life: Work, Play, and Place in the Alabama Mill Villages of the West Point Manufacturing Company." *Perspectives in Vernacular Architecture* 9 (2003): 135–50.

Boger, Lorise C. *The Southern Mountaineer in Literature: An Annotated Bibliography*. Morgantown: West Virginia University Library, 1964.

Bolsterli, Margaret Jones, et al., "Soul Food." In Edge, *Foodways*, 104–7.

Bower, Anne L. "Bound Together: Recipes, Lives, Stories, Reading." In Bower, *Recipes*, 1–14.

———, ed. *Recipes for Reading: Community Cookbooks, Stories, Histories*. Amherst: University of Massachusetts Press, 1997.

Brillat-Savarin, Anthelme. *Physiology of Taste*. Translated by M. F. K. Fisher. New York: Knopf, 1972.

Brown, Martin, and Peter Philips. "Craft Labor and Mechanization in Nineteenth-Century American Canning." *Journal of Economic History* 46, no. 3 (September 1986): 743–56.

Buck, Charles Neville. *When "Bear Cat" Went Dry*. New York: Grosset and Dunlap, 1918.

Bureau of Labor Statistics. "Inflation Calculator." www.bls.gov. Accessed 1 September 2008.

Byerly, Victoria. *Hard Times Cotton Mill Girls: Personal Histories of Womanhood and Poverty in the South*. Ithaca: ILR Press, Cornell University, 1986.

Caldwell, Erskine. *Tobacco Road*. New York: Grosset and Dunlap, 1932.

Calhoun, Richard James, and John Caldwell Guilds, eds. *A Tricentennial Anthology of South Carolina Literature, 1670–1970*. Columbia: University of South Carolina Press, 1971.

Cameron, Ardis. "When Strangers Bring Cameras: The Poetics and Politics of Othered Places." *American Quarterly* 54, no. 3 (2002): 411–35.

Campbell, John C. "From Mountain Cabin to Cotton Mill." *Child Labor Bulletin* 2, no. 1 (May 1913): 74–84.

———. *The Southern Highlander and His Homeland*. Compiled and edited by Olive Dame Campbell. New York: Russell Sage Foundation, 1921.

Campbell, Olive Dame. Diary, MS, 1 February 1909. John Charles and Olive Dame Campbell Papers #3800, Southern Historical Collection, Louis Round Wilson Library, The University of North Carolina at Chapel Hill, Chapel Hill, North Carolina.

Carlton, David L. *Mill and Town in South Carolina, 1880–1920*. Baton Rouge: Louisiana State University Press, 1982.

Cavanagh, Catherine Frances. "Stories of Our Government Bureaus." *Bookman* 34 (September 1911): 52–60.

Chambers, Lenoir. "Stop-watches Led to Textile Strikes." *New York Times* (7 April 1929): E1, 6.

Civil Rights Digital Library. "Barker, Mary Cornelia, 1879–1963." http://crdl.usg.edu /people/b/barker_mary_cornelia_1879_1963/. Accessed 10 August 2010.

Cixous, Hélène. "The Laugh of the Medusa." In *New French Feminisms*, edited by Elaine Marks and Isabelle de Courtivron. New York: Schocken, 1981.

Cleghorn, Sarah N. "Canned Childhood." In *Poems of Child Labor*, edited by National Child Labor Committee, 14. New York: National Child Labor Committee, no. 316, 1924.

Clendinen, Dudley. "Free Farmers' Paper Binds Georgians." *New York Times* (9 September 1986): A10.

Cobb, James C., and Michael V. Namorato, eds. *The New Deal and the South*. Jackson: University Press of Mississippi, 1984.

Cogdell, Virgie C. "Report of Mississippi Normal College Canning Club for 1913," Agricultural Narrative and Statistical Reports from State Officers. Microfilm Rolls 1–2, 1909–1917. Special Collections Department, Mitchell Memorial Library, Mississippi State University, Starkville, Mississippi.

Cohen, Lizabeth. *Making a New Deal: Industrial Workers in Chicago, 1919–1939*. Cambridge: Cambridge University Press, 2007.

Cohen, Michael M. "Jim Crow's Drug War: Race, Coca-Cola, and the Southern Origins of Drug Prohibition." *Southern Cultures* 12, no. 3 (2006): 55–79.

Cole, Karen. "Tending the Southern Vernacular Garden: Elizabeth Lawrence and the Market Bulletin." In *Such News of the Land: U.S. Women Nature Writers*, edited by Thomas S. Edwards and Elizabeth A. De Wolfe, 160–69. Hanover, N.H.: University Press of New England, 2001.

Collins, Carvel. "The Literary Tradition of the Southern Mountaineer, 1824–1900." Reprinted from *The Bulletin of Bibliography* 17, nos. 9–10 (September–December 1942; January–April 1943). North Carolina Collection, Louis Round Wilson Library, University of North Carolina at Chapel Hill, Chapel Hill, North Carolina.

Cooke, Grace MacGowan. "The Capture of Andy Proudfoot." In *Southern Lights and Shadows*, edited by William Dean Howells and Henry Mills Alden, 1–24. New York: Harper and Brothers, 1907.

———. *The Power and the Glory: A Novel of Appalachia*. Edited by Elizabeth S. D. Engelhardt. Boston: Northeastern University Press, [1909] 2003.

———. "The Spy." *Munsey's Magazine* 34 (1905–1906): 473–80.

Cooper, Anna Julia. *A Voice from the South*. Schomburg Library of Nineteenth Century Women Writers. Oxford: Oxford University Press, [1892] 1988.

"County Extension Workers, 1905–1945." A85–149, Box 1, James E. Tanner Papers, Special Collections Department, University Archives, Mitchell Memorial Library, Mississippi State University, Starkville, Mississippi.

Cowdrey, Albert E. *This Land, This South: An Environmental History*. Lexington: University Press of Kentucky, 1983.

Cresswell, Stephen. *Rednecks, Redeemers, and Race: Mississippi after Reconstruction, 1877–1917*. Jackson: University Press of Mississippi for the Mississippi Historical Society, 2006.

Creswell, Mary E. "The Home Demonstration Work." *Annals of the American Academy of Political and Social Science* 67 (September 1916): New Possibilities in Education, 241–49.

Crim, [Miss] Matt. "The Strike at Mr. Mobley's." *Century* 50 (July 1895): 378–84.

Cromer, Marie Samuella. Newspaper Clippings and Letters. Scrapbook, Marie Samuella Cromer Papers, South Caroliniana Library, University of South Carolina, Columbia, South Carolina.

Crow, Martha Foote. *The American Country Girl*. New York: Frederick A. Stokes, 1915.

Crumpacker, Bunny. *The Sex Life of Food: When Body and Soul Meet to Eat*. New York: St. Martin's, 2006.

"Curb Market Provides Good Outlet for Farm Product." Advertisement, 11 May 1937 (handwritten date). Henderson County Genealogical and Historical Society, Hendersonville, North Carolina.

Dabney, Joseph E. *Smokehouse Ham, Spoon Bread, and Scuppernong Wine: The Folklore and Art of Southern Appalachian Cooking.* Nashville: Cumberland House, 1998.

Dame, Daisy Gertrude. Papers. Letters. 4331, Southern Historical Collection, Louis Round Wilson Library, University of North Carolina at Chapel Hill, Chapel Hill, North Carolina.

Daniel, Pete. *Standing at the Crossroads: Southern Life in the Twentieth Century.* New York: Hill and Wang, 1986.

Dargan, Olive Tilford. Pseud. Fielding Burke. *Call Home the Heart: A Novel of the Thirties.* Introduction by Alice Kessler-Harris and Paul Lauter. New York: Feminist Press, [1932] 1983.

———. *A Stone Came Rolling.* New York: Longman's, Green, 1935.

Davis, Edward H., and John T. Morgan. "Collards in North Carolina." *Southeastern Geographer* 45, no. 1 (2005): 67–82.

Dicke, Tom. "Red Gold of the Ozarks: The Rise and Decline of Tomato Canning, 1885–1955." *Agricultural History* 79, no. 1 (2005): 1–26.

Douglas, Mary. *Food in the Social Order: Studies of Food and Festivities in Three American Communities.* New York: Russell Sage Foundation, 1984.

Dredge, Bart. "Contradictions of Corporate Benevolence: Industrial Libraries in the Southern Textile Industry, 1920–1945." *Libraries and the Cultural Record* 43, no. 3 (2008): 308–26.

Duke's Mayonnaise. "Duke's History: A True Southern History." http://www.dukesmayo.com/about.asp. Accessed 22 July 2010.

Duke's Sandwich Company. "About Us." http://www.dukesandwich.com/pages/about-us. Accessed 22 July 2010.

Dunaway, Wilma. *First American Frontier: Transition to Capitalism in Southern Appalachia, 1700–1860.* Chapel Hill: University of North Carolina Press, 1996.

Dunne, Robert. *A New Book of the Grotesques: Contemporary Approaches to Sherwood Anderson's Early Fiction.* Kent, Ohio: Kent State University Press, 2005.

DuPuis, E. Melanie. *Nature's Perfect Food: How Milk Became America's Drink.* New York: New York University Press, 2002.

Durand, Loyal, Jr. "'Mountain Moonshining' in East Tennessee." In *Baseball, Barns, and Bluegrass: A Geography of American Folklife,* edited by George O. Carney, 120–28. Lanham, Md.: Rowman and Littlefield, 1998.

Dykeman, Wilma. *The French Broad.* Newport, Tenn.: Wakestone Books, [1955] 1999.

Eaker, Imogene. Conversation with the author, Brevard, North Carolina, 6 June 2005. Notes in author's possession.

Edge, John T., ed. *Foodways,* vol. 7 of *The New Encyclopedia of Southern Culture.* General editor, Charles Reagan Wilson. Chapel Hill: University of North Carolina Press, 2007.

———. *A Gracious Plenty: Recipes and Recollections from the American South*. New York: HP Books, 1999.

———. "Lunch Counters (Civil Rights Era)." In Edge, *Foodways*, 77–79.

Eelman, Bruce W. "Entrepreneurs in the Southern Upcountry: The Case of Spartanburg, South Carolina, 1815–1880." *Enterprise and Society* 5, no. 1 (2004): 77–106.

Effland, Anne. "Migrant Labor." In Walker and Cobb, *Agriculture and Industry*, 178–81.

Egerton, John. *Southern Food: At Home, on the Road, in History*. Chapel Hill: University of North Carolina Press, 1993.

Elie, Lolis Eric, ed. *Cornbread Nation 2: The United States of Barbecue*. Chapel Hill: University of North Carolina Press, 2004.

Elliott, Blanche Hanks. "Autobiography." Blanche Hanks Elliott Papers. MC 1272, Box 2, Folder 1, Special Collections, University of Arkansas, Fayetteville, Arkansas.

———. "Women in Different Sections." Blanche Hanks Elliott Papers. MC 1272, Box 2, Folder 2, Special Collections, University of Arkansas, Fayetteville, Arkansas.

Ellis, William E. "Moonshine." In *Tennessee Encyclopedia of History and Culture*. Nashville: Tennessee Historical Society, 1998; online, University of Tennessee Press, 2002. http://160.36.208.47/FMPro?-db=tnencyc.fp5&-format=tdetail .htm&-lay=web&entryname=moonshine&-recid=33578&-find=. Accessed 15 June 2005.

Engelhardt, Elizabeth S. D. *Republic of Barbecue: Stories Beyond the Brisket*. With Marsha Abrahams et al. Foreword by John T. Edge. Austin: University of Texas Press, 2009.

———. *The Tangled Roots of Feminism, Environmentalism, and Appalachian Literature*. Athens: Ohio University Press, 2003.

———. "Writing That Old Moonshine Lit: Gender, Power, and Nation in Unexpected Places." *Journal of Appalachian Studies*, 13, nos. 1–2 (Spring/Fall 2007): 49–74.

Enstad, Nan. *Ladies of Labor, Girls of Adventure: Working Women, Popular Culture, and Labor Politics at the Turn of the Twentieth Century*. New York: Columbia University Press, 1999.

Etheridge, Elizabeth W. *The Butterfly Caste: A Social History of Pellagra in the South*. Westport, Conn.: Greenwood, 1972.

Evans, Mari-Lynn et al., eds. *The Appalachians: America's First and Last Frontier*. New York: Random House, 2004.

"Everyone Knows." *Farmer's Wife* (October 1923). In McKimmon, Conceit Book,

1915–1930, P.C. 234.23, McKimmon Papers, North Carolina State Archives, Raleigh, North Carolina, USA.

Farr, Sidney Saylor. *Appalachian Women: An Annotated Bibliography*. Lexington: University Press of Kentucky, 1981.

"Federation of Woman's Clubs Transacts Mass of Business," *Greensboro News*, 9 May 1924. In McKimmon, Conceit Book, 1915–1930, P.C. 234.23, McKimmon Papers, North Carolina State Archives, Raleigh, North Carolina.

Fendelman, Helaine, and Joe Rosson. "An Old Biscuit Table Is Worth Some Dough." www.hgtv.com/hgtv/ah_antique_appraisals/article/0,1801,HGTV_3081_26881 78,00.html. Accessed 15 November 2004.

Ferris, Marcie Cohen. "Gender and Food." In Edge, *Foodways*, 58–62.

———. *Matzoh Ball Gumbo: Culinary Tales of the Jewish South*. Chapel Hill: University of North Carolina Press, 2005.

Fetterley, Judith, and Marjorie Pryse. *Writing Out of Place: Regionalism, Women, and American Literary Culture*. Urbana: University of Illinois Press, 2003.

Fields, Annie (Mrs. James T. Fields). *How to Help the Poor*. Boston: Houghton Mifflin, 1884.

Fisher, Abby. *What Mrs. Fisher Knows about Old Southern Cooking*. San Francisco: Women's Co-op, 1881. http://digital.lib.msu.edu/projects/cookbooks/html/books/book_35.cfm. Accessed 15 June 2010.

FitzSimons, Frank L., Sr. "Henderson County Curb Market," *Heritage of Henderson County*, 25–26. Henderson County Genealogical and Historical Society, Hendersonville, North Carolina.

Flagg, Fannie. *Fried Green Tomatoes at the Whistle Stop Café*. New York: Random House, 1987.

Floyd, Janet, and Laurel Forster. "The Recipe in Its Cultural Contexts." In *The Recipe Reader: Narratives—Contexts—Traditions*, edited by Janet Floyd and Laurel Forster, 1–14. Burlington, Vt.: Ashgate, 2003.

Forderhase, Nancy K. "Eve Returns to the Garden: Women Reformers in Appalachian Kentucky in the Early Twentieth Century." *Register of the Kentucky Historical Society* 85, no. 3 (1987): 237–61.

Fox, John, Jr. *The Trail of the Lonesome Pine*. New York: Charles Scribner's Sons, 1908.

Fox, Minnie C., compiler. *The Blue Grass Cook Book*. New York: Fox, Duffield, 1904. http://digital.lib.msu.edu/projects/cookbooks/html/books/book_57.cfm. Accessed 15 November 2010.

Frost, William Goodell. "Our Contemporary Ancestors in the Southern Mountains." *Atlantic Monthly* 83 (March 1899): 311–19.

Furman, Lucy. *Mothering on Perilous*. New York: Macmillan, 1923.
———. *The Quare Women: A Story of the Kentucky Mountains*. Boston: Atlantic Monthly Press, 1923.
Gabaccia, Donna. *We Are What We Eat: Ethnic Food and the Making of Americans*. Cambridge: Harvard University Press, 1998.
Gabbard, Alex. *Return to Thunder Road: The Story Behind the Legend*. 2nd ed. Lenoir City, Tenn.: Gabbard Publication, 2000.
Gantt, Patricia M. "Taking the Cake: Power Politics in Southern Life and Fiction." In *Cooking Lessons: The Politics of Gender and Food*, edited by Sherrie A. Inness, 63–85. Lanham, Md.: Rowman and Littlefield, 2001.
Garden Club Cook Book. McGehee, Ark.: Stuart Printing Co., 1936. Special Collections, University of Arkansas, Fayetteville, Arkansas.
Garvey, Ellen Gruber. *The Adman in the Parlor: Magazines and the Gendering of Consumer Culture, 1880s to 1910s*. New York: Oxford University Press, 1996.
"Gastonia Mob Kills Woman in Volley Fired at Strikers." *New York Times* (15 September 1929): 1, 26.
Gielow, Martha S. *Old Andy, the Moonshiner*. Washington, D.C.: W. F. Roberts, 1909.
Gill, George Creswell. *Beyond the Blue Grass: A Kentucky Novel*. New York: Neale, 1908.
Gilman, Charlotte Perkins. *Women and Economics: A Study of the Economic Relation Between Men and Women as a Factor in Social Evolution*. Berkeley: University of California Press, 1998.
Gilmore, Glenda Elizabeth. *Gender and Jim Crow: Women and the Politics of White Supremacy in North Carolina, 1896–1920*. Chapel Hill: University of North Carolina Press, 1996.
Goodrich, Frances Louisa. *Mountain Homespun*. New Haven: Yale University Press, 1931.
Gordon, Jean, and Jan McArthur. "American Women and Domestic Consumption, 1800–1920: Four Interpretive Themes." In *Making the American Home: Middle-Class Women and Domestic Material Culture, 1840–1940*, edited by Marilyn Ferris Motz and Pat Browne, 27–47. Bowling Green: Bowling Green State University Popular Press, 1988.
Gray, Richard. "A Southern Writer and Class War in the Mountains: Grace Lumpkin's *To Make My Bread*." In *Reading Southern Poverty between the Wars, 1918–1939*, edited by Richard Godden and Martin Crawford, 179–91. Athens: University of Georgia Press, 2006.
Green, Charlotte Hilton. "Daughters of the New South," *Forecast*, June 1922. In

McKimmon, Conceit Book, 1915–1930, P.C. 234.23, McKimmon Papers, North Carolina State Archives, Raleigh, North Carolina.

Green Acre Bahá'í School, Retreat, and Conference Center. "History." http://www.greenacre.org/index.php?option=com_content&view=category&layout=blog&id=9&Itemid=5. Accessed 10 August 2010.

Green 'N' Growing Project, http://www.lib.ncsu.edu/specialcollections/greenngrowing/timeline/1910.html. Accessed 25 August 2008.

Greeson, Jennifer. "Expropriating the Great South and Exporting 'Local Color': Global and Hemispheric Imaginaries of the First Reconstruction." *American Literary History* 18, no. 3: 496–520.

Gregory, James N. *The Southern Diaspora: How the Great Migrations of Black and White Southerners Transformed America*. Chapel Hill: University of North Carolina Press, 2005.

Haber, Barbara. *From Hardtack to Home Fries: An Uncommon History of American Cooks and Meals*. New York: Free Press, 2002.

Hagood, Margaret Jarman. *Mothers of the South: Portraiture of the White Tenant Farm Woman*. New York: Norton, 1977.

Hale, Grace Elizabeth. *Making Whiteness: The Culture of Segregation in the South, 1890–1940*. New York: Vintage, 1999.

Hall, G. Stanley. *Adolescence: Its Psychology and Its Relations to Physiology, Anthropology, Sex, Crime, Religion and Education*. 2 vols. New York: Appleton, 1904.

Hall, Jacquelyn Dowd. "Disorderly Women: Gender and Labor Militancy in the Appalachian South." *Journal of American History* 73 (September 1986): 354–82.

Hall, Jacquelyn Dowd, et al. *Like a Family: The Making of a Southern Cotton Mill World*. New York: W. W. Norton, 1987.

Hapke, Laura. *Daughters of the Great Depression: Women, Work and Fiction in the American 1930s*. Athens: University of Georgia Press, 1995.

———. *Tales of the Working Girl: Wage-Earning Women in American Literature, 1890–1925*. New York: Twayne, 1992.

Harkins, Anthony. *Hillbilly: A Cultural History of an American Icon*. New York: Oxford University Press, 2004.

Harris, Carmen V. "Grace under Pressure: The Black Home Extension Service in South Carolina, 1919–1966." In Stage and Vincenti, *Rethinking Home Economics*, 203–28.

———. "'Well I just generally bes the president of everything': Rural Black Women's Empowerment through South Carolina Home Demonstration Activities." *Black Women, Gender, and Families* 3, no. 1 (Spring 2009): 91–112.

Harris, Jessica. *Beyond Gumbo: Creole Fusion Food from the Atlantic Rim*. New York: Simon and Schuster, 2003.

Harris, Joel Chandler. "At Teague Poteet's: A Sketch of the Hog Mountain Range." In *Mingo and Other Sketches in Black and White*, 37–168. Boston: Houghton Mifflin, [1884] 1898.

Hatley, Donald W. "Calling the Cotton Press." http://www.louisianafolklife.org/LT/Articles_Essays/calling_the_cotton_press.html. Accessed 15 July 2010.

Hawkins, Richard. "The Baltimore Canning Industry and the Bahamian Pineapple Trade, c. 1865–1926." *Maryland Historian* 26, no. 2 (1995): 1–22.

Heinemann, Ronald. "Ella G. Agnew, 1871–1958." *Encyclopedia of Virginia*. Edited by Brendan Wolfe. Virginia Foundation for the Humanities. http://www.Encyclopedia Virginia.org/Agnew_Ella_G_1871–1958. Accessed 29 July 2010.

Heyward, Du Bose. *Angel*. New York: George H. Doran, 1926.

Hickey, Georgina. *Hope and Danger in the New South City: Working-Class Women and Urban Development in Atlanta, 1890–1940*. Athens: University of Georgia Press, 2003.

Hine, Darlene Clark. "Rape and the Inner Lives of Black Women in the Middle West." *Signs* 14, no. 4 (Summer 1989): 912–20.

Hine, Lewis. "Child Labor in Gulf Coast Canneries: Photo-Graphic Investigation Made February, 1911." *Annals of the American Academy of Political and Social Science*, 38, Supplement: Uniform Child Labor Laws (July 1911): 118–22.

History of Home Demonstration Work, 1914–65 and Extension Homemaker Work, 1966–1977 in Arkansas. 1978. Special Collections, University of Arkansas, Fayetteville, Arkansas.

Hochschild, Arlie. *The Second Shift: Working Parents and the Revolution at Home*. New York: Viking, 1989.

Hoffschwelle, Mary S. "'Better Homes on Better Farms': Domestic Reform in Rural Tennessee." *Frontiers: A Journal of Women Studies* 22, no. 1 (2001): 51–73.

———. *Rebuilding the Rural Southern Community: Reformers, Schools, and Homes in Tennessee, 1900–1930*. Knoxville: University of Tennessee Press, 1998.

Holzer, Scott. "The Modernization of Southern Foodways: Rural Immigration to the Urban South during World War II." *Food and Foodways* 6, no. 2 (1996): 93–107.

Huber, Patrick. *Linthead Stomp: The Creation of Country Music in the Piedmont South*. Chapel Hill: University of North Carolina Press, 2008.

———. "Mill Mother's Lament: Ella May Wiggins and the Gastonia Textile Strike of 1929." *Southern Cultures* 15, no. 3 (Fall 2009): 81–110.

Huie, William Bradford. *Mud on the Stars*. Tuscaloosa: University of Alabama Press, [1942] 1996.

Hunter, Jane H. *How Young Ladies Became Girls: The Victorian Origins of American Girlhood.* New Haven: Yale University Press, 2002.

Hurston, Zora Neale. *Their Eyes Were Watching God.* New York: Perennial Classics, [1937] 1998.

Inness, Sherrie. *Dinner Roles: American Women and Culinary Culture.* Iowa City: University of Iowa Press, 2001.

Inscoe, John. *Race, War, and Remembrance in the Appalachian South.* Lexington: University Press of Kentucky, 2008.

Jakle, John A., and Keith A. Sculle. *Fast Food: Roadside Restaurants in the Automobile Age.* Baltimore: Johns Hopkins University Press, 2002.

Jellison, Katherine. *Entitled to Power: Farm Women and Technology, 1913–1963.* Chapel Hill: University of North Carolina Press, 1993.

Jensen, Joan M. *With These Hands: Women Working on the Land.* Old Westbury, N.Y.: Feminist Press, 1981.

Jensen, Joan M., and Anne B. W. Effland. "Introduction." *Frontiers* 22, no. 1 (2001): iii–xvii.

Johnson, Joan Marie. *Southern Ladies, New Women: Race, Region, and Clubwomen in South Carolina, 1890–1930.* Gainesville: University Press of Florida, 2004.

Jones, Jacqueline. *Labor of Love, Labor of Sorrow: Black Women, Work and the Family, from Slavery to the Present.* New York: Vintage, 1985.

Joyce, R. Edwin, Jr. "The Carrie Chapman Catt Citizenship Course: Inside Stories about the Federal Departments, Prohibition Unit." *Woman's Journal* 5, no. 35 (1921): 936, 942.

Kantrowitz, Stephen. "Youngest Living Carpetbagger Tells All: Or, How Regional Myopia Created 'Pitchfork Ben' Tillman." *Southern Cultures* 8, no. 3 (2002): 18–37.

Kaplan, Amy. *Anarchy of Empire in the Making of U.S. Culture.* Cambridge: Harvard University Press, 2002.

Kaplan, Amy, and Donald Pease, eds. *Cultures of United States Imperialism.* Durham: Duke University Press, 1993.

Keuchel, Edward F. "Master of the Art of Canning: Baltimore, 1860–1900." *Maryland Historical Magazine* 67, no. 4 (Winter 1972): 351–62.

Knight, Louise. *Citizen: Jane Addams and the Struggle for Democracy.* Chicago: University of Chicago Press, 2005.

Kraut, Alan M. *Goldberger's War: The Life and Work of a Public Health Crusader.* New York: Hill and Wang, 2003.

Lacy, Allen. "Introduction." In Lawrence, *Gardening for Love*, 1–22.

Lang, Amy Schrager. *Syntax of Class: Writing Inequality in Nineteenth-Century America*. Princeton: Princeton University Press, 2003.

Lanier, Parks. "Kit Brandon's Choice." In *Critical Essays in Appalachian Life and Culture*, edited by Rick Simon et al., 76–83. Boone, N.C.: Appalachian Consortium, 1982.

Laurel Cook Book. Prepared by the Women of St. John's Guild in the Year of 1900. Edited by Mrs. George Gardiner. Revised and Reprinted in 1910, 1914, 1933, and 1949. Special Collections, Mississippi State University, Starkville, Mississippi.

Lawrence, Elizabeth. *Gardening for Love: The Market Bulletins*. Edited by Allen Lacy. Durham: Duke University Press, 1988.

———. *A Garden of One's Own: Writings of Elizabeth Lawrence*. Edited by Barbara Scott and Bobby J. Ward. Chapel Hill: University of North Carolina Press, 1997.

———. *The Little Bulbs: A Tale of Two Gardens*. Durham: Duke University Press, 1986.

———. *A Southern Garden: A Handbook for the Middle South*. Chapel Hill: University of North Carolina Press, 1942.

Leonardi, Susan J. "Recipes for Reading: Summer Pasta, Lobster a la Riseholme, and Key Lime Pie." *PMLA* 104, no. 3 (1989): 340–47.

Levenstein, Harvey. *Revolution at the Table: The Transformation of the American Diet*. Berkeley: University of California Press, 2003.

London, Jack. *The Call of the Wild*. New York: Macmillan, 1903.

Longone, Janice Bluestein. "'Tried Receipts': An Overview of America's Charitable Cookbooks." In Bower, *Recipes*, 17–28.

Louisiana Department of Agriculture and Farming. "The Market Bulletin." http://www.ldaf.state.la.us/portal/News/MarketBulletinCurrent/tabid/165/Default.aspx. Accessed 15 July 2010.

Lucas, Margaret M., ed. and comp. *Ozark Canners and Freezers Association Progress Report*. (Springfield, Mo.?): The Association, 1963. Special Collections, University of Arkansas, Fayetteville, Arkansas.

Lumpkin, Grace. *To Make My Bread*. Introduction by Suzanne Sowinska. Urbana: University of Chicago Press, 1995.

Mancini, J. M. "'Messin' with the Furniture Man': Early Country Music, Regional Culture, and the Search for an Anthological Modernism." *American Literary History* 16, no. 2 (2004): 208–37.

Manring, Maurice M. *Slave in a Box: The Strange Career of Aunt Jemima*. Charlottesville: University Press of Virginia, 1998.

Marks, Harry M. "Epidemiologists Explain Pellagra: Gender, Race, and Political Economy in the Work of Edgar Sydenstricker." *Journal of the History of Medicine* 58 (January 2003): 34–55.

Marquis, Margaret. "'When de Notion Strikes Me': Body Image, Food, and Desire in *Their Eyes Were Watching God*." *Southern Literary Journal* 35, no. 2 (2003): 79–88.

Marrs, Aaron W. "Railroads and Time Consciousness in the Antebellum South." *Enterprise and Society* 9, no. 3 (September 2008): 433–56.

Martha White Flour. "History and Heritage." http://www.marthawhite.com/about/history_heritage.aspx. Accessed 15 July 2010.

Massy, Elaine, State Girls' Club Agent, and J. E. Tanner, State Boys' Club Agent. *Year Book for Boys' and Girls' 4-H Clubs of Mississippi 1925*. 4-H Club folder, Vertical File, University Archives, Special Collections Department, Mitchell Memorial Library, Mississippi State University, Starkville, Mississippi.

Mattingly, Carol. *Well-Tempered Women: Nineteenth-Century Temperance Rhetoric*. Carbondale: Southern Illinois University Press, 1998.

Maurer, David W. *Kentucky Moonshine*. With Quinn Pearl. Lexington: University Press of Kentucky, 1974.

McCleary, Ann E. "'Seizing the Opportunity': Home Demonstration Curb Markets in Virginia." In *Work, Family, and Faith: Rural Southern Women in the Twentieth Century*, edited by Melissa Walker and Rebecca Sharpless, 97–134. Columbia: University of Missouri Press, 2006.

McCulloch-Williams, Martha. *Dishes and Beverages of the Old South*. Knoxville: University of Tennessee Press, [1913] 1988.

McElroy, Lucy Cleaver. *Juletty: A Story of . . . Old Kentucky*. New York: Thomas Y. Crowell, 1901.

McGill, Robert. "Red Gold Ozark Tomatoes." *OzarksWatch* 9, no. 1 (1996): 23–25.

McKee, Kathryn, and Annette Trefzer. "Local Literatures, Global Contexts: The New Southern Studies." *American Literature* 78, no. 4 (2006): 677–90.

McKimmon, Jane Simpson. Papers. P.C. 234, North Carolina State Archives, Raleigh, North Carolina.

———. *When We're Green We Grow*. Chapel Hill: University of North Carolina Press, 1945.

McPherson, Tara. *Reconstructing Dixie: Race, Gender, and Nostalgia in the Imagined South*. Durham: Duke University Press, 2003.

McWhirter, Ollie Dean. *The Work of Miss Susie V. Powell*. Master's Thesis, Department of Sociology and Rural Life, State College, Mississippi (now Mississippi State University), 1964.

McWilliams, Mark. "Distant Tables: Food and the Novel in Early America." *Early American Literature* 38, no. 3: 365–93.
Miles, Emma Bell. Diary, TS, 8 May 1915. Miles (Emma Bell) Papers, Hist. C. acc. 43, Chattanooga–Hamilton County Bicentennial Library, Chattanooga, Tennessee.
———. *The Spirit of the Mountains*. Edited by David E. Whisnant. Knoxville: University of Tennessee Press, [1905] 1975.
Miller, Stephen. "Marvin 'Popcorn' Sutton, 1946–2009: Legendary Tennessee Moonshiner Plied His Trade to the End." *Wall Street Journal* (23 March 2009): A12.
Miller, Wilbur R. *Revenuers and Moonshiners: Enforcing Federal Liquor Law in the Mountain South, 1865–1900*. Chapel Hill: University of North Carolina Press, 1991.
Mintz, Sidney W. *Sweetness and Power: The Place of Sugar in Modern History*. New York: Penguin, 1985.
———. *Tasting Food, Tasting Freedom: Excursions into Eating, Culture, and the Past*. Boston: Beacon, 1996.
"Miss Powell Writes Best Club Essay." *Jackson Daily News*, 1936. Susie V. Powell (1869–1952) Vertical File, Special Collections, Mississippi State University, Starkville, Mississippi.
Monk, Linda R. "A Plague of Cornbread." *Gravy* 34 (Winter 2009): 2–4.
Moore, Danny. "'To Make the Best Better': The Establishment of Girls' Tomato Clubs in Mississippi, 1911–1915." *Journal of Mississippi History* 63, no. 2 (2001): 101–18.
Morley, Margaret. *The Carolina Mountains*. Boston: Houghton Mifflin, 1913.
Mullett, Mary. "Women and the Automobile." *Outing Magazine* 48, no. 4 (July 1906): 500–2.
Murfree, Mary Noailles. Pseud. Charles Egbert Craddock. *In the Tennessee Mountains*. Boston: Houghton Mifflin, 1884.
Nash, Ilana. *American Sweethearts: Teenage Girls in Twentieth-Century Popular Culture*. Bloomington: Indiana University Press, 2006.
National Library of Medicine Encyclopedia. "Pellagra." http://www.nlm.nih.gov/medlineplus/ency/article/000342.htm. Accessed 15 February 2010.
Neal, Bill. *Bill Neal's Southern Cooking*. Revised edition. Chapel Hill: University of North Carolina Press, 1989.
"Negroes Make Progress." (Memphis) *Commercial Appeal*, 21 December 1923. Mississippi Cooperative Extension Folder, 1910–1939, Vertical File, University Archives, Mississippi State University, Starkville, Mississippi.
Neuhaus, Jessamyn. *Manly Meals and Mom's Home Cooking: Cookbooks and Gender in Modern America*. Baltimore: Johns Hopkins University Press, 2003.

Newlyn, Andrea. "Challenging Contemporary Narrative Theory: The Alternative Textual Strategies of Nineteenth-Century Manuscript Cookbooks." *Journal of American Culture* 22, no. 3 (Fall 1999): 35–47.

Nickles, Shelley. "'Preserving Women': Refrigerator Design as Social Process in the 1930s." *Technology and Culture* 43, no. 4 (2002): 693–727.

Nicole di Bona Petersen Collection. "More about Advertising Cookbooks and the Advertising Cookbooks Collection." Duke University Digital Collections, Duke University Libraries. http://library.duke.edu/digitalcollections/eaa/cookbooks.html. Accessed 10 August 2010.

O'Connor, Flannery. *The Complete Stories*. New York: Farrar, Straus and Giroux, [1946] 1986.

O'Malley, Michael. *Keeping Watch: A History of American Time*. New York: Viking, 1990.

O'Neill, Molly. "A 19th-Century Ghost Awakens to Redefine 'Soul.'" *New York Times*. http://www.nytimes.com/2007/11/21/dining/21cook.html?pagewanted=1. Accessed 15 July 2010.

Opie, Frederick Douglass. *Hog and Hominy: Soul Food from Africa to America*. New York: Columbia University Press, 2008.

———. "Molasses-Colored Glasses: WPA and Sundry Sources on Molasses and Southern Foodways." *Southern Cultures* 14, no. 1 (2008): 81–96.

Ownby, Ted. *Subduing Satan: Religion, Recreation, and Manhood in the Rural South, 1865–1920*. Chapel Hill: University of North Carolina Press, 1990.

Page, Dorothy Myra. *Gathering Storm: A Story of the Black Belt*. New York: International, 1932.

———. *Southern Cotton Mills and Labor*. New York: Workers Library, 1929.

Patnode, Randall. "'What These People Need is Radio': New Technology, the Press, and Otherness in 1920s America." *Technology and Culture* 44, no. 2 (2003): 285–305.

Peacock, James. *Grounded Globalism: How the U.S. South Embraces the World*. Athens: University of Georgia Press, 2010.

Peck, Elizabeth S. "Katherine Pettit." In *Notable American Women, 1607–1950: A Biographical Dictionary*, vol. 3, edited by Edward T. James, 56–58. Cambridge: Belknap Press, 1971.

Peiss, Kathy. *Cheap Amusements: Working Women and Leisure in Turn-of-the-Century New York*. Philadelphia: Temple University Press, 1986.

Penzler, Otto, ed. *Pulp Fiction: Crimefighters*. London: Quercus, 2006.

Philips, E. Val. To Blanche Hanks Elliott, 17 September 1917 and 10 October 1917. Blanche Hanks Elliott Papers. MC 1272, Box 1, Folder 1, Special Collections, University of Arkansas, Fayetteville, Arkansas.

Piggly Wiggly. "About Us." http://www.pigglywiggly.com/about-us. Accessed 10 August 2010.

Pittenger, Mark. "A World of Difference: Constructing the 'Underclass' in Progressive America." *American Quarterly* 49, no. 1 (1997): 26–65.

Pitts, Buren, Louis W. Courtney III, and Virginia Clapp. "The Princely Tomato: Down Memory Lane." *Northern Neck of Virginia Historical Magazine* 50, no. 1 (December 2000): 5947–52.

Pollan, Michael. *The Omnivore's Dilemma: A Natural History of Four Meals*. New York: Penguin, 2007.

Pool, Maria Louise. *In Buncombe County*. Chicago: Herbert S. Stone, 1896.

Poole, William Frederick. *Poole's Index to Periodical Literature, 1802–1906*. 6 vols. Gloucester, Mass.: Peter Smith, 1963.

Powell, Susie V. Annual Reports. Agricultural Narrative and Statistical Reports from State Officers. Microfilm Rolls 1–2, 1909–1917. Special Collections Department, Mitchell Memorial Library, Mississippi State University, Starkville, Mississippi.

———. "How 4-H Club Work Started in Mississippi." 1939. Susie V. Powell Vertical File, University Archives, Special Collections Department, Mitchell Memorial Library, Mississippi State University, Starkville, Mississippi.

———. "Report of the Home Economic Extension Work for Mississippi, 1914–1915." Mississippi Cooperative Extension Folder, 1910–1939. Vertical File, University Archives, Mississippi State University, Starkville, Mississippi.

Prenshaw, Peggy Whitman. "Introduction: Special Double Issue on the Texts of Southern Food." *Southern Quarterly* 30, nos. 2–3 (Winter-Spring 1992): 6–12.

Presbyterian Women's Cook Book. Compiled and edited by the Women of the Brevard-Davidson River Presbyterian Church, December 1950.

Price, Theodore H., and Richard Spillane. "The Commissioner of Internal Revenue as a Policeman: His Work in the Suppression of the Traffic in Moonshine Whisky, 'Dope,' and Counterfeit Butter." *Outlook* 120 (27 November 1918): 498ff.

Randolph, Mary. *The Virginia House-wife: Or, the Methodical Cook: A Facsimile of an Authentic Early American Cookbook*. New York: Dover, 1993.

Rankin, Thomas. "MoonPies." In Edge, *Foodways*, 199–200.

Reader's Guide to Periodical Literature. 28 vols. New York: H. W. Wilson, 1900–1965.

Reck, Franklin M. *The 4-H Story: A History of 4-H Club Work*. Ames: Iowa State College Press, 1951.

Reed, John Shelton. "Barbecue Sociology: The Meat of the Matter." In Elie, *Cornbread Nation 2*, 78–87.

Rehder, John. *Appalachian Folkways*. Baltimore: John Hopkins University Press, 2004.

Reid, Debra. *Reaping a Greater Harvest: African Americans, the Extension Service, and Rural Reform in Jim Crow Texas*. College Station: Texas A&M University Press, 2007.

Reid, T. Roy. "Factors Limiting Contacts, Spread of Influence, and Results in Home Demonstration Work." September 2, 1931. Dorris Vick Collection. MC 961, Box 1, Special Collections, University of Arkansas, Fayetteville, Arkansas.

Reitano, Joanne. "Working Girls Unite." *American Quarterly* 36, no. 1 (Spring 1984): 112–34.

The Rest Room and Library Cook Book (Complied [sic] *by the Ladies of the Sorosis Club)*. Monticello, Arkansas, 1924. Special Collections, University of Arkansas, Fayetteville, Arkansas.

Richardson, Angelique, and Chris Willis, eds. *The New Woman in Fiction and in Fact: Fin-de-Siècle Feminisms*. New York: Palgrave, 2001.

Rieff, Lynne A. "'Go Ahead and Do All You Can': Southern Progressives and Alabama Home Demonstration Clubs, 1914–1940." In *Hidden Histories of Women in the New South*, edited by Virginia Bernhard et al., 134–52. Columbia: University of Missouri Press, 1994.

Rollins, William, Jr. *The Shadow Before*. London: V. Gollancz, 1935.

Romalov, Nancy Tillman. "Mobile and Modern Heroines: Early Twentieth-Century Girls' Automobile Series." In *Nancy Drew and Company: Culture, Gender, and Girls' Series*, edited by Sherrie A. Inness, 75–88. Bowling Green: Bowling Green State University Popular Press, 1997.

Romines, Ann. "Reading the Cakes: *Delta Wedding* and the Texts of Southern Women's Culture." *Mississippi Quarterly* 50, no. 4 (September 1997): 601–17.

Roosevelt, Theodore, and Acting Attorney General Charles M. Russell. *Presidential Records*. 4 September 1907–44–69. In *CIS Index to Presidential Executive Orders, pt. 1, April 30, 1789 to March 4, 1921, George Washington to Woodrow Wilson*. 10 vols. 1907.

Rosborough, Mae Blakeley. "Extension Activities During Twenty Year Period in Southeast Arkansas." MC 1145, Box 6, Folder 5, Arkansas Cooperative Extension Service Records, Special Collections, University of Arkansas, Fayetteville, Arkansas.

Rosengarten, Theodore. *All God's Dangers: The Life of Nate Shaw*. New York: Vintage, 1974.

Rotundo, E. Anthony. *American Manhood: Transformations in Masculinity from the Revolution to the Modern Era*. New York: Basic, 1993.

Rydell, Robert W. *All the World's a Fair: Visions of Empire at American International Expositions, 1876–1916*. Chicago: University of Chicago Press, 1984.

Salzman, Jack, David D. Anderson, and Kichinosuke Ohashi, eds. *Sherwood Anderson: The Writer at His Craft*. Mamaroneck, N.Y.: Paul P. Appel, 1979.

"Saturday, May 30." (Hendersonville, N.C.) *Times News* (20 May 1925). Henderson County Genealogical and Historical Society, Hendersonville, North Carolina.

Sauceman, Fred. "Social Class and Food." In Edge, *Foodways*, 102–4.

Scharff, Virginia. *Taking the Wheel: Women and the Coming of the Motor Age*. New York: Free Press, 1991.

Schneir, Miriam, ed. *Feminism in Our Time: The Essential Writings from World War II to the Present*. New York: Vintage, 1994.

Schocket, Eric. "Undercover Explorations of the 'Other Half,' or the Writer as Class Transvestite." *Representations* 64 (Autumn 1998): 109–33.

Scott, Anne Firor. *Making the Invisible Woman Visible*. Urbana: University of Illinois Press, 1984.

———. *Natural Allies: Women's Associations in American History*. Urbana: University of Illinois Press, 1991.

"Seven Men Accused in Gastonia Killing of Woman Striker." *New York Times* (16 September 1929): 1, 12.

Shannon, Anna. "Biographical Afterword." In Dargan, *Call Home the Heart*, 433–46.

Shapiro, Henry D. *Appalachia on Our Mind: The Southern Mountains and Mountaineers in the American Consciousness, 1870–1920*. Chapel Hill: University of North Carolina Press, 1978.

Shapiro, Laura. *Perfection Salad: Women and Cooking at the Turn of the Century*. New York: Farrar, Straus, Giroux, 1986.

———. *Something from the Oven: Reinventing Dinner in 1950s America*. New York: Penguin, 2004.

Silber, Nina. *The Romance of Reunion: Northerners and the South, 1865–1900*. Chapel Hill: University of North Carolina Press, 1993.

Simon, Bryant. *A Fabric of Defeat: The Politics of South Carolina Millhands, 1910–1948*. Chapel Hill: University of North Carolina Press, 1998.

Simonson, Robert. "Moonshine Finds New Craftsmen and Enthusiasts." *New York Times* (4 May 2010). www.nytimes.com/2010/05/05/dining/05white.html?_r=1&scp=3&sq= whiskey&st=cse. Accessed 15 July 2010.

Sinclair, Upton. *The Jungle*. New York: Doubleday, Page, 1906.

Smith, Andrew F. *The Tomato in America: Early History, Cookery, and Culture*. Columbia: University of South Carolina Press, 1994.

Smith, Margaret Supplee, and Emily Herron Wilson. *North Carolina Women: Making History*. Chapel Hill: University of North Carolina Press, 1999.

Smith-Rosenberg, Carroll. *Disorderly Conduct: Visions of Gender in Victorian America*. New York: Knopf, 1985.

Southern Foodways Alliance. *Appalachia: Exploring the Land and the Larder.* http://www.southernfoodways.com/sym_03.shtml. Accessed 15 July 2010.
"Southern Summer School for Women's Workers in Industry." Mary Cornelia Barker Papers. Manuscript, Archives, and Rare Book Library, Robert W. Woodruff Library, Emory University. 0528-018.tif. http://larson.library.emory.edu/marbl/DigProjects/swh/images/Barker%20528/0528-018.pdf. Accessed 10 August 2010.
Sowinska, Susan. "Grace Lumpkin (1891–1980)." *New Georgia Encyclopedia.* www.georgiaencyclopedia.org/nge/Article.jsp?id=h-2473. Accessed 15 July 2010.
Stage, Sarah, and Virginia B. Vincenti, eds. *Rethinking Home Economics: Women and the History of a Profession.* Ithaca: Cornell University Press, 1997.
Stanonis, Anthony J. "Just Like Mammy Used to Make: Foodways in the Jim Crow South." In *Dixie Emporium: Tourism, Foodways, and Consumer Culture in the American South*, edited by Anthony J. Stanonis, 208–33. Athens: University of Georgia Press, 2008.
Stewart, Bruce E. "'When Darkness Reigns Then Is the Hour to Strike': Moonshining, Federal Liquor Taxation, and Klan Violence in Western North Carolina, 1868–1872." *North Carolina Historical Review* 80, no. 4 (October 2003): 453–74.
Stoddart, Jess. *Challenge and Change in Appalachia: The Story of Hindman Settlement School.* Lexington: University Press of Kentucky, 2002.
Stoler, Ann Laura. *Along the Archival Grain: Epistemic Anxieties and Colonial Common Sense.* Princeton: Princeton University Press, 2009.
Stone, May, and Katherine Pettit. *The Quare Women's Journals: May Stone and Katherine Pettit's Summers in the Kentucky Mountains and the Founding of the Hindman Settlement School.* Edited by Jess Stoddart. Ashland, Ky.: Jesse Stuart Foundation, 1997.
Stoneley, Peter. *Consumerism and American Girls' Literature, 1860–1940.* Cambridge: Cambridge University Press, 2003.
Strasser, Susan. *Never Done: A History of American Housework.* New York: Pantheon, 1982.
Streeter, Amy Evans. "Hot Tamales and the Mississippi Delta." *The Tamale Trail.* Southern Foodways Alliance. http://www.tamaletrail.com/. Accessed 10 August 2010.
Talbott, Mary Hamilton. "Splendid Work by Girls' Canning Clubs." *New York Times* (16 March 1913): SM16.
Tanner, James E. "Concerning Miss Powell's Resignation." A85–149, Box 3, James E. Tanner Papers, Special Collections Department, University Archives, Mitchell Memorial Library, Mississippi State University, Starkville, Mississippi.

———. "County Extension Workers, 1905–1945." A85-149, Box 1, James E. Tanner Papers, Special Collections Department, University Archives, Mitchell Memorial Library, Mississippi State University, Starkville, Mississippi.

———. "Food Preservation." A85-149, Box 4, James E. Tanner Papers, Special Collections Department, University Archives, Mitchell Memorial Library, Mississippi State University, Starkville, Mississippi.

———. "Mississippi Extension Service Among Negroes." A85-149, Box 4, James E. Tanner Papers, Special Collections Department, University Archives, Mitchell Memorial Library, Mississippi State University, Starkville, Mississippi.

———. "Miss Powell's Letter." A85-149, Box 3, James E. Tanner Papers, Special Collections Department, University Archives, Mitchell Memorial Library, Mississippi State University, Starkville, Mississippi.

———. Newspaper Clippings. A85-149, Box 3, James E. Tanner Papers, Special Collections Department, University Archives, Mitchell Memorial Library, Mississippi State University, Starkville, Mississippi.

———. *The Places of the 4-H Club Boy in the Extension Program*. A&M College, Mississippi Annual Extension Workers Meeting, December 11, 1929. James E. Tanner Vertical File, University Archives, Special Collections Department, Mitchell Memorial Library, Mississippi State University, Starkville, Mississippi.

Tarbox, Gwen Athene. *The Clubwomen's Daughters': Collectivist Impulses in Progressive-Era Girl's Fiction, 1890–1940*. New York: Garland Publishing, 2000.

Tartan, Beth. "Community Cookbooks." In Edge, *Foodways*, 41–45.

Taylor, Joe Gray. *Eating, Drinking, and Visiting in the South: An Informal History*. Baton Rouge: Louisiana State University Press, 1982.

Taylor, Welford Dunaway. *Sherwood Anderson*. New York: Frederick Ungar, 1977.

Thompson, Holland. "Life in a Southern Mill Town." *Political Science Quarterly (1886–1905)* 15, no. 1 (March 1900): 1–13.

Todd, Mark. "Memories of Silvermont Mansion Shared." *Transylvania Times*, 25 May 2010. http://www.transylvaniatimes.com. Accessed 10 August 2010.

Tomato Club Songs. "See How We Can." Agricultural Narrative and Statistical Reports from State Officers. Microfilm Rolls 1–2, 1909–1917. Special Collections Department, Mitchell Memorial Library, Mississippi State University, Starkville, Mississippi.

Troubetzkoy, Amelie Rives. *Tanis, The Sang-Digger*. New York: Town Topics, 1893.

Trubek, Amy B. *The Taste of Place: A Cultural Journey into Terroir*. Berkeley: University of California Press, 2008.

Tullos, Allen. *Habits of Industry: White Culture and the Transformation of the Carolina Piedmont*. Chapel Hill: University of North Carolina Press, 1989.

Turner, William H. "The Demography of Black Appalachia: Past and Present." In *Blacks in Appalachia*, edited by William H. Turner and Edward J. Cabbell, 237–61. Lexington: University Press of Kentucky, 1985.

"Uncle Sam Starts a Juvenile Class in Agriculture." *New York Times* (4 August 1912): SM13.

"Unique Entertainment." Newspaper Clipping, 4 June 1915. In McKimmon, Conceit Book, 1915–1930, P.C. 234.23, McKimmon Papers, North Carolina State Archives, Raleigh, North Carolina.

University of North Carolina at Chapel Hill. "Myra Page Papers, 1910–1990." Finding Aid, Biography. www.lib.unc.edu/mss/inv/p/Page,Myra.html. Accessed 15 July 2010.

University of Vermont. "Sarah Norcliffe Cleghorn Papers." Finding Aid, Biography. http://cdi.uvm.edu/findingaids/collection/cleghorn.ead.xml. Accessed 10 August 2010.

Van Vorst, Mrs. John [Bessie], and Marie Van Vorst. *The Woman Who Toils: Being the Experiences of Two Gentlewomen as Factory Girls*. New York: Doubleday, Page, 1903.

Van Vorst, Marie. *Amanda of the Mill*. Indianapolis: Bobbs-Merrill, 1904.

von der Heide, Mary, and Emily Pronovost. "Dazelle Foster Lowe," Green 'N' Growing. www.lib.ncsu.edu/specialcollections/greenngrowing/essay_foster_lowe.html. Accessed 10 August 2010.

Vorse, Mary Heaton. *Strike!* New York: H. Liveright, 1930.

Walker, Melissa. "Agriculture." In Walker and Cobb, *Agriculture and Industry*, 3–29.

———. *All We Knew Was to Farm: Rural Women in the Upcountry South, 1919–1941*. Baltimore: Johns Hopkins University Press, 2000.

Walker, Melissa, and James C. Cobb, eds. *Agriculture and Industry*, vol. 11 of *The New Encyclopedia of Southern Culture*. General editor, Charles Reagan Wilson. Chapel Hill: University of North Carolina Press, 2007.

Walsh, Margaret. "Gender and the Automobile in the United States." *Automobile in American Life and Society*. www.autolife.umd.umich.edu/Gender/Walsh/G_Overview.htm. Accessed 15 June 2010.

Warner, Melanie. "Wal-Mart Eyes Organic Foods." *New York Times*. http://www.nytimes.com/2006/05/12/business/12organic.html. Accessed 15 November 2010.

Warnes, Andrew. *Hunger Overcome?: Food and Resistance in Twentieth-Century African American Literature*. Athens: University of Georgia Press, 2004.

———. *Savage Barbecue: Race, Culture, and the Invention of America's First Food*. Athens: University of Georgia Press, 2008.

Warren, Maude Radford. "She 'Lifted' Sixty-six Counties: The Story of Jane S. McKimmon's Work in North Carolina." *Country Gentleman* (29 June 1918). In McKimmon, Conceit Book, 1915–1930, P.C. 234.23, McKimmon Papers, North Carolina State Archives, Raleigh, North Carolina.

Wayne State University. "Mary Heaton Vorse Papers." Finding Aid, Biography. http://www.reuther.wayne.edu/files/LP000190.pdf. Accessed 10 August 2010.

"We Buy Polk Salad." Otto Rayburn Collection. MS R19, Box P, Special Collections, University of Arkansas, Fayetteville, Arkansas.

Welty, Eudora. *The Collected Stories of Eudora Welty*. Orlando: Harvest, 1980.

West, Elizabeth Cassidy. "'Yours for Home and Country': The War Work of the South Carolina Woman's Committee." *Proceedings of the South Carolina Historical Association* (2001): 59–68.

Whisnant, David. *All That Is Native and Fine: The Politics of Culture in an American Region*. Chapel Hill: University of North Carolina Press, 1983.

White, Deborah Gray. *Too Heavy a Load: Black Women in Defense of Themselves, 1894–1994*. New York: Norton, 1999.

White, Ray Lewis. "The Original for Sherwood Anderson's *Kit Brandon*." *Newberry Library Bulletin* 6 (1965): 196–99.

Whitlow, Louise, chairman. *Susie Virginia Powell: Pioneer Woman Educator of Mississippi*. Compiled by Alpha Chapter, Committee on Pioneer in Education, 1957. Special Collections Department, Mitchell Memorial Library, Mississippi State University, Starkville, Mississippi.

Wilkinson, Alec. *Moonshine: A Life in Pursuit of White Liquor*. New York: Knopf, 1985.

Williams, Cratis D. "New Directions: Folk or Hillbilly?" In *An American Vein: Critical Readings in Appalachian Literature*, edited by Danny L. Miller, Sharon Hatfield, and Gurney Norman, 1–12. Athens: Ohio University Press, 2005.

Williams, Michael Ann. *Great Smoky Mountains Folklife*. Jackson: University Press of Mississippi, 1995.

Williams-Forson, Psyche A. *Building Houses Out of Chicken Legs: Black Women, Food, and Power*. Chapel Hill: University of North Carolina Press, 2006.

Williamson, Jerry. *Hillbillyland: What the Movies Did to the Mountains and What the Mountains Did to the Movies*. Chapel Hill: University of North Carolina Press, 1995.

Wilson, Charles Reagan. "Biscuits." In Edge, *Foodways*, 122–25.

Wilson, Clyde. "Holland Thompson." In *Dictionary of North Carolina Biography*, edited by William S. Powell. Chapel Hill: University of North Carolina Press, 1979–1996. Online at Documenting the American South. http://docsouth.unc.edu/nc/Thompson/bio.html. Accessed 15 February 2010.

Wilson, Emily Herring. *No One Gardens Alone: A Life of Elizabeth Lawrence.* Boston: Beacon, 2004.
———, ed. *Two Gardeners: Katharine S. White and Elizabeth Lawrence, A Friendship in Letters.* Boston: Beacon, 2002.
Wilson, Kathleen Curtis. *Uplifting the South: Mary Mildred Sullivan's Legacy for Appalachia.* Johnson City, Tenn.: Overmountain Press, 2006.
Wilson, R. S. "My dear Mr. [Bradford] Knapp." 12 February 1916. Agricultural Narrative and Statistical Reports from State Officers. Microfilm Rolls 1–2, 1909–1917. Special Collections Department, Mitchell Memorial Library, Mississippi State University, Starkville, Mississippi.
Wintle, Sarah. "Horses, Bikes and Automobiles: New Woman on the Move." In Richardson and Willis, *The New Woman in Fiction*, 66–78.
Wolfe, Margaret Ripley. "Sherwood Anderson and the Southern Highlands: A Sense of Place and the Sustenance of Women." *Southern Studies* 3 (Winter 1992): 253–75.
Womble, Walter L. *Love in the Mists.* Raleigh: Edwards and Broughton, 1892.
Woolson, Constance Fenimore. "Up in the Blue Ridge." In *Rodman, the Keeper: Southern Sketches*, 276–339. New York: D. Appleton, [1878] 1880.
Yaeger, Patricia. *Dirt and Desire: Reconstructing Southern Women's Writing, 1930–1990.* Chicago: University of Chicago Press, 2000.
Year Book for Girls' Home Demonstration Clubs, Mississippi 1924. Mississippi Cooperative Extension Folder, 1910–1939. Vertical File, University Archives, Special Collections Department, Mitchell Memorial Library, Mississippi State University, Starkville, Mississippi.

INDEX

Addams, Jane, 55, 146; Hull House, 214n6
African Americans, 11, 57, 65, 107-8, 115, 178; clubwomen, 27, 79-80, 114; Anna Julia Cooper, 52-53; critiques of gender and class by, 147, 170, 188, 215n31; foodways, 12, 52, 60, 113, 176, 232n29; friendship with white women, 109-11, 174, 198, 224n43; girls, 88, 90, 103; Great Migration, 65, 77, 87, 106, 169; mill communities and, 142, 145, 157, 230n64; moonshine, 25, 45, 212n43; rights as citizens, 33, 85-87, 128, 180; stereotypes of, 37-38, 124, 181; tomato clubs, 88, 90, 103, 106-12, 216n1, 223n37; Lucy Wade, 110-11; Booker T. Washington, 96, 107; women as cooks, 9, 11, 13, 78, 181; women in domestic service, 54, 65, 69-70, 171, 181. *See also* Fisher, Abby; Jeanes teachers; Lowe, Dazelle Foster; Oliver, Alice Carter
Agnew, Ella G., 85, 91, 107-8, 112-13
agriculture in the South, 15, 21, 85-87, 101, 122, 160-61; African Americans and, 96, 107, 109, 111, 218n6; agribusiness, 172; curb and farmers' markets, 183-90; early extension work, 79, 92, 161, 216n1; economic instability in, 65, 126-28, 131, 168; extension agents, 92-93, 104-5, 111-15, 177, 195; *Farmer's Wife*, 78-79; farm girls' cultures, 83-89, 115-17; gardens, 13, 148-49; migrant workers in, 120, 171, 232n29; monoculture in, 96, 115, 126-27, 140, 161; *Progressive Farmer*, 106, 156; sharecropping and tenant farming, 17, 86-90, 95, 131; state market bulletins, 18, 194-202; subsistence and small farms, 1-2, 12, 24, 31, 41-43, 86. *See also* United States Department of Agriculture (USDA)
Alabama, 4, 60, 64, 194, 200; foodways of, 7; Tuskegee, 96, 107
Amanda of the Mill (Van Vorst), 133-34, 136-40, 141, 151, 162
American Woman's Home (Stowe), 54, 76
Anderson, Sherwood: *Beyond Desire*, 141, 146, 159, 162; biography, 145-46, 211n33; *Kit Brandon*, 25-26, 39-49, 84, 116, 146, 155
Angel (Heyward), 24-25
Appalachia: African American Appalachians, 65, 70; authors from, 24, 48-49, 142-45; class and, 40, 64, 68, 74, 87, 167; extractive industry in, 43-44, 86; families in, 1-3, 11, 65-67, 155-57, 147; female stereotypes, 32, 35, 47-48, 105, 115; foodways, 5, 7, 15, 58, 60, 70, 75-76; girls from, 17, 40, 45, 91, 97; invention of, 4, 6, 8, 124; isolation, 37, 41-44, 133-35, 171; male stereotypes, 22, 25-26, 29; mountains, 16, 78-79, 162, 185, 202; philanthropy in 53-55, 84-85; separate race, 11, 38-39, 46, 56-57, 64, 146; women from, 51, 59-63, 69-74

Arkansas, 7, 25, 43, 188; cookbooks from, 175, 177, 179-82, 194; curb markets in, 165, 174, 184; home demonstration in, 107, 112-13, 120-22

Asian cultures, 12, 57, 211n28

"At Teague Poteet's" (Harris), 35, 37, 84, 208n13

automobiles, 41-44, 46-48, 105, 109, 116, 167

Baltimore, Maryland, 94-95, 125

beaten biscuit crusade, 22, 51, 58, 78-79, 88-91, 97

beaten biscuits: ingredients and equipment needed, 64-65, 67-68; recipe for, 59, 69

Beecher, Catharine, *American Woman's Home*, 54, 76

Beyond Desire (Anderson), 141, 146, 159, 162

Beyond the Blue Grass (Gill), 27, 29-30, 32

Call Home the Heart (Dargan), 129-30, 137, 144-45, 154-62, 165

Campbell, John, 63, 64, 226n7; *The Southern Highlander and His Homeland*, 63, 66

Campbell, Olive Dame, 56, 63, 64, 66, 74

"Capture of Andy Proudfoot, The" (Cooke), 60, 71

Caribbean, 12, 25, 181

Carolina Mountains, The (Morley), 60-61, 75-76

Cavanagh, Catherine Frances, 27, 30-33, 39, 42, 49, 208n11

civil rights, 170-72, 180; civil rights cake, 175, 180-82

class: class-bread hierarchy, 61-67; feminist methods and, 15, 202; fluidity in, 39-48, 103; idea of "the South" and, 4, 12, 168-69; interclass alliances, 25, 89, 105, 107-17, 174, 198; leisure and, 72-75, 136, 145; middle class, 11, 59, 69-70, 99, 124-25, 161; race and, 10, 171-72, 176, 178, 188; teen girls and, 34, 36-39, 122, 161-62; tensions between, 130, 145, 180-82, 190, 205n8. *See also* Lang, Amy; Yaeger, Patricia

consumer culture, 8-10, 16-17, 22, 89, 132; advertising and, 14-15, 39, 95-97, 175, 179-80; consumer desire, 6, 44-45, 141, 148, 156, 223n34; consumer goods, 36, 44, 66-68, 132-33, 159; corporations, 28-31, 88, 169-70, 173, 188, 205n8; creation of national market, 25, 52, 72-74, 84, 95; failure of, 77, 117, 122; female consumers, 10, 13, 77-78, 94, 136, 177; girls and women as items to be consumed, 33, 38, 39, 139, 153, 160; mail-order catalogs, 14, 43, 68, 105, 132, 177-78; moonshine and, 39-49, 167; resistance to, 161, 168, 185; role of mills in, 134-35, 140, 152-54, 230n64; women as advertisers, 194-96, 199-202

cookbooks: history of, 175-77; scholarship about, 177-79, 181-82

Cooke, Grace MacGowan, 53; "The Capture of Andy Proudfoot," 60, 71; *The Power and the Glory*, 72-73; "The Spy," 209n14

Cooper, Anna Julia, 52-53

Copenhaver, Eleanor, 146, 226n13

cornbread: ingredients and equipment needed, 65-66, 68; recipes for, 59-60

cotton, 3, 87, 95-96, 121-26, 140, 149; in Deep South, 7, 124, 131, 195; mills, 48, 85-86, 124-25, 133, 145, 157-58

Crim, Miss Matt, 53; "The Strike at Mr. Mobley's," 61

Cromer, Marie Samuella: biography, 85, 88, 113-14, 119-21, 123; founding of tomato

clubs, 83-87, 90-91, 99-100, 108; goals for tomato clubs, 93-94, 96, 102, 106
curb markets: development of, 183-85, 189

Dame, Daisy, 24, 25, 56, 207n6
Dargan, Olive Tilford: biography, 141, 144, 147; *Call Home the Heart*, 129-30, 137, 144-45, 154-62, 165; *A Stone Came Rolling*, 154, 228n35
Dishes and Beverages of the Old South (McCulloch-Williams), 59, 69, 73, 170, 176
Duke's mayonnaise, 2, 9-11, 78

écritures féminines, 202-3
Egerton, John, 10
Elliott, Blanche Hanks, 120-21, 165, 174, 184, 224n43, 225n2

feminism, 8, 18; feminist 15, 98-101, 146, 202-3; antifeminist, 61
Fisher, Abby, 69, 77, 176; *What Mrs. Fisher Knows about Old Southern Cooking*, 69, 176
Florida, 7, 25, 69, 125, 171, 194
food companies, southern, 9-10, 205n8; beverages, 9, 159, 173; grains, 3, 9; grocery stores, 169-70, 173. *See also* Duke's mayonnaise
4-H movement, 9, 87-88, 97, 113, 116; history of, 94, 105
Furman, Lucy, 54; *Mothering on Perilous*, 56, 74-75; *The Quare Women*, 56, 67

Gabaccia, Donna, 10, 205n8
Gardening for Love (Lawrence), 193-99, 201-2
Gathering Storm (Page), 125, 130, 134-35, 139, 152-54, 162

gender, 4, 10, 134; essentialism, 202-3, 212n44; fluidity of, 40, 45-48, 209n14; food as gendered, 8, 12-15; nostalgia and, 26-32; race and, 11, 106-9, 171; rural issues in, 89, 93-94, 113
Georgia, 69, 88, 143; Atlanta, 86, 170; foodways, 5, 7; market bulletins, 194, 196, 198; mills in, 128, 133, 146, 226n13; moonshine in, 16, 35, 37, 44, 212n43
Gielow, Martha S., 33, 210n20; *Old Andy, the Moonshiner*, 34-39, 42, 46, 49, 84
Gill, George Creswell, 49, 208n11; *Beyond the Blue Grass*, 27, 29-30, 32
Gilmore, Glenda Elizabeth, 109-10
girls' culture: African American girls, 88, 90, 103, 112; domesticity and, 9, 58, 59, 155-56; education and, 35-39, 52-55, 101-4, 113, 167-68, 226n13; friendship between, 105, 116-17, 146, 188-89, 225n2; invention of, 22, 33-34, 49, 115, 132; money and, 28, 32, 92-94, 97-101, 127, 162; politics and citizenship of, 104-8; tomato club girls, 83-92; wildness of, 16, 32, 35-38, 42-45, 210n22; workers, 10, 17, 119-22, 133, 150. *See also* girls' studies
girls' studies, 33-34, 37-38, 211n31
Goldberger, Joseph, 125-27, 130, 132, 140, 157-58
Golden Apples (Welty), 201-2
Great Depression, 39, 46, 106, 168

Hale, Grace, 172-73
Harris, Joel Chandler, 48-49; "At Teague Poteet's," 35, 37, 84, 208n13
Heyward, Du Bose, 207n6; *Angel*, 24-25
Hindman Settlement School, 54-59, 61-63, 65-72, 74-75, 79, 156
Hine, Darlene Clark, 110

INDEX

immigration: immigrant foodways, 12, 55, 205n8; migrant laborers, 120, 171, 232n29; Scots-Irish, 1, 24; social Darwinism and, 37-39, 49, 167; teen girls and, 33-34, 222n33
In Buncombe County (Pool), 59, 63-64, 75-76
Inness, Sherrie, 178, 181

Jeanes teachers, 107-8, 111, 216n1, 223n37
Jewish cultures, 12
Juletty (McElroy), 27-32, 38, 42, 46, 84, 209n14
Jungle, The (Sinclair), 14, 95, 130, 226n13

Kaplan, Amy, 57-58
Kentucky, 18-19, 144; Berea College, 57; bluegrass region in, 53, 69, 171, 176; eastern region in, 51, 146, 172; foodways, 7, 15; Hindman Settlement School, 54-59, 61-63, 65-72, 74-75, 79, 156; moonshine in, 16, 24, 27-32
Kit Brandon (Anderson), 25-26, 39-49, 84, 116, 146, 155
Knapp, Seaman A., 83-84, 86, 99, 107-8, 216n1

labor, 10, 65, 87, 95; of African Americans, 12, 69, 78; child labor, 53, 119-20, 128, 134, 225n1; disposable bodies, 41-49; domestic, 16, 54, 74, 182; feminist labor historians, 98-99; girls, 120-22, 132; right-to-work states, 170-71; southern labor fiction, 17, 22, 141-47, 168; strike violence, 39-40, 130, 137, 146, 154, 160; unions, 133, 142-47, 149, 151-52, 162; women and, 16, 41-49, 100-1, 106
Lang, Amy, 62-63, 215n37
Latino/a cultures, 12, 155, 171, 181, 232n29

Lawrence, Elizabeth, 18, 203, 232n4; *Gardening for Love*, 193-99, 201-2
leisure, 64, 85, 99, 101, 119, 225n1; class and racial-codes in, 52, 68-72, 73, 136, 145, 168
Levenstein, Harvey, 10, 55, 205n8
"Life in a Southern Mill Town" (Thompson), 123, 126-27, 159
Loray Mill (Gastonia, N.C.), 130, 137, 141, 154-55
Louisiana, 7, 25, 44, 170, 194-95, 232n3
Lowe, Dazelle, 108-10, 223n40
Lumpkin, Grace: biography, 141, 143, 162; *To Make My Bread*, 130, 135-37, 139-40, 143-44, 147-52

market bulletins, 194-96, 232n3
masculinity, 13, 34, 56, 78, 112, 183-84; stereotypes of, 25-29, 46, 146
McCulloch-Williams, Martha, 53; *Dishes and Beverages of the Old South*, 59, 69, 73, 170, 176
McElroy, Lucy: biography, 48-49, 208n11; *Juletty*, 27-32, 38, 42, 46, 84, 209n14
McKimmon, Jane S.: curb markets, 170, 174, 184-90, 194, 196, 199-200; farmers' institutes demonstrations, 78-80, 156; tomato clubs, 19, 83-93, 96, 98-103, 105-14; *When We're Green We Grow*, 102, 170, 184-90, 194, 196, 199-200
McPherson, Tara, 7, 172; lenticular logic, 205n4
Miles, Emma Bell, 53, 77; *Spirit of the Mountains*, 66, 70-71, 75, 76-77
"Mill Mother's Lament" (Wiggins), 141-42
Mississippi, 7, 15, 17, 19, 188-89; cookbooks from, 176, 181; market bulletins, 193-95, 197-98, 201-2; tomato clubs, 83-85, 87-94, 97-98, 100, 103-7, 111-15

moonshine: historical reasons for, 23-25, 207n2; recipes, 22-23, 206n1; stereotypes of, 25-26. *See also* Whiskey Rebellion (of 1794)

Moore, Virginia, 85, 91

Morley, Margaret, 53; *The Carolina Mountains*, 60-61, 75-76

Mothering on Perilous (Furman), 56, 74-75

Native American cultures, 11, 176; Cherokee, 5, 105, 200, 205n2

New Women, 16, 26-29, 33, 39, 42, 49; in the South, 22, 27, 53, 167

North Carolina, 1-7, 11-13, 15-19, 36, 170; Asheville, 59, 60, 75, 144; biscuits in, 59-61, 65, 75-76, 78-80; Brevard, 1, 2, 179-81; Charlotte, 86, 99, 194, 196; cookbooks, 165, 174, 179-80; curb markets, 183-90; Gastonia, 127, 128, 130, 141, 146, 170; Hendersonville, 1, 183-85, 232n29; market bulletins, 194-202; mills in, 123-28, 130-32, 134-37, 139-62, 170-71; moonshine in, 24-25, 31, 32, 43-44, 212n43; Raleigh, 32, 86, 196; tomato clubs, 83-94, 96-103, 105-117. *See also* Lawrence, Elizabeth; McKimmon, Jane

nostalgia, 57; anti-nostalgia, 44; food and, 1, 6, 8-9, 15; gender and, 26-32, 116; invented South and, 52, 78, 172-3, 190, 197-98; plantation nostalgia, 3-4, 12, 69, 170

Old Andy, the Moonshiner (Gielow), 34-39, 42, 46, 49, 84

Oliver, Alice Carter 88, 111

Page, Dorothy Myra: biography, 141, 145, 147, 171; *Gathering Storm*, 125, 130, 134-35, 139, 152-54, 162; *Southern Cotton Mills and Labor*, 145

pellagra: causes of, 76, 122, 125-26; gender and race differences, 157-58, 226n6; symptoms of, 124; treatments for, 126-27, 162, 169

Pettit, Katherine: biography, 53-59, 146, 213n4; resistance to, 74, 156; rhetoric of corn versus wheat, 32, 61-72, 78-79, 95

Pool, Maria Louise, 53; *In Buncombe County*, 59, 63-64, 75-76

Powell, Susie V.: resignation of, 225n48; tomato clubs, 84-85, 87-92, 93-94, 98, 100-5, 111-15; women's talk, 188-89

Power and the Glory, The (Cooke), 72-73

Progressive Era activism, 26, 52-53, 57-59, 73; decline of, 42, 111, 128, 157; *Progressive Farmer*, 106, 156; rhetoric of, 14, 16, 22, 31-32, 66, 99; southern, 54, 213n3

Prohibition Era, 29, 42

Quare Women, The (Furman), 56, 67

race and racial ideologies, 17, 87, 147, 205n4, 205n8; "Dixie ailment," 145; ethnicity, 4, 34, 45, 55, 181, 223n37; interracial work, 89, 104-12, 142, 176-82, 198; lynch mob violence, 3, 40, 230n64; poor whites and "white trash," 12, 26, 124, 169, 188; "race suicide," 37, 211n28; racism, 33, 105, 110-11, 127, 168, 172; whiteness, 3, 11, 42, 57-58, 72; white privilege, 13, 36-39, 85-87, 110, 170, 230n64

railroads, 14, 68, 96, 136, 186; masculinity and, 29, 46, 61, 63

Rollins, William, Jr.: biography, 146; *The Shadow Before*, 141, 146-47

segregation, 10, 147, 175, 178, 181, 232n29; Jim Crow, 3, 33, 69, 85-87; plantation nostalgia, 3-4, 12, 69, 170; resistance to, 89, 109, 216n1

sexism, 34, 127, 146, 153, 216n1; sexual abuse 42, 147; sexual harassment, 134, 140
sexual pleasure, female, 42, 45, 89, 167-68, 209n14; food and, 71-72, 166, 202; perceived as dangerous, 33, 39, 155
Shadow Before, The (Rollins), 141, 146-47
Shapiro, Laura, 55, 71
Sinclair, Upton, 146; *The Jungle*, 14, 95, 130, 226n13
Smith-Lever Act (1914), 113, 219n10
South, the: global and transnational, 4, 7-8, 10, 11, 15, 205n5; idea of, 4-8, 13, 41, 49, 169, 171-73
South Carolina, 1, 32, 194; African Americans in, 87, 108-9, 111; Aiken County, 83-85, 90; foodways, 2, 5, 7; Greenville, 9-10, 78; identity, 106, 113-15, 119-21; mills in, 123, 131, 133-34, 136-40, 142-43; tomato clubs, 17, 86-88, 93-96, 99, 102. *See also* Cromer, Marie Samuella
Southern Cotton Mills and Labor (Page), 145
Southern Highlander and His Homeland, The (Campbell), 63, 66
Southern School for Women Workers in Industry, 128-29, 146, 226n13
Spirit of the Mountains (Miles), 66, 70-71, 75, 76-77
"Spy, The" (Cooke), 209n14
Stoler, Ann Laura, 180-81
Stone, May: biography, 53-59, 146, 213n4; resistance to, 74, 156; rhetoric of corn versus wheat, 32, 61-72, 78-79, 95
Stone Came Rolling, A (Dargan), 154, 228n35
Stowe, Harriet Beecher, *American Woman's Home*, 54, 76
Strike! (Vorse), 125, 141, 146, 151-52
"Strike at Mr. Mobley's, The" (Crim), 61

Tanis, the Sang-Digger (Troubetzkoy), 61, 63, 71, 72
technology, 4, 8, 10, 15, 72, 199; anthropomorphized, 138-40; chemistry in, 22-23, 92-97, 102, 168, 170, 200; faith in, 9, 17, 89, 116, 161; standardizing time, 134-37, 140, 186, 200, 226n13; transportation and, 14, 105, 173, 205n8. *See also* railroads
Tennessee, 31, 120, 194; authors from, 5, 60, 142, 176; biscuits and, 66, 70-77; foodways, 7, 169; moonshine in, 16, 40-44; tomato clubs, 85
terroir, 7, 189-90
Texas, 4-5, 7, 25, 216n1, 223n37
Thompson, Holland, 123-27, 132, 225n5; "Life in a Southern Mill Town," 123, 126-27, 159
To Make My Bread (Lumpkin), 130, 135-37, 139-40, 143-44, 147-52
tomato clubs: creation of, 83-89; definition of, 90-92; evolution into 4-H, 113
Troubetzkoy, Amelie Rives, 53, 72; *Tanis, the Sang-Digger*, 61, 63, 71, 72

United States Department of Agriculture (USDA), 17, 88, 103, 106, 173, 216n1

Van Vorst, Bessie, 133; *The Woman Who Toils*, 133-34
Van Vorst, Marie: biography, 130, 132-33; *Amanda of the Mill*, 133-34, 136-40, 141, 151, 162; *The Woman Who Toils*, 133-34
Virginia, 9, 145, 146, 176, 194; biscuits and, 61, 63, 69, 72; foodways, 4, 7; moonshine in, 24, 43, 47-48; tomatoes and, 85, 107, 112, 223n37

Vorse, Mary Heaton: biography, 145-56; *Strike!*, 125, 141, 146, 151-52

Welty, Eudora, 179, 193-94, 201; *Golden Apples*, 201-2
What Mrs. Fisher Knows about Old Southern Cooking (Fisher), 69, 176
When We're Green We Grow (McKimmon), 102, 170, 184-90, 194, 196, 199-200
Whiskey Rebellion (of 1794), 23-24, 206n1
Whitmire, Iva Sanders, 1-2, 6, 13, 51-52, 58, 180
Wiggins, Ella May, 128-29, 130, 141-43, 145, 146; "Mill Mother's Lament," 141-42
Williams-Forson, Psyche, 11, 171, 188

Woman Who Toils, The (Van Vorst and Van Vorst), 133-34
Women's Christian Temperance Union (WCTU), 25, 42
women's clubs, 14, 54, 183-84, 213n3, 219n12; African American clubwomen, 79-80; cookbooks by, 3, 174-77, 180-82; General and State Federation of Women's Clubs, 55, 91-92, 104, 108, 115; Junior League, 174-75, 220n13; mill-supported, 128, 150; southern clubs, 53, 109-10, 112

Yaeger, Patricia, 7, 147, 152, 153, 160-61, 230n64

www.ingramcontent.com/pod-product-compliance
Lightning Source LLC
Chambersburg PA
CBHW011744220426
43666CB00018B/2893